Transcommuna___ˌ

From the Politics of Conversion
to the Ethics of Respect

Transcommunality

From the Politics of Conversion to the Ethics of Respect

John Brown Childs

Temple University Press
Philadelphia

Temple University Press, Philadelphia 19122
Copyright © 2003 by Temple University
Published 2003
Printed in the United States of America

∞ The paper used in this publication meets the requirements of the
American National Standard for Information Sciences—Permanence
of Paper for Printed Library Materials, ANSI Z39.48-1984.

Library of Congress Cataloging-in-Publication Data

Childs, John Brown.
    Transcommunality : from the politics of conversion to the ethics
of respect / John Brown Childs.
        p.   cm.
    Includes bibliographical references and index.
    ISBN 1-59213-004-6 (cloth : alk. paper) — ISBN 1-59213-005-4 (pbk. :
alk. paper)
    1. Pluralism (Social sciences).   2. Community.   I. Title.

HM1271 .C48 2003
307–dc21   2002074211

ISBN 13: 978-1-59213-005-4 (pbk. : alk. paper)

091208

Contents

Transcommunality

From the Politics
of Conversion
to the Ethics of Respect

For Arthur Childs,
Red Clay Keeper of the Memories

Ntunnaquômen, máttapsh yóteg awássih, cuttaunchemókous.

[I have had a good dream, come sit by the fire, warm yourself, I will tell my story.]

—From the Algonkian language of my
Massachusêuck ("Massachusett") ancestors

◆ ◆ ◆

So [the Peacemaker] passed from settlement to settlement finding that men desired peace and would practice it if they knew for certainty that others would practice it too.

But first, after leaving the hunters [the Peacemaker] sought the house of a certain woman who lived by the warrior's path which passed between the east and the west.

When [the Peacemaker] arrived, the woman placed food before him and, after he had eaten, asked him his message.

"I carry the Mind of the Master of Life," he replied, "and my message will bring an end to the wars between east and west."

"How will this be?" asked the woman, who wondered at his words, for it was her custom to feed the warriors passing before her door on their way between the east and the west.

"The Word that I bring," he said, "is that all peoples shall love one another and live together in peace...."

"Thy message is good," said the woman, "but a word is nothing until it is given form and set to work in the world. What form shall this message take when it comes to dwell among men?"

"It will take the form of the longhouse," replied [the Peacemaker], "in which there are many fires, one for each family, yet all live as one household under one chief mother. ... They shall be the *Kanonsionni*, the Longhouse. They shall have one mind and live under one law. Thinking will replace killing, and there shall be one commonwealth."

—The Message of the Peacemaker to the Mother of the
Nations, during the creation of the Haudenosaunee
or "Iroquois" Confederacy (circa 14th century)

First Words

A MAJOR PROBLEM of the twenty-first century will be the crisis of diverse, often competing, social/cultural identities among people uprooted by corrosively powerful global economic combines. This crisis will be significant not just in itself, but because it has the direct consequence of undermining coordinated resistance to the destructiveness of globalized systems of power. In an era rushing toward mindless materialism, propelled by powerful, unfeeling economic syndicates that uproot body and soul, more and more people will seek refuge in compartmentalized forms of social identity. However, the search for safety in such sealed compartments is by itself largely illusory. Fragmented, isolated, and unknowing of, or hostile to, one another, people are more, not less vulnerable to the very forces of destruction from which they seek escape.

Yet the strong desire for rooted affiliation is *not* the source of the problem. The real difficulty is not that people feel the need for such grounded affiliation in a culture, religion, community, cosmology, or philosophy. Rather, as Simone Weil, writing in the dark days of exile from Nazi domination, observed in her book *The Need for Roots*, "To be rooted is perhaps the most important and least recognized need of the human soul" (1952, 41).[1] The real dilemma we face is the lack of constructive and mutually respectful interaction among those diverse settings, rather than the diversity itself.

Confronted and often confounded by a crushing, globalizing monoculture that is supported by willing national elites, and

7

imposed from the core regions of economic power, we are not becoming better-connected peoples despite "mass communications." Instead, we are being broken down into ever more atomized elements, subordinated as mere uncommunicating parts of "mass culture." Some of these compartmentalized and fractured groupings take the form of rabid and genocidal nationalisms, as in the former Yugoslavia, Rwanda, and Guatemala, often with the compliance or direct support of some western nations. The elite construction of this globalization rotates most of us around a dense negative center of gravity, the content of which is determined by those with power, but which does not provide pathways for positive horizontal communication among the many peoples of the world. With the notable and partial technological exception of the Internet (which of course requires electricity and money),[2] along with some forms of popular culture that draw from the wells of resistance,[3] and of various nongovernmental conferences and convocations (that also require money), vast millions of peoples, many of them impoverished and struggling against essentially the same homogenizing global forces, have little or no way of corresponding with one another, no matter how much their daily situations correspond in terms of poverty and subordination.[4] So the corrosive equation we face is one of:

HOMOGENIZATION + FRAGMENTATION = SUBORDINATION

By contrast, the reality of highly diverse communities, organizations, cosmologies, and philosophies that *are* in resistance to this domination indicates that heterogeneity is an important basis from which to work for a just world. Certainly such heterogeneity cannot be ignored or marginalized. In this sense the dialectically opposite equation to the one above is:

HETEROGENEITY + COOPERATION = RESISTANCE AND FREEDOM

I propose that there is a way to both maintain particularistic rooted affiliations and create broad constellations of inclusive cooperation that constructively draw from such diversity. I call this way of cooperation *transcommunality*.

1

Introduction

TODAY, HUGE AND GROWING systems of economic domination continue their profit-driven bulldozer crush across the world. As some small portions of national populations are absorbed into affluent class positions, increasing numbers of people are relegated to disease-ridden paramilitary-controlled backwaters of the free-market mainstream. From rain forests to sweatshops, from Siberia to the Amazon, from the hydroelectric dam flooding of the Indigenous lands of the Sami in Scandinavia and the Cree in Québec to the chemically wrecked bodies of young women working in the U.S.-owned electronics factories in northern Mexico—from all the compass points, in a staggering variety of forms, the global economy is corrosively impacting nature and humans. Marx and Engels assailed capitalism's "uninterrupted disturbance of all social conditions" and its "everlasting uncertainty and agitation"—condemnations that can be applied even more emphatically today than when they wrote those words in the 1848 *Communist Manifesto.*[1] Technological improvements in political networking now tie ever larger sections of national and local political elites into the structural roles of eager administrative servants and armed guardians for megabusiness enterprise as it rips away the very air and earth upon which millions of species of living beings depend. In many parts of the world, thousands of desperate people flee their homes to seek temporary relief in near slave labor conditions of factories that produce luxury items for the

affluent. Workers in the "developed world" find their jobs obliterated as business syndicates move their operations to those areas
of highest maximum labor exploitation. In numerous sprawling
megacities, hundreds of thousands of castaways live in the back
alleys of despair. Indigenous peoples, whose sacred ancestral lands
have been in place for centuries, face acceleration of this century's
disruption as giant corporations, armored by governmental pro-
tections, strip-mine and clear-cut the soul of the earth. For Indigenous peoples, the technological "progress" of the expansionary
capitalist "free market" brutally equals cultural extinction in an
equation that has lasted for centuries.[2]

In this global house of crisis, with its many different rooms in
which the instruments of torture and death are varied in technology but ultimately lead to destruction, we need alliances
among the myriad communities and organizations that are resist-
ing devastation on thousands of different fronts in distinct ways
around the world. Consequently, a key practical issue is what kinds
of productive relationships among these often highly different
struggles can be established, without simply duplicating the hierarchies of power and domination with which we are contending.
If such egalitarian alliances are not created, then the world will
lack what could well be the only major effective barrier to rapa-
cious technological/economic undertakings that corrode the
entirety of existence from the air and oceans to the earth, and
from body to soul.

I propose that around the world many are poised on the edge
of an important development within which is emerging a twenty-
first-century mode of organizing for justice and dignity that I
call *transcommunality*. By transcommunality I mean the constructive and developmental interaction occurring among distinct
autonomy-oriented communities and organizations, each with its
own particular history, outlook, and agenda. This interaction,
developed through interpersonal relations of people engaged in
common tasks, is producing working groups of activists whose
roots are in communities and organizations, but who also form
bridges among diverse peoples as they address substantial, albeit
often varied corrosive dilemmas—from economic crisis to envi-

ronmental degradation, from Indigenous land rights to the organizing of workers across national borders. It is to the facilitation
of transcommunal cooperation that this essay is aimed.

Transcommunalists do not employ a "melting pot approach"
in which particular community and organizational allegiance is
obliterated in order for cooperation to occur. On the contrary,
transcommunal activists are effective at bridging diverse community and organizational positions precisely because they emerge
from and work within distinctive communal and organizational
settings. Rather than being an abstract call for "unity," transcommunality relies on concrete interpersonal ties growing out of what
I refer to as *shared practical action* from diverse participants. From
such practical action flows increasing communication, mutual
respect, and understanding.

Transcommunality must be distinguished from an inward-
focused identity politics (common to many vanguard leftist and
ethnic-nationalist leadership elites) that consciously cuts off its participants from contact with others in the name of racial, ethnic, or
ideological claims of purity. By contrast, a transcommunal identity politics celebrates and asserts distinctive and essential com-
munity/organizational allegiances that can serve as multiple bases
for common action with others. Such politics recognizes what
Denis-Constant Martin calls the capacity of particularistic vantage
points to simultaneously express universalistic elements such as
justice and freedom (1994, 35). Consequently, transcommunality
emphasizes a constant process of negotiational construction of
organization among diverse participants, rather than an imposed
monolithic system. Such negotiated action involves the recognition
that dispute and difference, sometimes profound, must be accepted
as a basic aspect of the "human condition" rather than being constrained through top-down, police-like controls.

Transcommunality at its best avoids the pitfalls of unifying
philosophies that attempt to reconcile all differences, usually
through force, about which Isaiah Berlin (1957) warned us. The
transcommunal emphasis on negotiation/renegotiation recognizes that differences of perspective can only be effectively addressed if such viewpoints are respected while simultaneously

their partisans have the frameworks within which they can actually speak to and come to know one another.[3]

Transcommunality is not a utopian abstraction if by "utopia" we mean that which does not exist.[4] Transcommunal cooperation is both an historic reality and a living mode. In my own involvement with community organizations around the United States, such as the California-based Barrios Unidos, Stop the Violence/Increase the Peace, and the Milagros Education Project, I see activists who work cooperatively across "race," "ethnic," and other lines to negotiate peace and nonviolence with youth in the street. In 1993 at the National Gang Peace Summit held in Kansas City, I saw hundreds of young women and men from rival street organizations around the country, where many different African American, Latino, Native American, and white communities work together for an end to violence. Today there are thousands of examples of such transcommunal action among a wide variety of groups worldwide. Such efforts are just part of a widening set of overlapping constellations of wide varieties of activists, organizations, and institutions—all rooted in and proud of their particular affiliations while also being able to reach out to others. My offering here is to illuminate this transcommunal way of thinking and acting.

Given the heterogeneity of organizing actions around the world, the question before us is no longer Lenin's famous Vanguard party slogan, "What is to be done?" with its implication that some one group or person must develop THE answer. Rather, in an environment of multifaceted modes of action, we are now faced with the different question of "What is being done?" This question implies multiple answers, all being worked out in diverse settings that are being impacted in many ways by powerful globalizing forces. So a different line of inquiry immediately develops. "What is being done, and how?" How can we enhance cooperation among diverse peoples struggling for justice and freedom in a wide variety of ways and situations? Transcommunality, rather than bypassing or obliterating multiplicity, offers a conceptual framework that opens up ways of cooperation and communication among diverse approaches and ways of thought.

2

Red Clay, Blue Hills

In Honor of My Ancestors

> In every place visited among the Sakalava we found
> events and names recalled by tradition still living in
> memory . . . we have heard the Sakalava invoke these
> names in all important activities of their social life and
> recall with pride these events.
>
> —Charles Guillain (1845)
> on the cultures of Madagascar

BEFORE PROCEEDING with this discussion of transcommunality, I will speak about my ancestors. It is from them that I have received the desire to contribute to the best of my ability to what I hope is constructive cooperation leading to justice, equality, and peace in the world. I owe it to them to make these comments. That which I say in these pages flows from two great currents, the African and the Native American, whose conflux runs through my family and infuses my spirit today. In 1992, when my wife, my mother, and I went to visit my family in Marion, Alabama, my cousin Arthur Childs, who had served as a lieutenant in World War II in Burma and who was family story-teller, took us immediately to the cemetery, where in the midst of red clay dust he told us the histories of those who had passed on.

My great-great-great-great-great-great-grandmother known as "the Princess" to her captors, was born in Madagascar, the large island nation peopled by populations from the Pacific and Africa. As detailed in Horace Mann Bond's book *Black American Scholars*, around 1748 the Princess, a member of the Madagascan royal family, was on board a French ship bound for France, where she apparently was to be educated in a convent school. Their ship was captured by privateers from the English American colonies. My ancestress found herself in chains in Philadelphia, from where she was sold into slavery in Virginia in 1749. She later became the "property" of Thomas Burke who moved from Virginia to Hillsboro, North Carolina, where he became governor during the War for Independence. Beginning in 1835 most of the descendants of the Princess established their families in the red clay country of Marion, in Perry County, Alabama, where they were moved when their owning white families left North Carolina for Alabama (Bond, 1972, 36). The history handed down within both the Burke family and my family is that when "the 'Princess' was brought first to Virginia where she began her career as a slave, the other slaves acknowledged her royal origin and gave her the respectful homage due to one of her background" (Bond, 1972, 35).

After Emancipation, my father's forebears, Stephen Childs and family, created the "Childs Bakers and Confectioners, Growers, and Shippers" store on Main Street in Marion. This store became an important part of the African American community there. My father, born in the midst of what had been a core slave-holding region, was named after John Brown, the revolutionary fighter who gave his life in the battle against slavery.

Marion is where in 1867 my relatives, James Childs and Alexander H. Curtis, along with seven other Black men, founded the first African American school in that area, the Lincoln Normal School. This school provided a crucial foundation for African American educational and community development that had impact beyond Perry County and Alabama. The Lincoln Normal School's purpose according to its African American founders was "to afford the means of education to the largest practicable number of applicants, preference being given to those preparing to teach" (Childs, 1991, 29). Because of the denial of effective educational facilities to African Americans, the founders of Lincoln Normal invited white, former anti-slavery activists from the Congregational Church's American Missionary Association to be the initial teachers at Lincoln Normal (ibid., 29–30, and Bond, 1972, 40–41). These teachers were housed in a building that had originally been a headquarters of the local Ku Klux Klan.

The school, as Bond points out, provided a *"complete* social and moral as well as educational community" (1972, 40). Among the original aspects of that community were textbooks praising the war against slavery and such abolitionist activists as Frederick Douglas. Bond says the school's "Northern textbooks, including 'Union' songs and anti-slavery poems, and readings and declamations extolling the heroes of the anti-slavery movement, did not endear the institution to the local whites. . . . Poems by Whittier and orations repeated from Charles Sumner and Frederick Douglas, and songs such as 'The Battle Hymn of the Republic' . . . taught a kind of history that must have been unpalatable to the local attitudes" (ibid., 41).

Lincoln Normal went on to become an influential African American educational institution. Of the importance of the school, Bond observed that "when we note Perry County, Alabama—that from statistics of illiteracy of the population, of farm tenancy among the Negroes, and of abysmally low per capita public school expenditures for the Negro population . . . the conclusion is inescapable, that doctorates emerged from such areas because of the intervention of such 'mission' schools as the Lincoln Normal School" (Bond, 1972, 97–98). Among my relatives influenced by Lincoln Normal through his mother Roberta Childs Hastie, who graduated from there, was Judge William Henry Hastie (Sc.J.D., Harvard), the civil rights advocate and Howard University law school professor. Hastie became the first African American federal circuit court of appeals judge in U.S. history in 1937. In 1932 he had joined what came to be called President Roosevelt's "Black Cabinet" of African American advisors on New Deal issues. Judge Hastie also served as a civilian aide to the secretary of war. He resigned that position in 1943 to protest racial segregation in the military and continued to be an important voice for civil rights.

In his overview of the effect of Lincoln Normal on successive generations, Horace Mann Bond called it "the best predominately Negro secondary school this country has ever known" (1972, 42).

In the midst of Ku Klux Klan terrorism country, my Childs family relations, along with other African Americans in Marion, worked to create Lincoln Normal School as a sustaining community despite a dangerous, often lethal environment of racial oppression. They sought to use their roots in the rural and small-town deep South as a basis for construction of a bastion of justice and dignity.

I was born in 1942, in Boston, Massachusetts, in the Roxbury area. As a small child I lived in a housing project called Bataan Court. My Roxbury birthplace is only a few miles north of a state recreational park in the Blue Hills. There in the Blue Hills is a body of water called by its Native American name of Punkapoag, which means the "Place of the Fresh Water Pond." Punkapoag is where some of my mother's Native American ancestors once lived. My relations were members of the Algonkian Confederacy known as the Massachusett, or to be more precise "Massachu- sêuck," which means "The Place of the Big Hills." The Massa- chusett nation was an egalitarian confederacy comprising several communities such as the Punkapoag, the Nipmuck, the Nepon- set, and the Wesaguset.[1]

Neighbors of the Wampanoag, these ancestors of mine encoun- tered Europeans under the command of Giovani de Verrazano in 1524. Verrazano described the Massachusett as a "most beautiful" people who were "sweet and gentle, very like the manner of the ancients." They were, he observed, expert sailors who can "go to sea without any danger," in boats made "with admirable skill" (Brasser, 1978, 78). Almost one hundred years later, in 1614, Cap- tain John Smith described their land as "the paradice of all these parts" (Salwen, 1978, 170). This "paradice" was soon decimated by the wave of epidemics that ravaged many of the New England Indigenous peoples as larger ships carrying more Europeans brought diseases such as smallpox, to which Native peoples had no immunity. Importantly, the elders and the children were most vulnerable. The loss of their lives destroyed the capacity of many nations to continue. The Massachusett people were particularly hard hit this way. Their population plummeted from an estimated 30,000 to a mere few hundred by the mid 1650s. By that time, the surviving members of those nations that had been decimated were forcibly concentrated into small villages called "Praying Towns," where they were supposed to adapt to and adopt Christianity. One of these towns was Punkapoag. In Punkapoag, the Native peoples worked to establish a sanctuary from the pressures around them. But whether by force or inclination, the conversion to Christianity of these Native peoples offered virtually no protection from the anti-Indian waves of racism and hysteria among whites.

Many of the Praying Town inhabitants, the so-called "Praying Indians," although they provided men to serve in colonial militias (against the French), were attacked, dispersed, and killed by their English neighbors. For those who survived, and for their descendants, such atrocities clearly drew the final bloody message that their ancient homelands were no longer the richly textured environments of deeply rooted free life but had to a large degree become the places of tears. Many Narragansett, Pequod, Mohegan, Massachusett, and others were now exiles. Once a coherent cultural entity, the Punkapoag community of the Massachusett confederacy, with its members forced into exile, and finding intermarriage with other peoples the only means to survival, ceased to exist as a social whole.

Responding to long decades of cultural erosion and terrorism directed against them, a gathering of Christian Native peoples, including some of my ancestors, under the leadership of Rev. Samson Occom, a Mohegan man and a Presbyterian minister who had struggled against great odds to attain his "calling," sought and were generously given land by the Oneida nation in what is now New York State. In 1774 they were adopted as "the younger brothers and sisters" of the Oneida in a ceremony at Johnson Hall in upper New York State. A Wampum belt commemorating this event unfortunately is now lost. The Oneida are one of the five original nations of the Haudenosaunee or "Iroquois" Confederacy, of which we will hear more later. In upstate New York, south of Lake Oneida, Rev. Occom and his followers created the settlement of "Brothertown" that they hoped would allow them to (re)create a homeland free from subjugation. Brothertown, also known by its Algonkian name of *Eyamquittoowauconnuck* ("The Place of Equal People"), and its nearby Mahican counterpart of New Stockbridge were in effect the first in a long line of visionary "utopian communities" in upper New York State, although these Native American antecedents to that later nineteenth-century white cultural movement are not usually credited as such.

My Native American ancestors, whose family name had become "Burr," intermarried with the Oneida. Eventually in the early 1800s, they moved back to their ancestral homeland of Massachusetts.[2] Eli and Saloma Burr, my great, great, great grandfather and grandmother, settled in the western part of Massachusetts near Springfield. Eli and Saloma, and their children Vianna, Fidelia, Alonzo, and Albert, are listed in the 1868 Massachusetts State "Indian" census as Oneida people. Eli's grandfather had been an "Oneida chief," according to these state records. Eli and Saloma's children married African Americans. One of the grandchildren, James Burr, became well-known as an African American inventor.

A 1915 obituary in the Massachusetts *Springfield Republican* noting the death of one of their grandsons, John Burr, contains information that could have only come from the Burrs, namely, that his ancestors were originally from "Ponkapog," Massachusetts, and that they had been adopted by the Oneida in the 1700s. So, well over one hundred years after their ancestors had left New England for the Oneida sanctuary of Brothertown, the Burrs still carried the memories both of their Massachusett origins and of the importance of their adoptive Oneida homeland.

From these currents of Massachusêuck, Brothertown, Oneida, and Africa came my mother, Dorothy Pettyjohn, who was born in Amherst, Massachusetts, and became a teacher. As a young woman in the 1930s, she went to "Cotton Valley" in Alabama to teach in a school for impoverished, rural, African American children, not far from Marion and its Lincoln Normal School. It was there that she met and married my father. So the waves of oppression crashing over many peoples, driven from their land, forged them into complex syntheses of memory and belonging that link Africa and Native America for me.[3]

In 1835, Alexis de Tocqueville's soon to be famous, vast overview of the young United States, *Democracy in America*, was published. Among his otherwise astute descriptions based on his travels in "America," de Tocqueville inaccurately pictures what he calls "the three races of the United States." These are, he says, "the white or European, the Negro, and the Indian," which he claims are always distinctly separate populations. Concerning "the Negro" and "the Indian," he writes that these "two unhappy races have nothing in common, neither birth, nor features, nor language, nor habits" (1960, 343).

If this assertion by de Tocqueville were true, then I could not exist, given my African and Native American currents that have flowed together. My family relations cannot be compartmentalized into these rigid, sealed-off categories suggested by de Tocqueville. Nor can the depths of their courage be plumbed by his superficial description of the "unhappy races," no matter how terrible their tribulations as they have flowed through so many valleys of oppression. Today I recognize that from Punkapoag in Massachusetts, and Brothertown in New York State, to Lincoln Normal School in Alabama, my relations were among those establishing roots in what they hoped would be sustaining communities that could buffer people against the forces of hatred, while offering solid ground for justice and dignity. I know that my connection to my ancestors is not only genealogical, as important as that is. My connection to them is also that of the spirit. I have for many years worked alongside those trying to create places of freedom from injustice. I continue to do so today, both in my community work and in the development of the concept of transcommunality. I now understand, after years of my own internal development, with guidance from elders and friends, that this work of mine is propelled by those currents flowing from the springing hopes of my ancestors.

I do not feel like one of those "crossing border hybrids" now so much discussed by scholars who examine postmodernity. Nor does the older Latin American term "Zambo," for "half black/half Indian," describe how I know myself. It is not in such a divided fashion that I recognize my existence. To the contrary, in the language of my Algonkian ancestors, *Noh Neen*—I am a man—who stands at *newichewannock*—"the place between two strong currents." Without these two distinct streams there can be no such in-between place. But this place is real and complete unto itself. In the same way, I emerge a full man, not a simple bifurcated halfling, from the two strong currents of Africa and Native America. It is this *newichewannock* that marks the place of my spirit, and that propels me today.[4]

3

Emplacements of Affiliation

Emplacements of Affiliation and Their Linkages

TRANSCOMMUNAL COOPERATION emphasizes coordinated heterogeneity across "identity lines"—not only of "ethnicity," "race," "class," and "gender," but also of organizationally, philosophically, and cosmologically diverse settings. Transcommunality entails a changed way of thinking, a paradigm shift or, to use the Andean Indigenous terminology, *Pachakuteq*, "a change of direction" (Delgado, 1994, 1). Transcommunality moves beyond the classic Eurocentric, progressive emphasis on homogenizing unity based on the leadership of a "vanguard party," while also escaping from aimless ever-splintering relativism of the postmodern perceptions of diversity and multiculturalism. As Gilles Deleuze says, in another context, it is not enough to say "Long live the multiple" (1993a, 29).

There is no doubt as to the tremendous discipline and courage that many vanguard groups have maintained in the face of often brutal and overwhelming odds. However, much Euro-based progressive political thought is impressed with the seal of the tradition of conversion of one's neighbors to one's own particular perspective, generally viewed as the only accurate position. This approach involves, as Gemma Corradi Fiumara says, the "illusion that we can speak to others without being able to listen" (1990, 29). Important parts of Marxist practice, for all its heroic and courageous developments, are heirs to the politics of conversion, and this should be addressed directly. Conversionary politics requires its adherents to assert a distinct set of beliefs to which others, if they are to be partners in the struggle for justice, must convert. By contrast, transcommunality emphasizes a general ethics of respect in which mutual recognition and acceptance of diverse, even divergent perspectives occur among partners. Transcommunality sees distinct group locations with their often clear-cut boundaries and well-developed internal senses of communal integrity as essential. It is precisely from these clearly defined, rooted locations that diverse communities can reach out to one another, creating constellations of cooperation that reinforce rather than undermine a positively interactive heterogeneity.[1]

These ethics of respect can lead to some transformation of interacting participants as they learn more about one another. However, this transformation is not a one-sided conversion to a single perspective, but rather involves an opening up to shared understandings. My development of the concept of transcommunality, drawing in large part from many Indigenous models of alliances in the Americas, offers a flexible approach in which the autonomy of cooperating participants rather than uniformity is key. This transcommunal approach entails a *Pachakuteq*-like "change of direction" as described by Guillermo Delgado, from a lineal worldview in which one group presumes to lead the rest along a single path, to a more circular orientation in which there are many different angles of approach, all of which can lead to the same central position but all of which have their own distinct locations.[2]

Consequently, for transcommunal activists, diversity need not be a barrier to cooperation. Rather, diversity is absolutely essential for any effectively coordinated multitude of positions. As John Calmore points out, "in a multicultural society ... justice will develop from the diverse views" of those in different arenas of struggle (1995, 1233). Once this premise is accepted, a key issue becomes that of developing a framework within which diverse activists in multiple positions can work together without losing the unique essence of their being that is crucial to their strength, which itself is necessary in order for them to be effective as bridges to one another. Transcommunality offers such a framework. Transcommunality is a method that incorporates fusion and fission, structure and fluidity. It allows for a high degree of diversity, autonomy, *and* coordination of its participants. This coordination involves a particular form of dialogue similar to that described by Tzvetan Todorov, which is "animated by the idea of a possible progression in the discussion." Such dialogue, says Todorov, "does not consist in the juxtaposition of several voices but in their interaction" (1993, 52). In parallel, bell hooks describes the essential equality of a dialogue that "implies talk between two subjects, not the speech of subject and object. It is a humanizing speech, one that challenges and resists domination" (1989, 131).

Transcommunality does not negate the communities and perspectives from which interacting participants emerge. Rather, it involves a form of responsiveness in which the participants' mutual awareness of each other is enhanced and modified. Such interaction is similar to that dialogue described by Patricia Hill Collins in which "everyone has a voice, but everyone must listen and respond to other voices in order to be allowed to remain in the community." Collins asserts that sharing "a common cause fosters dialogue and encourages groups to transcend their differences" (1990, 236–237). Similarly, transcommunality entails a process of self-transformation among its participants as they interact and communicate with one another.

But transcommunality is not only "dialogic" in the sense of speaking and listening, as important as they are. Transcommunality also entails constant learning through continuous interaction of diverse participants, which in turn builds mutual trust and understanding, both as to what kinds of relations are possible, but also as to what kinds of relations are not possible.[3] Such progressive transformation of distinct, interacting participants in common projects does not require a melting-pot's boiling-down of distinctions into a single homogenized whole. *Mutual learning and transformation are only possible precisely because there really are different vantage points based on distinctive experiences.* As Mikhail Bakhtin points out, none of us can engage in such a pure empathy with another that we lose our own identities in the process. Bakhtin says, "If I actually lost myself in the other instead of two participants there would be one." This would be an "impoverishment of being" (1993, 16).

In contrast to such "impoverishment," transcommunality offers an *enrichment* of social being through its emphasis on autonomous participants whose interaction reaffirms their sense of distinctive, rooted affiliations while also nourishing shared identity among them.[4] The glue holding these transcommunal ties together is that of face-to-face interpersonal relationships of mutual trust, built up through *shared practical action,* in which people from what I call different *emplacements of affiliation* can work together around shared tasks and objectives.

The open, inclusionary approach of transcommunality emphasizes the creation of shared structures and outlooks through negotiations among diverse participants, rather than being a priori and imposed from one source. Different activists, rooted in their own distinctive community and institutional settings, form the foundations for interaction. The solid ground of cultural, social, philosophical, and organizational affiliations allows for transcommunal bridges to be built. Martin Luther King Jr. proposed such transcommunal outlooks in his book *Where Do We Go From Here: Chaos or Community.* King asserted the necessity of an African American people who would "be mindful of enlarging the whole society." He argued that "we must not overlook the fact that millions of Puerto Ricans, Mexican Americans, Indians and Appalachian whites are also poverty-stricken. Any serious war against poverty must of necessity include them" (1967, 156).

King was moving toward addressing the lack of positive relationship among racial/ethnic groups, which is a historically important dilemma for those working on the creation of cooperation. The interaction of many racial/ethnic groups is often limited at best and hostile at worst. For those trying to organize inter-racial/ethnic cooperation, the decades of inequality, oppression, and the corrosive influence of authoritarian divide-and-rule strategies create tremendous difficulties in shaping positive interaction.

However, there is another equally significant area of concern for those seeking to act transcommunally. This involves gaps among fundamentally distinct emplacements of affiliation. An *emplacement* is a site of collective life shared by a group of people that provides them with a rooted and demarcated sense of shared perspective and affiliation. An emplacement may be geographically located (or from the point of view of some communities, spiritually located in a particular geographical setting). Or an emplacement may involve dispersed members who nonetheless feel solid commonality based on "sites" defined in terms of religious, ideological, philosophical sets of shared beliefs, values, and objectives. Such affiliations are not exactly "identities." In fact, that term, as in "identity politics" carries with it too much psychological baggage. For example, "multiple identities" rings of mental disorder. However, "multiple affiliations" comes more easily to the lips insofar as people can have such pluralistic affiliations, perhaps arranged in rank order of significance or perhaps arranged equally. So emplacements of affiliation are places and organizational environments of belonging that are experientially fundamentally significant to those involved and which may or may not involve some degree of exclusivity vis-à-vis other affiliations.

"Emplacement" means of course "place" and "placing" of something or someone in a given location, and implies a fortification, a defensive position. The reality of human society and history is not only that we live in places or have memory of significant places. Most of those places are also in some way "fortified." By fortified, I do not necessarily mean by weapons (although that can be the case). Rather I mean the fortifications of distinctive group symbols, ceremonies, holi(holy)days, food, clothing, music, jokes. These symbol-walled hill forts constitute most communal identities. There are the fences (perhaps, to use the phrase in

Robert Frost's poem, "good fences" under some circumstances) that constitute a key part of human life. Such "fortified" emplacements are not necessarily aggressive, nor must they be hostile toward those outside the fencing (although such hostility obviously can and does happen). But those within such settings clearly mark off certain moments and spaces as their own that others either cannot enter, or can enter only with permission or at certain times. Useful to note is that the equivalent Spanish term *emplazamiento* also can mean a summons—a call to the plaza, the place. In this communicative sense of calling people together, "emplacement" also is of value to any discussion of cooperation and communication.

Thinking transcommunally requires a pragmatic recognition of this fundamental fortified-place aspect of human communal existence. *Places* and the consciousness attached to them are, as Arif Dirlik says, "integral to the human experience" (2001, 15). He adds that such places are not simply locations/moments but are constantly produced by human activity. As Dirlik emphasizes, we must work with this basic reality. We do not need to try to wish it away in order to talk about the relationship between pluralism and cooperation. That wishful route leads, at its worst, toward obliterative state policies aimed at crushing distinctive cultures and communities in the name of unity. By contrast, transcommunal action draws from the strength of many such pluralistic and distinctive fortified places rather than trying to bypass or evaporate them. This drawing from multiple emplacements of affiliation gives transcommunality its practical rather than simply utopian dimension, and its embracing outlook rather than a closed-fist, dogmatic, conversionary perspective.

Certainly, emplacements of affiliation are significant in part because each has its own distinct "rules of the game" and its unique goals, methods, and outlooks. For example, those who work on issues such as violence against women, child labor, or environmental destruction can be said to have distinctive organizational/goal-oriented/philosophical emplacements of affiliation. Those working from left and labor perspectives of necessity have as a central organizing worldview the significance of class in general and of working-class status in particular. When they wrestle with the questions of bringing members of different racial/ethnic groups together, it is primarily within the context of their "working-class identity" vis-à-vis the owners of the means of production. So we can imagine a multiracial, labor-oriented emplacement in which organizers have managed to bring together Latinos, African Americans, and Asian Americans. But such organizing is reasonably premised on the basis that all those involved in the particular alliance are essentially workers who face the same fundamental conditions in the workplace and confront the same companies. For example, efforts by the United Electrical Workers to build bridges between U.S. (Anglo, African American, and Latino) workers and their colleagues in Mexico are now underway since the implementation of the North American Free Trade Agreement in 1994. The key unifying feature is their shared status as electrical workers, employed at the same company, General Electric. Basic objectives, essential worker outlooks, and similar conditions (albeit with different wage structures and work conditions north and south of the border) characterize this situate form of organizing.

However, there are other significant emplacements energized by very different concerns. In a multitude of such settings, other objectives, outlooks, and ways of life are often importantly different from those of the labor activists. As the Gramscian scholar Renate Holub points out: "The working class . . . no longer seems to constitute the backbone of the present nation-state. . . . Impulses for radical democratic politics will, therefore, no longer emanate from the working class . . . but from the formation of new social and cultural groups that pursue various liberatory and emancipatory agendas" (1992, 175–176). I basically agree with my friend Renate Holub but must add that an important portion of what she calls the "impulses for radical democratic politics" are not completely "new." Rather, many such impulses are rooted in ancient traditions. I am thinking here in particular of many forms of Indigenous activism around the world as but one of such rooted "impulses" for freedom.

Indigenous Activism

> Thomas thought about all the dreams that were murdered here,
> and the bones buried quickly just below the surface.
> —Sherman Alexie, *Reservation Blues* (1995, 7)

Many Indigenous[5] activists from the Arctic to Argentina, and across
the Pacific into Asia and Africa, emphasize not "class" and "individual human rights" as central issues, but focus instead on *community-based* land and on *free determination* to decide whether and
to what degree integration and separation from the nation-state
should take place. They focus as well on spiritual power.[6] The land,
which is ancestral, is a place of spiritual strength and renewal and
cannot be viewed from such perspectives as just a material object.
A sense of spiritual infusion alongside genealogical rootedness in
a particular place, combined with a deep concern for autonomy
or sovereignty, becomes more salient than "class" in such settings.
To be more exact, the very distinction between "spiritual" and
"material" does not apply to many such outlooks. Rather, these
dimensions are fused in complex and fluid ways.[7] Moreover, an
intense concern for sovereignty of Indigenous cultures at one level
is quite the opposite of the globalistic views of many leftists and
environmentalists who often critique sovereignty and "identity politics" as a source of chauvinism and a barrier to cooperation. By
contrast, for many Indigenous communities and peoples we might
say that "cultural justice" rather than the more commonly used
term "social justice" would be more accurate as the rallying cry.
These distinctive Indigenous outlooks must be recognized if we are
to organize shared frameworks between labor and those who are
struggling for sovereignty of their ancestral territory.

Often, many urban left and labor activists, already struggling
to make some significant contributions to the relationship
between categories of "worker," "ethnicity," and "race," are generally oblivious to the significance of these communities, their
traditions, and the dilemmas which they face. Guillermo Delgado,
writing about Indigenous community activism in Latin America,
observes that many leftist "popular" movements emphasize the

centrality of the urban/working class, but often marginalize and miss the salience that land, autonomy, dignity, and spiritual perspectives can have for many Native peoples: "From an Indigenous point of reference, Indigenous peoples' histories remain colonial when reduced to class. Class is not everything. . . . Indigenous histories are not just about exclusion; above all they are about land" (1994, 6).[8]

Many Indigenous scholars also point to the significance of spiritually and kinship infused understandings that are quite different from western economic-materialistic models of human society and "nature." As Jack Forbes informs us, there is a "closeness of Native Americans to the natural world and to animal life." This closeness, he says, is not just one of an individualistic experience but also involves "good acts" that involve the well-being of others (1992, 29 and 155). Rebecca Adamson, president and founder of the First Nations Development Institute, observes: "The indigenous understanding has its basis in spirituality, in a recognition of the interconnectedness and interdependence of all living things. . . . The 'environment' is perceived as a sensate, conscious entity suffused with spiritual powers through which the human understanding is only realized in perfect humility before the sacred whole" (1996, 64).

Similarly, the Indigenous emphasis on ancestral space is clear in Hawaiian sovereignty activist Haunani-Kay Trask's observation that "In our genealogy, Papahanaumoku—earth mother—mated with Wekea—sky father—from whence came our islands, or *moku*. Out of our beloved islands came the taro, our immediate progenitor, and from the taro our chiefs and peoples." Consequently, "Our relationship to the cosmos" is "familial," Trask says: "If we husband our lands and waters, they will feed and care for us. In our language, the name for this relationship is malam 'aina: care for the land who will care for all family members in turn" (1993, 82–83).

In parallel fashion, Mapuche leader Aucan Huilcaman notes that in Chile, their Indigenous conception of land is "connected in a substantial manner with being human and with our own

nature. Our conception of territory is a physical space where the
Mapuche people should have control, planning power, and autonomy to exercise free self-determination" (1994, 18). Winona
LaDuke, president of the Indigenous Women's Network, emphasizes the importance of land and communal self-determination
when she writes:

> Today native people have four percent of their original land base
> and on our lands we have two-thirds of the uranium resources in
> the United States and one-third of the western low sulfur coal
> resources. We also have vast oil reserves in our territories, for
> example, the Arctic National Wildlife Refuge and the Gwich'in
> Territory in Alaska. Obviously, in the case of the dams we have
> vast water resources on our lands. The implications in an era of
> energy junkies, in a society that consumes way beyond its capac-
> ity, are devastating for our communities. (1991, 17)

Matthew Coon-Come, Grand Chief of the Grand Council of
the Cree of Québec, pointed to the close connections of his people with the land in a forum on environmental destruction: "I am
here with others from my area. Our people from Whapmagoos-
tui, Waswanipi, and Waskaganish are hunters and trappers, people who really live off the land. I am only one among many who
believe in speaking for Mother Earth, for who can speak better
than the ones who have lived with the animals and been tied to
the land?" (1991, 7). In the report *Status and Rights of the James Bay
Cree*, Coon-Come emphasizes the way in which these fundamental perspectives on territory are so crucial "to the right of self-
determination." The nation-states of the western hemisphere, he
says, "have denied our rights, denied even that we have these
rights, denied that we are peoples who posses the right of self-
determination" (Grand Council of the Cree, 1994, 33).

In Australia, Gordon Pablo, elder and spokesperson of the
Wuthathi People, says: "People think that we want money, that
we want compensation or royalties. *We want the land only.* . . . If
these developments do go ahead, it will break the heart of we traditional people because the land is our mother. . . . I said to Mrs.
Warner, Minister for Aboriginal Affairs, 'How would you feel if

someone chopped up your mother in front of you?'" Also for Pablo, as is not uncommon with many Native peoples, maintenance of language and culture is fundamental to the protection of the land: "I bin thinking about my people at Injinoo, especially about the younger ones. They seem to have lost the language and culture. That is why I made up my mind to come back to my hometown where I bin born. I am now Language Co-ordinator at Injinoo....My aim is to record all this Wuthathi language before it is lost" (1992, 99–100, 106).

The artist Thancoupie, from Far North Queensland, Australia, similarly describes herself in terms of intense relationship with the land, which in turn is directly entwined with her culture: "My art and my politics interlock.... My designs are from this country, from this land, and that's political. I've used my foot in my designs, and my foot rests firmly on this ground, and my clay is made from this soil, and the Aboriginal struggle for this soil, this ground, this country—so that's political. I record the law and culture of my people in my art—law and culture that existed long before other people came to this country carrying their guns and their Bibles" (1993, 136).

As Inés Hernández-Avila, of the University of California, Native American Studies program, points out: "The removal and attempted alienation of Native peoples from their ancestral land bases by government forces almost always ensures cultural genocide. The land bases give form and sustenance to Native cultures; the ceremonial, spiritual life of any Native culture is guided intimately by the land base as teacher as well as provider" (1996, 336).

For many Indigenous communities, albeit in highly varied ways and diverse contexts that demonstrate their complex heterogeneity and distinct locations and histories, there are strong connecting threads of concern and outlook that emphasize the struggle for spiritually infused land, and communal self-determination as an ever tangible and fundamental fact of life. This core orientation is often dangerously misunderstood by many predominately white progressives, for whom ethnic / cultural identity often is perceived as a "backward" barrier to working-class unity, which

is asserted to be *the* primary engine of "progress." Of course both
the assertion of the centrality of the (primarily European/North
American) industrial working class and the acceptance of the concept of "progress" are questionable from many Indigenous viewpoints. As Winona LaDuke says: "I consider myself a conservative. I think that most Native people are very conservative, and
their conservatism comes from their perception that the immen-
sity of cultural, technological, social, and ecological change that
has occurred in the last 50 years is not conservative at all! It is
entirely radical and frightening" (1998, 74).[9]

Importantly, LaDuke's self-description of "conservative" clearly
cannot be reduced to a simple position along the usual "left to
right" spectrum. I hear in her use of that term a conservatism that
flows from people's history and lives and which is neither left nor
right. Kinship with those gone before infuses this usage. Growing
out of this emphasis on kinship is a concern for future generations, and for the well-being of the earth on which they must live.
This future-oriented conservatism that is resistant to global
destruction makes tradition a vital element. Robert Warrior suggests that "Traditions make the future a possibility, just as they did
for the people with whom the traditions originated" (1995, 106).
For such Indigenous perspectives, tradition can be a foundation
for the future. As Denis-Constant Martin observes, in many settings tradition is active and alive. Tradition, he says, "transforms
itself without ceasing. . . . In this sense, tradition consists of inno-
vations that are rooted in a specific terrain . . . that is produced by
tradition itself" (1992, 18 [my translation]).

By contrast, for much western-originated progressive thought,
the move toward the future has often required a dramatic break
with the traditional or "backward" past.[10] From the Jacobins of the
French Revolution, with their creation of a new calendar starting
from "Year One" to the Soviet "New Man" and "New Woman,"
the past is perceived as a dead weight to be discarded. Obviously,
arguments can be made for such perspectives; consider the bar-
barity of slavery and servitude that can hardly be justified in the
name of "tradition." The "traditional" in some generalized abso-

lute abstract sense is not sacrosanct, static, and perfect.[11] By the same token, programs that seek to totally destroy the past in the name of constructing a perfect future are hardly beyond reproach, as twentieth-century history with its Hitlers and Stalins instructs us. From a transcommunal perspective, the task is not for one group or person to say which vantage point is more "accurate" in an abstract universalistic sense, but rather to determine how partisans of such fundamentally distinct outlooks can work together in mutual respect.

For many on the left, the Indigenous emphasis on tradition may seem "conservative" in a negative sense of being on the "right-wing end" of the political spectrum. By contrast, those Indigenous views that emphasize conserving culture and tradition can often be seen as efforts to accentuate that which is *central* to a people, rather than being on the end of a political spectrum. For many Indigenous activists the conceptual framework is circular and three dimensional rather than having the linear restrictions of "the political spectrum." From this perspective, the center is a spiritual-cultural point of reference. It is a doorway open to all directions, north to south, east to west, and down into the earth as well as up to the heavens, so anchoring a wide variety of ways of being. In short, there are cosmological, or if you wish, paradigmatic differences between these more circular Indigenous outlooks and those that employ the lineal spectrum running from left to right as a description of the world.

Far from "backward," the resistance potential of such tradition-oriented thinking is, as Maivăn Clech Lăm points out, an important dimension of the global struggle for justice. Lam notes that much Indigenous activism has had "remarkable" success in precisely the areas of struggle considered by many within classic Marxism as secondary or "superstructural," namely the cultural, the legal, and the spiritual: "Columbus has been debunked; the world has suddenly learned that not all indigenous peoples are dead, that many in fact are actively seeking the restoration of lands and resources. . . . Finally, indigenous peoples have also conspicuously participated in, and often led, global countercultural campaigns against consumerism, particularly of the kind that directly implicate the resources of their homelands" (1996, 261).

Similarly, Stefano Varese points out that the underlying impetus of Indigenous movements for self-determination, communal land, and continuity with the past of the ancestors directs a radical impulse at the very nation-state elites now carrying out the bidding of global economic syndicates. Varese writes: "The project of Indian liberation movements . . . clearly calls for the subversion and radical reorganization of the 'national' spaces, the total recuperation of the interrupted history, the 're-Indianization' of vast sectors of the population of the continent, and the unity of the continental Indian population." All of this "radical" project, which is concomitantly "conservative" and "traditional," involves, says Varese, "Recognizing multiplicity as the framework of knowledge and of existence and the interaction of differences as the only appropriate environment for the construction of civilization" (1982, 40).

In our terms here, such an emphasis on *interactive* multiplicity is transcommunal and stands opposed to smothering globalizing homogeneity of the powerful, as well as to the disintegrative fragmentation of meandering intellectualistic approaches to "diversity." As we can see from LaDuke, Warrior, and Varese, such Indigenous emphases on multiplicity can incorporate the conservative and the radical as well as the fluid and the structural. In many settings, the essential conceptual distance between such basic circular and lineal outlooks blunts the ability of many leftists to respect and appreciate the significance of such Indigenous outlooks and activisms. In one interview, Nilo Cayuqueo, Mapuche activist and organizer of the South and Meso-American Indian Information Center, points out that when Indigenous peoples cannot be placed along an anti- or pro-left spectrum, their own unique locations tend to be dismissed by the left. Cayuqueo says of the Mapuche activists: "We're not anticommunist, we're not anti-Marxist, or pro-Marxist. What we want is to be able to work together for our common interest, which is anti-imperialist. But [the left is] not willing to recognize the Indian people as being oppressed, they just see them as another social category. . . . What we have is a conception of the world that is completely different from the European conception. I am not saying that Indian societies are perfect, but our system or organization is humanistic" (1982, 101–102). From a similar angle, Guillermo Delgado argues that class-centric urban progressives in Latin America are often unable to grasp the significance of such perspectives and approaches among Indigenous peoples for self-determination. Consequently, he says, many such activists often tend to wrongly fault "the ethnic and autonomous movements for being separatist." Such viewpoints lead not to cooperation, says Delgado, but to repeated efforts on the part of some progressives to constrain expectations and hopes for Indigenous territorial autonomy (1994, 6).

Concurrently, Atencío Lopez, secretary of the Kunas Unidos por Napguana in Nicaragua, says, "The struggle of Indigenous peoples . . . has always been obscured by non-Indigenous political groups, especially by guerrilla movements that have swept it under their ideological class struggle" (1994, 21). Ward Churchill's overall assessment of this issue is that Marxism "in its present form at least, offers us far worse than nothing. With friends such as these we are truly doomed." Churchill also points out that an "increasing number of thoughtful Marxists have broken with at least the worst of Marxian economism, determinism, and human chauvinism." Those who have done so, he says, "may possess the potential to forge mutually fruitful alliances with American Indians and other indigenous peoples." Churchill then raises the logical question of whether those who do so will be "viewed as Marxists any longer" (1996, 479). I concur with the importance of this question. But, as we shall see in the later discussion of elements of transcommunality such as autonomy, mutual respect, and transformation, I believe it is possible for those possessing quite different standpoints to work together for freedom and justice, defined not from one center, but from many angles of perspective.[12]

This gap between, on one side, many essentially secular progressive organizations whose affiliations are with an ideology of socialism and, on the other side, many spiritually infused and self-determination-oriented Indigenous communities is an important distinction that requires a respectful understanding of the differently rooted sites involved.[13] If any relationship is to exist across these very different arenas, this gap must be bridged in ways that allow for mutual respect of the different positions. To paraphrase Nilo Cayuqueo, we can all be against tyranny, but with a high degree of variation that can include some coming from Marxist and others from traditional outlooks. Respect is vital if the generally urbanized left is to link itself with the energetic grassroots networks of Indigenous activism that are, as Guillermo Delgado and Susan O'Donnell point out, "rekindling" the extensive "communication and trade links that existed in the Americas before the arrival of the Europeans" (1995, 35).

Interminglings of activists with roots in diverse emplacements can take place. But such interactions necessitate mutual respect among their participants. In turn, mutual respect requires that predominately white progressive forces discard their own colonial outlooks that often continue the marginalization of precisely those populations that face subjugation targeting their race/ethnicity/gender. Assuming such transformation, some degree of interaction among those opposed to tyranny is possible and can be significant. For example, in the late-twentieth century, the James Bay Cree nation mounted a highly successful campaign to fight the HydroQuébec dam project that would destroy their lands. The Grand Council of the Cree of Québec effectively enlisted an array of environmentalist organizations and other non-Indigenous allies in Canada and the United States. Simultaneously, the Cree people maintained their central position of shaping the content and direction of their struggle. The allies played useful but supporting and secondary roles under the direction of the Cree people (Tokar, 1995, 50).[14]

Another major example of an Indigenous movement that can address progressive allies through its critical analysis of the global economic system, while also being rooted in ancient culture and tradition, is the Mayan "Zapatista" liberation army or EZLN in

Chiapas, Mexico. The EZLN staunchly opposes the damaging impacts of global capitalism and its agencies of legitimization such as the North American Free Trade Agreement and the International Monetary Fund. Simultaneously, the EZLN is rooted in centuries of Mayan distinctiveness and resistance to oppression. Consequently, the EZLN cannot be reductively described as a "leftist movement." It is an Indigenous movement. Yet, in its resistance to global capitalism, the EZLN is an important example of how a political-economic analysis of the global economy that is congruent with basic left tenets can entwine with an Indigenous emphasis on sovereignty, culture, and the spiritual. The movement in Chiapas, as Carlos Fuentes suggests, "speaks a language that is fresh, direct, post-Communist" even as it draws from Indigenous communities that for centuries "have shown themselves to be true 'people of reason' who know how to govern themselves" (1997, 91).

Significantly from a transcommunal angle, the EZLN with its intermingled traditional / forward-looking orientation shows itself willing to reach out to supporters around the world, while doing so on its own terms. Such reaching out allows for "outsider" support that does not interfere with the internal developments of movements such as the EZLN. In true transcommunal form, the EZLN draws from its Mayan roots, while also embracing a widely inclusionary and outgoing constellation of supporters. As spokesperson Subcommandante Marcos pointed out about the Zapatista outreach, "We have helped create, at the side of men and women in the five continents, a great network . . . that is fighting to build a better world" (DePalma, 1998, 14).

Similarly, the Mapuche people of Chile in their important statement, the "Temuco-WallMapuche Declaration on the North American Free Trade Agreement, Indigenous Peoples, and Their Rights," analytically critique the "free trade" format as "serving to accumulate wealth for a small minority and to create poverty and exclusion for the great majority of Indigenous and non-Indigenous peoples." Moreover, the Mapuche activists see such so-called "free" trade as "a new form of expansion of colonialism and neocolonialism expressed in the economic sphere" (Aukin Wallmapu Ngulam, 1994, 1). Accordingly, the Mapuche reach out to a variety of groupings around the world, including predominately white environmentalists, nongovernmental organizations, and other social movements, as well as other Indigenous peoples. Their emphasis on the need for defense against globalizing capitalism and their reaching out to potential allies are simultaneously rooted in Indigenous foundations of Mapuche culture, history, land, and religion, and in the overall context of Indigenous realities. As Stefano Varese points out, such Indigenous emphases on land and freedom are directly related to resistance to globalized systems of power (1997, 19–35). Such relationships show the kinship of much Indigenous activism to what Gilles Deleuze calls modes of action/thought that can be both "archaic" and "up-to-date revolutionary" as they call into question "both the global economy of the machine and the assemblages of national states" (1993a, 256).

Indigenous Rooted Cosmopolitans

Cross-border outreachings by rooted Indigenous communities perform a transcommunal solution to the dualistic dilemma between local and global activism outlooks, described by Jonathan Friedman in his excellent overview of Indigenous organizing. Friedman accurately distinguishes between social justice–oriented, "cosmopolitan" leadership groups that seek to "reorganize the world," and more locally grounded Indigenous communities that resist the global power structure where it hits them. As Friedman notes, even such locally rooted places of resistance are being "globalized in channels of international political organization that have amplified their voice" (2001, 68). But given the world orientation and outreaching approach of many Indigenous activists such as the Cree, Mapuche, and EZLN, to name but a few, I would go farther than my colleague. These Indigenous organizations, with their confederacy-formatted intertwining of many different locations and levels, are capable of being cognizant of the world

structure and the necessity of transforming it, not simply resist-
ing it where they are. They can be rooted and cosmopolitan at the
same time.

The EZLN statement quoted above makes clear that they see
their Indigenous struggle not just as local but rather as also creating "a great network . . . that is fighting for a better world." This
kind of intermingling, as Arif Dirlik points out, entwines "globalization" and "localization." Such intertwining by community-
based movements is clearly an indication of complex transcommunal capabilities to interweave centuries-old Indigenous Mayan
self-determination struggles with today's globalized "cosmopolitan" issues (Dirlik, 2001).

Similarly, the 1992 Mapuche "Temuco-Wallmapuche Declaration" speaks to the threat to the world of "free trade" while also
being deeply concerned with Indigenous issues. This declaration
clearly takes the cosmopolitan concern with world restructuring
into the local and the local into the cosmopolitan in a supple and
significant way. The declaration states in part: "We invite the
organizations, movements, groups and ecological parties and
other political parties to continue strengthening their relations
with the Indigenous Peoples, in facing the continental and global
assault of neoliberalism, based on productive accumulation of
material, putting the future of humanity and the planet at risk"
(Aukin Wallmapu Ngulam, 1992, 4).

The Cree, Mapuche, and EZLN also illustrate one of the most
effective assets provided by reflective outside allies who recognize
the limitations and baggage of their position: they can make the
hidden visible. Such a productive opening up of the externally
enforced and debilitating isolation of community activists engaged
in direct localized (town, region, hamlet, forest) struggles can be
an important resource. To be forcibly isolated is to be ever more
vulnerable to an oppression that hides itself from the rest of the
world, thus increasing its strength.

From the Cree and the Mayan movements to the original
peoples of Australia, contacts with outside allies can blunt the
impact of at least some of the direct oppressive forces that they

face. Minimally they can make the news of killings, torture, and other atrocities visible beyond national borders and so place local elites in the uncomfortable position of responding to pressure from around the world. The struggle against apartheid in South Africa of necessity took its main form there. But that main struggle was clearly assisted, as Nelson Mandela noted after his release from prison, by secondary support around the world. Similarly, during some work I did in the U.S. Civil Rights Movement in Alabama in 1965, I was struck by the fact that the black people there did not need to be "organized." They already had organization of various kinds. What they did need were links to the outside world that could end their isolation, which left them at the mercy of an entire political/legal system that supported white terrorism of the Ku Klux Klan. By bringing the South, especially the rural areas, into the viewing range of the people of United States and the world, the Civil Rights Movement was able to make a local struggle into a globally linked one, which in turn made that local struggle much more potent.

Simultaneously, the particular realities and needs of the people there remained central. As the local activist Fannie Lou Hamer said of the necessity for local community self-determination of social/political objectives, "'Cause you see, if we are free people as Negroes, if we are free then I don't think you're supposed to tell me how much of my freedom I am supposed to have" (1981, 47). Directly involved activists and supporting allies all need to be on guard against the tendency of allies from the "core" regions, and those in domestically dominant social positions, to automatically assume superior attitudes even while they try to be useful. Criticism and self-criticism as well as alertness to one's own position in society are all essential if mutual respect is to be developed and maintained. Also, it is worth noting that the links should not always be one way from "north to south." Those fighting for justice in countries such as the United States can use the same type of alliance support from "outside" for the same reasons.

Many Indigenous activists, such as those among the Mayans of Guatemala and Chiapas, and the Cree of Canada, show that they can treat leftist and "progressive" analyses of the nation-state and global capitalism with respect, while drawing from and maintaining their own historical and spiritual/cultural roots. Are white, secular, cosmopolitan progressives willing to work respectfully with such developments around the world?

Shantytown Organization

Similar cleavages can be seen between urban cosmopolitan progressives and those millions of people laboring in the emplacements of underground or "informal" economies outside the mainstream of capitalism's institutions. Although they work long hours and at often dangerous jobs, most of these people are usually excluded from the category of "worker." Not "officially" employed, and not receiving paychecks, they are marginalized analytically. For example, not usually included as workers are those whose labor is that of systematic picking at the mountains of "trash" cast off by the affluent in cities such as Rio de Janeiro, Lagos, and New York. Much of this "trash" can be retrieved, used, and traded by those with the skills and the organization to do it. As Jorge G. Castañeda points out, the left in Latin America generally found that its singular class focus ran up against much more multifaceted social situations: "The left has always been troubled by a central theoretical paradox: its Marxist origins and inclinations have led it to accentuate *class*, while the incipient configuration of a class structure in Latin America, and the numerical weakness of the working class in particular have led it to place a great emphasis on *the people*. . . . The proliferation of grass roots movements compounded this difficulty: the 'new' social protest was not class-based" (1994, 235).

In recognizing such multiplicities, even the rearrangement of the categories "work" and "workers" must take place. As André Gorz argues, "The struggles that lead along the lines of work maintain their importance but the workers movement cannot ignore other struggles, taking place on other terrains, that have a growing importance in society, in the reconquest by men and women of power in their life. . . . The union movement cannot be indifferent to the women's movement . . . and it must take into account its own orientations[;] . . . the union movement cannot be indifferent any longer to the struggle of populations against the invasion of their neighborhoods by megatechnologies" (1988, 271 [my translation]). Moreover, Gorz states, "The right of people to govern themselves with sovereignty and their mode of cooperation with others is everything. It cannot be accomplished on the terrain of work . . . to the detriment of other struggles on other terrains" (1988, 271 [my translation]).

Clearly many "working people" are part of complex organizational structures that permeate the dense marginalized metropolitan areas of Africa, Asia, and Latin America, and parts of the United States (for example, on the El Paso/Juarez junction of the U.S.-Mexico border). Inside these sprawling zones are intricate, multidimensional grassroots networks. In the midst of the chronic crisis of the dispossessed that marks these settlements, there is a vitality that defies exact labeling and certainly does not fit exactly into the category of working class, although many of the shantytown inhabitants are or were in that class. As David Hecht and Maliqalim Simone observe about such areas in parts of metropolitan Africa:

> Impoverished communities often settle and build on government or private land without the clear legal right to do so. These are so called "popular neighborhoods". . . . They produce informal, and often illegal, associations, alliances, strategies and practice that provide an infrastructure for the community and a measure of functional autonomy. . . . While inept and unstable governments come and go these popular neighborhoods mostly endure. Their so called "frontline technologies" are particularly effective in gathering and disseminating information, they expand networks beyond the neighborhood, and channel resources back into it, facilitating most of the community's exchange and distribution of goods and services. (1994, 15–16)

Similarly, Thomas Angotti reminds us that in many Latin American cities, "Large community-based movements arose to stop displacement and secure basic urban services. These movements have forged coalitions that play a significant role in local and national politics" (1995, 17).[15]

The category of "worker" is even complicated for those who appear at first glance to be inside the industrial mainstream (being union members and factory workers) while being marginalized in other significant ways that do not fit their apparent belonging to the working class. For example, Laura Corradi's work among immigrant North African workers in Italy informs us: "Almost all of the immigrants interviewed were factory workers, productive and disciplined with a regular job, a regular work permit, a regular position in the eyes of the State and of Capital. . . . They lived in housing arrangements somewhat anomalous, if they had housing at all. In fact, some of them slept in train stations, some in public gardens, in cars, in tents or in abandoned houses with no doors or windows, no electric power, water and heat" (1993, 3). Also, observes Corradi, those who lived in such housing "were the most vulnerable for bashing and other racist backlash." For these "productive and disciplined" full-time factory workers, issues of regular housing and racism are at least as significant as workplace labor conditions. Corradi points out that in this setting it is a mistake to "see work and housing as separate items" and to give "a sort of priority to work." Instead, she says, for immigrant workers those two dimensions are combined in ways that are the exact opposite of the mainstream pattern for native-born Italian workers. For immigrants, being "a productive worker" is a necessary but not sufficient condition, given their housing situations, which "are schizophrenic" (1993, 3).

Similar and even more intensive conditions exist for thousands of factory workers in cities such as Bombay. Their homes are on the streets. The need for water is a present and central concern. Factory workers can also be "street people." For them, shelter and water are ever-present concerns. They live in a very different zone from that of most of their class counterparts in "the North." Consequently, they are essentially invisible to many progressives for whom the categories "worker" and "street person" can seem vast distances apart. In these situations, any action against the oppressive conditions of these workers will have to take into account housing and water as well as their workplace conditions.

The United States has few spatial equivalents to the extra-urban shantytown circles around most of its major cities, with the growing and notable exceptions of the important U.S.-Mexico border region. Nonetheless, similar patterns exist in the central "inner cities," where a variety of underground structures and grassroots groups thrive. It is in the inner cities that we see organizational responses to negative aspects of the "informal economy" such as youth violence, and to the unemployment and factory shutdowns that facilitate its development. In common with the often creative and potent shantytown organizations, there is great vitality among these inner-city groups. As James Jennings argues, in the midst of the marginalization of the ghetto there is "a capacity to alter radically the political landscape in favor of progressive social and economic policies" (1997, 13). So the creation of a coordinated, mutually supportive, social justice interaction inclusive of such shantytown emplacements requires awareness of the very existence of their distinct situations, along with a high degree of mutual respect for the particular agendas and objectives and the peoples within them. In sum, a transcommunal approach to distinctive emplacements of affiliation will be premised on some degree of self-transformation of participants as they learn to accept the fact that allies can have quite different concerns and outlooks. For the transcommunal activists, it may be pragmatically possible for at least some left, Indigenous, and shantytown organizations to work together, in some circumstances, assuming there is a fully equal participation of all those involved.

Such cooperation will require leftist partisans to accept that what they view as the significance of the urban working class may not be the conceptual center of gravity for the Indigenous organization, or that the very category of "worker" in shantytowns must be viewed from a different angle. The very language of resistance to global economic destruction that is employed in multiple, distinct emplacements will be quite different. So be it. They can still potentially be of service to each other. Indigenous activists confronting giant corporations can incorporate salient elements from a broad range of what Arif Dirlik (1996a) calls Marxist "diagnosis." These elements can illuminate how capitalism increasingly becomes more global and more centralized (one thinks especially of Lenin's great work, *Imperialism, the Highest Stage of Capitalism*). Simultaneously, the significance of ancestral land and of the spiritual forces that such land entails is also real for many Indigenous peoples, and this will have to be respected by the left activists if they want to engage in global cooperative organizing with those communities.[16] As Dirlik suggests, a wide variety of movements focused on different problems such as class, gender, and ethnicity "may learn from, and cross-fertilize one another while respecting their different identities" (1996b, 25). Similarly, in this more open sense of mutual respect and interaction, the term "transcommunal activist" can potentially embrace a socialist partisan, a shantytown former gang-leader turned community peace maker, and an Indigenous elder.

4

Learning from the Haudenosaunee

The Importance of Respect

THERE IS NOTHING fundamentally new about the mode of cooperation that is at the heart of transcommunality. We can learn from many historic and contemporary examples of the phenomenon.[1] Because of the wealth of detailed information available, I want to focus here on the system of thought and organization of the Haudenosaunee or "Iroquois" people. However, it is important to recognize that the Haudenosaunee are part of what Georges E. Sioui of the Department of Indian Studies at Saskatchewan Indian Federated College calls "the universality of Amerindian values" that runs like a great current through many Indigenous cultures of the Americas (1992, 23). For example, in North America alone, numerous examples of transcommunal outlooks can be found in such alliances as the Wabanaki (or Abanaki), the Massachusett, the Seminoles/Africans, and in the vast resistance movements among Native peoples that were the framework for the organizing of alliances by such leaders as the woman prophet Cocochee, Pontiac, Metacom or "King Philip," Tecumseh, Koacoochee or "Wild Cat," John Horse (one of the black Seminoles), Louis Riel (the Métis leader in Canada), and the many thousands of women and men who sustained them. The combination of autonomy and coordination is a fundamental aspect of many Native American societies.[2]

Simultaneously, it is important to note the limitations of such broadly encompassing currents. As my Cree colleagues Professors Maria Campbell and Winona Stevenson, also from the Saskatchewan Indian Federated College, inform us, it is important not to obscure the very high range of diversity among "Indigenous peoples" in the Americas (Campbell and Stevenson, 1998). The full range of the human condition, with all its attendant strengths and frailties, hostilities and kindness, equality and authoritarian hierarchy, can be found in Native American societies. Nonetheless, I also agree with Professor Sioui and other like-minded writers about common, albeit diversely lived, Indigenous currents such as the emphasis on an intense communal relationship with nature. This relationship is hard to express in English precisely because the connection is so entwined that to separate out "community" and "nature" can present an inaccurate picture of Native American life. So with both heterogeneity and common currents in mind, we can proceed.

The Haudenosaunee, an ancient people living in the part of North America that is now upper New York State and southeastern Canada, created a supple and superbly practical mode of complex organization well before Columbus stumbled into the "New World." The Haudenosaunee, in the classic form of their society, embody a spirit and mode of organization that I believe is very close to transcommunality. For those who may find transcommunality an unattainable, utopian way of life, such Indigenous alliances offer formative models of the creation of cooperation in the midst of conflict and communal difference. From my perspective, the Haudenosaunee are an important and instructive systemic example of transcommunal methods and outlooks for creating constructive communicative crossings of boundaries among diverse, even competing and hostile groups.

As I understand the work of scholars with Haudenosaunee roots and involvement, such as John Mohawk, Jake Swamp, Oren Lyons, Gerald Taiaiake Alfred, and Lynne Williamson, this word

for their culture means, in essence, "People of the Longhouse."
The Haudenosaunee dwellings were longhouses containing several families. Each family was connected to the family next to it.
But each had its own space, its own identity, and its own autonomy. The Haudenosaunee took this longhouse image of togetherness and autonomy and applied it to the geographic area that
is their historical territory. This land ran from the Seneca people
of the west, near what is now Buffalo, New York, through the land
of the Cayuga, the Onondaga, the Oneida, and the Mohawk, farthest east near what is now Albany, New York. West to east constituted the "Longhouse" of these nations, each linked to the others while maintaining its own space and autonomy.

Known also in English as the League or Confederacy of the Iroquois, this society exercised great influence on the history of English and French colonies, and on the United States, as numerous
scholars such as Bruce E. Johansen (1982), Vine Deloria (1992), and
Donald Grinde (1992) have argued.[3]

To say that the Haudenosaunee offer us a great deal of knowledge about how to act and organize transcommunally is not to
suggest that outsiders to this distinctive culture and history can
simply replicate it by reading about it. My approach here is not
one of attempted total emulation of the Haudenosaunee. Those
of us who are not Haudenosaunee can, I believe, understand some
elements and structures, and be inspired by them, while avoiding
the temptation of trying to achieve the obviously near impossibility of knowing completely what it feels like to be a person from
another culture. What is achievable is the more practical objective of drawing out universal implications from the classic Haudenosaunee social philosophy in order to illuminate useful approaches to global struggles for freedom and justice.

In taking this position I benefit from John Mohawk's understandings. Professor Mohawk says: "The political thought of the
Haudenosaunee deserves to be judged on its own merits, not as
an artifact of the past. We should investigate it today, question it,
expand on it, learn from it just as we would from any doctrine of

political thought" (1986, xv). Similarly, the Lumbee legal scholar
Robert A. Williams Jr. of the University of Arizona advises us, "in
our search for law and peace in today's multicultural world we can
derive value from efforts to reconstruct this important moment
in the history of North American indigenous and political
thought" (1996, 2).[4]

Concomitantly, I am fully aware of the imperative that my colleague, the Mohawk/Mississagua-descent scholar and community activist Lynne Williamson, notes when she says, "Native
groups expect to participate in developing solutions to global
problems. . . . However, for a great number of us, the first responsibility is to our own people" (1993, 287). Consequently, all of
those who from outside positions attempt to draw on various
forms of Indigenous knowledge must work, as Donald L. Fixico
says, "in a respectful manner that calls for a set of professional
ethics and scholarly responsibilities" (1998, 84). I trust and hope
that my writing meets this requirement.

Coordinating Autonomy

From a transcommunal perspective, we can view the Haudenosaunee as a significant example of a complex form of interaction
that accepts and celebrates autonomy of distinct groups while also
emphasizing cooperation and affiliation among those same participants. Obviously, every culture has its unique features and linkages that cannot be duplicated elsewhere. Moreover, no one has
ever created the perfect society that meets all of its own founding
ideals. The principles of peace became severely stressed as the Haudenosaunee, like many other Native Americans, sought to maintain themselves in the midst of power politics and economic conflict among Dutch, French, English, and Americans in the northern
regions of "North America," all of which enveloped and often
undermined Indigenous nations in a complex variety of ways.
Nonetheless, the Haudenosaunee, in their origin among what had
initially been five warring nations, creatively and constructively

addressed key problems related to maintaining cooperation in the midst of diversity, without centralized top-down domination by one group.

There is a vast amount of material on the Haudenosaunee and I will not attempt to survey it here, nor do I claim expert knowledge of this complex history. Essentially theirs is the story of a people who, early in their history, overcame a period of conflict and violence to create a community of cooperation among five distinct sovereign peoples, the Seneca, Cayuga, Oneida, Onondaga, and Mohawk. This confederacy emerged before the arrival of the Europeans. Significantly, the Haudenosaunee developed in direct response to what John Mohawk describes as "a time of great sorrow and terror for the Haudenosaunee. All order and safety had broken down completely." There was, he says, a "spiral of vengeance and reprisal, which found assassins stalking the northeastern woodlands in a never-ending senseless bloodletting" (1986, xvi). Similarly, the Haudenosaunee writer Tehanetorens notes this was a time in which "although related by blood, the five nations . . . became enemies of each other. They forgot the ways of the Creator, and fought among themselves and with others, bringing sorrow, destruction and death to each nation" (1976, 8).

During this terrible time, there appeared a man who became known as the "Peacemaker." The Peacemaker, as John Mohawk says, "sought out the most remarkable survivors of this random and undeclared war and he initiated discussions with them." In these discussions, the Peacemaker "offered the idea that all human beings possess the power of rational thought and that in the belief in rational thought is to be found the power to create peace." The Peacemaker asserted that "in the area of negotiations between nations, the most desirable goal would be not only a cessation of violence but the active interactions which could create a better world for everyone" (Mohawk, 1986, xvi, xvii).

The Peacemaker went from "village to village and nation to nation." He and his co-worker Hiawatha[5] met with support and opposition. In time, their work bore fruit in the cessation of hostilities, in the breaking of the cycles of vengeance, and most importantly in the development of "The Great Law of Peace." The Great Law of Peace was aimed not only at ending violence but at creating "active interactions which could create a better world for everyone" (Mohawk, 1986, xvii). The Great Law of Peace, as Paul Wallace points out, is more than a reaction against violence. Rather, the Great Law has constructive dimensionality aimed at creating a secure and sustaining environment. It is, he says, "not a defensive instrument dealing solely with safeguards against oppression and war. It is a positive thing, giving expression to the Five Nations way of life" (1986, 34). It is this Great Law of Peace and its implementation in Haudenosaunee society that tells us so much about the possibilities and approaches to transcommunal action.

A key image in the Great Law of Peace is the "clasping of hands" or the "linking of arms" of different peoples. As Robert A. Williams Jr. observes, these clasped hands indicated an acceptance of shared rights and obligations that tied diverse peoples together. "In Iroquois legal thought, the Great Peace was a natural state of communication, connection, solidarity and trust between all peoples, linking them together in reciprocating relations of trade, friendship, and goodwill" (1996, 7).

Paul Wallace in the *The White Roots of Peace* points out that the Great Law expresses the principle of unity in diversity, a principle that gives its distinctive strength to the Confederacy (1986, 34). The League or Confederacy of the Longhouse offered security to distinct multiple layers of group identities rather than requiring each nation, clan, and household to simply assimilate into a homogenous larger unit. In this sense, the very identity of the Confederacy is that of a society of cooperative diversity among many different but coordinated groups, rather than a reductionist, homogenizing unification.

Importantly, the symbols of the Confederacy, while visionary and far seeing in their intent, are also practical and grounded. Such symbols are used to emphasize the importance of both coordination and autonomy among its participating communities. According to Oren Lyons, Onondaga Faithkeeper and an American

Studies professor at the State University of New York at Buffalo, the ideology of the Confederacy "was complex," but its "symbols were easy to grasp" (1992, 39). Similarly, Paul Wallace notes the practicality of the message of the Peacemaker to the Five Nations that "We shall have one dish, . . . and we shall have a co-equal right to it" (1986, 34–35). The framing image of the Confederacy as "the Longhouse" consisted, as the Peacemaker indicated, of multiple yet coherently spaced "council fires." Their separateness was combined with constant interactions among those around each fire. Moreover, a longhouse can be added to and made longer. New compartments can be created, room can be made for others. Consequently, the overall Haudenosaunee structure of affiliations is not one of closure but of openness to an ever-larger population willing to live within its framework—the message of Peace.

Yet another key symbol in this openness to the world emphasized a rooted unity, that of "the Tree, under the shelter of which the Five Nations gathered." As the Tree grew, its roots extended, as did its branches, so it was open to a potentially ever-wider range of nations (Wallace, 1986, 37). Tehanetorens describes how the Peacemaker reminded the people "that other nations are to be invited to take shelter beneath the Tree" (1976, 36). While the ever-growing branches provided shelter to many, peace was always the prominent concern. Under the "white roots" of the Tree of Peace "are buried all weapons of war" (Mohawk Nation/ Akwasasne, 13).

The Haudenosaunee have their historic center among the Onondaga, in what is now central New York State. Onondaga is the very heart of the geographic/cultural "Longhouse" that symbolized the international linkages of these diverse peoples. The historian Matthew Dennis notes: " [The Peacemaker] and the civil chiefs planted a great Tree of Peace at Onondaga, the settlement of Thadodaho now designated as the Firekeeper. The evergreen 'Tree of the Great Long Leaves' (great white pine) sheltered the League" (1993, 94). Meetings of the great council of the League took place at the central or "heart" location of Onondaga. Today, Onondaga is still a vibrant element of the Haudenosaunee. In this sense the Onondaga habitat was indeed central to the Confederacy. But constitutionally, Onondaga is not a "capital" of a centralized hierarchical system that issues orders to subordinate units. To the contrary, it is the place for gathering and discussion by the representatives of the many-faceted Confederacy.

Classically, such debate was framed by protocols that managed both agreement and disagreement so that many voices could be heard but disruption avoided. As Matthew Dennis observes, Haudenosaunee debates and deliberations required "a measured, respectful, courteous manner" (1993, 95). As Lynne Williamson notes, "Disagreement was, as I understand it, handled by allowing different opinions to be openly debated although in a rational way" (1995). Moreover, as Williamson observes:

> Public speech provided a key dynamic within Haudenosaunee governance. Taking place when all are present in council in the longhouse, the recitation of the Great Law is spoken by leaders from memory in the original languages. . . . The beauty and power of the oratory, its ability to persuade and the evocative quality of the metaphors used, reinforce a sense of Haudenosaunee identity by narrating a common history of the people who are listening and participating. Even while we may be disagreeing or in debate, the essence of the words links us through archetypal principles. (1993, 285–286)

The intricately flexible diversity-as-unity of the classic Haudenosaunee mode of organization is constantly reinforced by direct interpersonal contacts, structured through complex ceremonies and protocols. In this vein the Great Council of the League met at Onondaga "not less than once a year, and being called by runners at short notice whenever important business arose" (Dennis, 1993, 43). Commonly recognized rules of conduct that contributed to clear-headed discussion and restraint of anger and violence are essential to the discourse of the diverse participants. "When you administer the Law," said the Peacemaker, "your skins must be seven thumbs thick. . . .Carry no anger and hold no grudges. Think not of yourselves, O chiefs, nor of your own generation. Think of continuing generations of our families, think of

our grandchildren and of those yet unborn, whose faces are coming from beneath the ground." Through the various expectations
of actual interpersonal conduct, the maintenance of a common
identity among its diverse peoples is made tangible rather than
abstract. Dennis notes the direct and daily use of the "symbols and
metaphors and the institutions and ritual practices bequeathed
by the Peacemaker to the Five Nations"; thus, "Peace was never
abstract or simply ideological; it was concrete and experiential"
(Dennis, 1993, 108).

Moreover, the broadly embracing sweep of the Confederacy
was rooted in local strengths, including those of the household,
and this in turn added to the respect accorded women in Haudenosaunee society. According to Dennis, "The Five Nations conceived of peace and enacted it in terms of domestic harmony—
within households [owachiras] and villages. . . . The *owachira* was
a domain controlled by women in the complementary relationship with men. . . . Women commanded great prestige and authority." With the women-centered household as an essential model,
the Haudenosaunee "extended the mechanism of domestic harmony" to maintain peace throughout their society (Dennis, 1993,
108–109).

The Haudenosaunee held onto many different levels of freedom and autonomy even while they acted effectively in concert
with each other. Oren Lyons writes: "Each of the communities of
the Haudenosaunee controlled its internal affairs independently
of the Confederacy Council while the Confederacy Council was
restricted to controlling affairs of a national or international character" (1992, 39). Notably, even "national or international" affairs
did not necessarily have to be agreed to by every community,
family, or individual. Rather, Haudenosaunee life was constantly
infused with a high degree of freedom to make decisions that
could diverge from those arrived at by the Council. Lyons continues: "Among the Haudenosaunee participatory democracy
meant that on some level every individual had a right to voice an
opinion and to agree or disagree on actions to be taken. . . . . In
fact, the Confederacy Council had no coercive power whatsoever

over its people. There was no permanent army, no police force, no insane asylums, and no jails. This meant that communities were free to disagree with the decisions of the Confederacy Council especially on trade issues" (1992, 39).

Similarly, as Matthew Dennis points out, local Haudenosaunee communities "enjoyed considerable autonomy." Moreover, the essential unity of the Haudenosaunee grew upward and outward from the many local roots, rather than being arbitrarily imposed by a central elite above. Dennis writes: "The decisions or non-decisions of the confederacy were the product of discussions in households, villages, and tribes throughout Iroquoia. These were the deliberations of ordinary men and women rather than specialized elites; the discourse of the League council was, then, only a reflection of the considered debates that characterized owachira, clan, town, and nation" (1993, 96).

Many Europeans, habituated to authoritarian, male-dominated societies with central governments, were often baffled by this grassroots democratic system in which women exercised key decision-making power; that emphasized multiple levels of autonomy; was devoid of a ruling elite; that was open to other nations and peoples; that strenuously sought to avoid anger and violence by emphasizing compassion, clear-headedness, and consensus rather than dictate and imposition.

As already indicated, there are distinctive features of Haudenosaunee culture and history that cannot be duplicated or simply imitated by outsiders. For example, the significance of kinship ties is not something that could be used to tie together African American and Latino inner-city organizations. Robert Williams reminds us of the genealogical elements in Haudenosaunee social thought: "The intricate system of clans and lineages provided the Iroquois with a ready-made structure for maintaining . . . cohesion of their multitribal confederacy" (1996, 28).

Yet this importance of kinship did not lead to anything like an emphasis on exclusionary "racial purity" so common in western culture. The Haudenosaunee genealogical orientation also allowed for adoption of many people from different Native American nations and from among Europeans. The Tuscarora people, driven out of North Carolina by colonialists who were attempting to enslave them, became the "sixth compartment" of the Longhouse in 1722. The Oneida reception of my Native ancestors, that I have already described, is another example of the inclusionary aspect in the Haudenosaunee understandings of the world. So, in its classic form, Haudenosaunee kinship can be extended (like the Longhouse compartments) in varying ways to a wide variety of "outsiders," assuming their willingness to live by the Great Law of Peace. Such flexibility is an example of transcommunally open, rather than closed, forms of collective identity.

Well before the European invasions of the Americas, the Haudenosaunee brilliantly created a highly flexible and coherently open democratic social system of great strength. In this system, they produced a supple and complex unity from diversity, while achieving an essentially egalitarian, multinational society that lives on today. From my vantage point, I see the Haudenosaunee as a highly developed and organized form of transcommunal thought, action, and organization. Their detailed cooperative arrangements, emphasizing both coordination and autonomy, offer importantly suggestive frameworks for both the visionary and the practical aspects of transcommunal life today.

5

Elements of Transcommunality

WITH THE HAUDENOSAUNEE as a pivotal conceptual framework, we can draw out key elements of transcommunality and schematically delineate them in the ways described below.

Words and Deeds

In classic Haudenosaunee society, respectful speech and listening form an essential path by which honest positions and feelings can be circulated within the society. The Mother of the Nations says to the Peacemaker that his "words are good," but then immediately she asks, "But what form will these words take when they come to be in the world?" Those who speak and those who listen are cognizant of the various requirements that mitigate against anger while also allowing full expression. However, the significance of interpersonal relations and constant ways of meeting from the household to the entire Confederacy over the issues of tactics, strategies, and objectives also tells us that direct interaction is vital in this social system. Similarly, transcommunality emphasizes the deed as well as the word. The word without the deed is one-dimensional and lacks the fullness that comes from real relationship. Abstract principles such as "community" or "brotherhood/sisterhood," while being important visionary signposts as to the direction in which to move, cannot of themselves achieve the sustained everyday actions that are the building blocks for such abstractions. It is for this reason that transcommunality is fundamentally experience based and action oriented.

Task-focused Outlooks

Transcommunal action is necessarily *task focused*. Those who come from different group locations do so in order to work with others to address some basic problem or dilemma. The formative task for the Haudenosaunee was the ending of violence and the creation of a way of life that would prevent such violence from developing again. Similarly, in many urban areas of the United States, cooperative groups are being formed among Asian American, African American, and Latino organizations to end youth violence in cities, with that pressing need as a primary task to accomplish. These peace activists emphasize the pragmatic necessity of transcommunal cooperation. As Khalid Shah, the director of the Los Angeles area peace organization Stop the Violence/Institute the Peace, says of their willingness to work with a range of people: "We don't worry about your religion or your color, or how much money you make. But we have one common goal and that is the issue of the violence that is killing us all. So if we can come together on that issue and make leadership accountable, then we can get some things done" (1996, 36). Similarly, Jitu Sidiki of the Black Awareness Community Development Organization said of that group's relationship to Latino peace activists in the parallel organization Barrios Unidos, "solidarity with Barrios Unidos and Latinos is necessary. What Barrios Unidos is doing affects what happens in African American communities (Childs, 1995, 2). Not abstractions but real ways of being characterize transcommunality.

Shared Practical Action

As they work to achieve common objectives, the members of the transcommunal group engage in *shared practical action*. The design and carrying out of tactics and strategies to achieve the tasks at hand result in cooperative work with pragmatic real-time aspects.

While carrying out this work, the interacting participants learn more about each other, rely on each other, and develop a commonly held body of knowledge based on their task-oriented actions/interactions. Common experience is developed through the process of the work. For example, Riva Kastoryano, writing about alliances among immigrants in France, points to the way in which a common struggle against racial and cultural discrimination provides an environment for cooperation across a wide variety of ethnic and religious lines. There are, she points out, a growing number of associations that are "religious, social, cultural [that] now represents the mosaic of diverse groups that form local collectivities in the ghetto. They unite young people, whatever their national or religious origin" (1996, 90 [my translation]).

Out of this "mosaic" interaction appear what I consider transcommunal activists who serve as bridges among these different groups. Kastoryano adds: "Intercultural mediators, and ghetto mediators appear now as new actors who regulate conflicts in the zones where there are the strongest concentrations of immigrants" (1996, 91). Similarly, I find among many of the urban organizations that work with youth in gangs the emergence of transcommunal activists who push for dialogue across ethnic/race lines. As with their counterparts in France, these transcommunalists do not make such assertions purely on the basis of abstract principles, but rather on the necessity of confronting common problems, in this case the problem of violence that undermines community vitality. As Khalid Shah said while lecturing in one of my classes, "There is no color line when it comes to violence, we all have to work together (Childs, 1997, 1). Such shared practical action serves both as an objective and as a method. To work together is an objective that can lead to a larger goal, such as combating racism or urban violence.

Numerous demonstrations against the inequities of "free trade," such as those in Seattle, Prague, Davros, and Québec, have brought together more and more diverse and interacting participants. One activist/observer noted that the Québec demonstration against free trade in the Americas was the most diverse and cross-border gathering up to that point. He states that the march and rally "brought out around 30,000 trade unionists from Canada, the U.S., Mexico, Haiti, Columbia, Brazil, as well as over 20,000 environmentalists, human rights campaigners, feminists, community organizers" (Chase, 2001, 2).

For cross-border activism, such as we saw in the Québec demonstration against free trade, the coming together around the common objective of simply being present and active in a specific location is another important initial form of shared practical action which in turn can lead to enhancement of future organizing.

Constructive Disputing

Shared practical action can lead to arguments and clashes within an association of transcommunalists. Differences of approach and outlook emerging out of distinct cultural backgrounds are unavoidable if the association is to be truly transcommunal. Indeed, *constructive disputing* is part of the growth of mutual knowledge of the individuals participating in the association. Such disputes are actually necessary to the well-being and continued growth of the transcommunal association. Disputing is necessary because it will often be the only densely concentrated way in which important, distinctive features of the members' ways of operating become clear.

Moreover, disputing is inevitable once we move beyond the abstractions of "unity" and "community" into the grit of everyday action. Through that action we expose how different we are to one another. Such exposure is vital if we are to really bridge the gaps between groups. This bridging cannot be built on the thin air of generalities but must be constructed on the concreteness of meaningful events that expand our mutual awareness of one another in the association. The issue here is not simply one of tolerance of different views and procedures. Rather it is recognizing that they exist first and foremost. Disputing can shed a great deal of light on that reality. In fact, constructive disputing can perform a vital function of making problems evident. Too often the embrace of progressive idioms such as "solidarity" smother real tensions. In such cases the problem is not that there is conflict, but that the sources of conflict are hidden. As Ivan Illich points out, a "convivial society" must recognize "the legitimacy of conflicting interests" (1973, 106).

Much can be learned here from Haudenosaunee protocols for discussion. John Mohawk, Matthew Dennis, Paul Wallace, Robert Williams, and others provide usefully detailed discussion on these methods. Dennis for example writes:

> Chiefs were cautioned to take no offense at anything said against them, or for any wrongdoing they might suffer. "Their hearts shall be full of peace and goodwill, their spirits yearning for the good of their people. Long suffering in carrying out their duties, [their] firmness shall be tempered with tenderness. The spirit of anger and fury shall find no lodgement in them and in all they say and do [they] shall exercise calmness. . . ." The League chiefs epitomized the Iroquois ideal of peace and harmony and provided examples of how every Iroquois should live. (1993, 96–97)

Importantly, the Haudenosaunee ideals are clearly practical and everyday in their applicability, rather than being abstract and remote. The concern expressed by the Mother of Nations to the Peacemaker that the Great Message of Peace must entail words that have "form" in the world was answered by systematic, practical means of reaching toward the ideals. A few rare and alert European observers could detect the distinctiveness of this approach that fused inner peace with social calmness. Dennis records Lafitau's comments on the Haudenosaunee: "Respect for human beings, which is the mainspring of their actions, serves no little to keep up their union. Each one, regarding others as masters of their own actions, lets them conduct themselves as they wish and judges only himself" (1993, 111). This system of containing disputes employed respect for the existence of different individual and group perspectives, an emphasis on leading by example in the use of "calmness," and a constant reminding that the overall good of the society depended on continued cooperation in the midst of difference.

Constructive disputing allows diverse and even competing/ conflicting concerns to be confronted and recognized without being suppressed. Constructive disputing breaks out of the negative circle of competition/conflict by reacting with shock-absorbing responses, such as those found among the Haudenosaunee, which included "sensitivity, condolence, atonement, forgiveness, restraint, circumspection, calmness, and peace" (Dennis, 1993, 111). Transcommunalists seek to integrate the elements from various, even competing, vantage points that are mutually assimilable, while avoiding damaging competition with those who differ from their outlooks. In the same vein, bell hooks suggests that confronting difference is vital to development of mutual understanding: "Fear of painful confrontation often leads women and men active in feminist movements to avoid rigorous critical encounter, yet if we cannot engage dialectically in a committed, rigorous, humanizing manner we cannot hope to change the world" (1989, 25).

Of course, constructive *disputing* can degenerate into a disruptive *conflict*. Unmanaged, dispute can push even the most transcommunally inclined people toward fission rather than fusion. To avoid fundamentally disruptive conflict, it is vital that the constructive function of disputing be clear to everyone, that there be constant mutual respect shown for the distinctiveness and intensity of different positions, and that everyone be deeply invested in the potential of making some degree of mutual accommodation to these positions while being ready to transform them to some extent also. But such avoidance of corrosive conflict should not be confused with a suffocating imposition of artificial harmony demanded in the name of unity. Transcommunal receptivity to some degree of dispute as positive requires an organizational willingness to be a melange of sometimes colliding positions.

This acceptance of a mix of distinct, even contentious outlooks is akin to those African outlooks described by Hecht and Simone in which fluidity and ambiguity are intimately connected to daily action. Such fluidity, they say, "may be according to many African cosmologies the very thing that offers them their only protection. African traditional societies, far from embedding individuals in stolid norms and procedures, generate their own highly plural and contradictory forms, engaging different peoples and activities over a broad landscape" (1994, 110).

Transcommunalists, engaged in constructive disputing and focused on common tasks, enact the larger transcommunal approach of maintaining distinct positions as they interact and so learn more about one another. This constant process of unification springing out of instructional tension occurs through the shared practical action of the participant activists. In turn, shared practical action is possible precisely because the transcommunalists thread together the tensions of their different, sometimes conflicting, positions with the common goals of peace, justice, and equality. Wole Soyinka, in his essay "Language as Boundary," describes a process very much like this when he writes of "an awareness" that "rediscovers eternal causes for human association and proceeds to build new entities held together [through a] recognizable identity of goals" (1988, 87). For our purposes here, we recognize these "new entities" as transcommunal associations created through interactive diverse participants who maintain their roots while linking up with one another.

In sum, given that differences can be very real and that consequently some dispute is probably inevitable, and indeed is necessary for further construction of the transcommunality itself, we must learn how to benefit rather than be disrupted by it.

The Necessity of Interpersonal Relations

Commonly developed experience, such as that involved in constructive disputing, entails deepening *interpersonal relations*. Face-to-face contacts develop into long-term relationships from this shared activity. In turn, such relationships allow for expansion of shared activity. Interpersonal relations, within which the participants build an increasing sense of trust and predictability with each other, are the tough but flexible silken threads upon which these small groups form, and upon which larger groups will depend. As Hawaiian sovereignty proponent Haunani-Kay Trask observes about nonindigenous (or *haole*) allies who can be trusted:

Of course long-time Hawaiian activists know the few *haole* exceptions.... We trust these people implicitly because they have
endured over the years in struggle after struggle. *Haole* who hon-
estly support us, do so without loud pronouncements about how
we feel or how they know just what we *mean*. Moreover, they readily acknowledge our leadership since they are present to support
us, not to tell us what to do and how to do it. These *haoles* are
trusted by Hawaiian activists precisely because their behavior over
the years speaks louder than any sympathetic public statements on
their part ever could. (1993, 251)

As Simone Weil notes, for fundamental cooperation to occur
there must be "not only good, but warm, genuinely friendly, and
... intimate relations" (1952, 206). Trust, as the Haudenosaunee
show so well, is a key element in such communication among
diverse peoples. Through tangible trust, built up through actual
experience of shared practical action, the predictability of transcommunal relationships and, therefore, their relative reliability
are formed.

Personal Transformation

Transcommunality's emphasis on the maintenance of one's core
affiliations, be they cultural, organizational, religious, philosophical, etc., is simultaneous with an emphasis on the transformative
impact that such interaction creates. All this involvement in shared
practical action, constructive disputing, and the building of interpersonal relations results in enhanced awareness of others who
were formerly distant and unknown. The aforementioned African
American and Chicano activists who work with youth to bring
peace to the streets of Los Angeles have transformed their understandings of one another and of each other's ethnic community.
They of course remain African American and Chicano, but they
are also something new in their transcommunal interaction and
mutual awareness. Similarly, such activists usually recognize that,
for many youth, membership in gangs is an effort to find social
sustenance and community, however misguided the outcome may
be. Consequently, these activists seek to emphasize these positive

inclinations among youth, while moving them in directions that are constructive rather than destructive.

The Haudenosaunee were highly alert to such transformative potentials as part of the way in which a society emphasizing coherence and diversity could develop, even in the face of skepticism and long-term hostilities among different peoples. As John Mohawk informs us, the Peacemaker's task was that of addressing those who lived out their anger, not avoiding them, because he saw their potential: "What do you say to a fellow who has been on countless headhunting forays? How do you convince him that a society, which has reached chaos, can be turned into a society, which provides safety and hope? How do you convince him that the thirst for revenge is the source of diminishment of his own human potential?" (Mohawk, 1986, xix).

The history of the Haudenosaunee tells of the great warrior Thadodaho, an Onondaga chieftain whose powers were feared by most. (There are several different transliteration spellings of the name Thadodaho; I am using a commonly accepted one.) For Thadodaho the way of war was the only path to follow. So strong was he, and so dangerous, that his hair was entwined with living snakes. Few dared approach him, and those who did died. But the Peacemaker and Hiawatha did not reject Thadodaho. They did not revile him as an implacable enemy. Rather, they sensed his potential for peace. With calming words they approached him, with the Great Message of Peace. Hiawatha "combed" the snakes from Thadodaho's head, and the mind of Thadodaho "was made straight" (Wallace, 1986, 29). Thadodaho was then chosen to preside over the great council of the Five Nations, and the Onondaga to this day pass on his name. In this history, Thadodaho does not stop being Onondaga. Nor does he stop being a strong and influential person. But his contact with thoughts of peace and cooperation transforms him. It is this combination of transformation and maintenance of core affiliations that is so significant for transcommunal activism.

Similarly, Luis Rodriguez, a former Los Angeles gang member who has become a successful author and advocate for peace among youth of all races, says to young people: "I tell you that you have the creativity, the potential. I've been where you are. I know you can do it" (Childs, 1996, 41).[1] In the Inuit autonomous land of Nunavut, Canada, community leader Mary Williams, who works with young people in trouble, says: "The Whites want a guilty person, in order to punish and enclose. What we find important, to the contrary among us Inuit, is the return to the harmony of the group that is vital for survival. This happens through dialogue, advice, reconciliation, and especially through reeducation about contact with nature. In any case through coercion in prison, the Whites construct criminals" (Cojean, 1998, 13 [my translation]).

As Abenaki writer Joseph Bruchac points out, belief in the positive transformational potential of even the most negative of opponents is a common feature of much Indigenous thought in the Americas: "There is also a strong tradition of redemption among native people. Rather than a fixed and permanent condition, 'evil' in a human being is often seen as a twisting of the mind. Every person contains both the 'good mind' and the confusion of the mind that is called 'bad' or 'evil' in the English language. Even monsters can be redeemed when their hearts are melted by the warmth of a fire" (1993, xiii).

In the midst of the economic marginalization of thousands, with unemployment rates of 90 percent in some inner-city, rural, and "reservation" settings of the United States, the attractions of gangs and "fast money" are powerful, and no one would claim that the battle for peace in the streets has been won. Nonetheless, from the Haudenosaunee Great Message of Peace to the work of activists such as Mary Williams and Luis Rodriguez, the potential for reconciliation and transformation through respectful interaction in a constructive social setting is vital to transcommunality.

Creation of Transcommunal Associations

The organizational structure of transcommunal associations develops out of increased communication and enhanced mutual understandings. Shared practical action, leading to interpersonal relationships, coalesces into associations that give these individuals a strong sense of group cohesiveness. Such groups may achieve formal status or may remain informal. Either way, they grow directly from face-to-face communication and work. As John Dewey suggests in *The Public and Its Problems:* "Interactions, transactions, occur de facto and the results of interdependence follow. But participation in activities and sharing in results ... demand communication as a prerequisite" (1927, 152).

Because transcommunal associations are built on the solid ground of constantly reinforced interpersonal trust, they can be shock absorbers that buffer their members from the pressures of group conflict. For example, long-term members of the Black/Korean Alliance in Los Angeles were able to maintain already established ties even in the aftermath of violent conflict between members of those two communities in 1992 (Choo, 1994).

The Propulsion of Vision

Simultaneously with its down-to-earth practicality, a visionary breadth propels the transcommunal association. The Haudenosaunee Peacemaker's practical protocol-oriented approach to cooperation made the ending of warfare among the Five Nations possible while it was fueled by the visionary desire for peace and well-being. In the same manner, a transcommunal association aims at nothing less than social justice, equality, and peace in a society that removes the grasping, materialistic power stranglehold of a few from the throats of the many. More immediate goals are oriented toward these principles. Consequently, a visionary grasp of the future fuels mundane matters such as organizing a meeting, a demonstration, or an educational event. The vision of egalitarian nonviolent life is what pulls the transcommunal activists toward the future while sustaining them with a profound sense of responsibility and possibility. In its merger of immediate, near-term, and distant objectives and principles, the transcommunal association avoids a sterile overemphasis on utopian dreams that have no connection with the real world. On the other side of that coin, transcommunality also escapes from the entrapment of a compulsively utilitarian outlook so locked into the status quo that it goes nowhere and changes nothing.

The pragmatic, visionary do-ability of transcommunal action links the immediately possible to more general goals and principles. This linking grounds the actions of transcommunalists. They know that at least some small initial victories not only are possible but probable, while the more long-range objectives are not lost sight of, so giving a profound future-oriented spirit to the daily struggle.

The Engaged/Disengaged Flexibility of Transcommunality

A key feature of transcommunal organization and action is its "On/Off" structural potential. A transcommunal organization does not require that all its distinctive groupings be in direct contact at all times. Rather, each group, facing its own particular local circumstances, works from and develops its own specific, context-rooted way of being. The multiple groups at many different levels can also call on one another or the entire organization for assistance, advice, and support when necessary. At the moment of such a call, dormant relationships are reawakened, and the larger organization becomes visible.[2]

This On/Off capability is of great value, for it allows each participating group to be directly responsive to its particular environment while also assuring that no one group is isolated and overcome by its local conditions. This dynamic structure also effectively functions to assist the classic Haudenosaunee in maintaining multiple layers of local and national affiliations, while also providing an overarching framework of the larger organization of the Confederacy "Longhouse" itself. This On/Off capability of organization requires highly sensitive forms of coordination among the varied participants who *step in* when called upon to do so, but who *do not step on* anyone in the process. The flexible potential to connect, disconnect, and reconnect as needed is an absolutely vital aspect of the mutual respect that participants from diverse, often quite different communities can employ.

Consequently, the transcommunal activists must always recognize that at certain moments and in certain settings, the best cooperation may be no cooperation. To stand aside, if requested to do so by a community, can be just as important as being directly involved. Recognition that boundaries created by communities can be very real and meaningful to those within them can require a respectful keeping of distance. The images of "crossing borders" and "blurring of genres" should not obscure the clarity of community distinctiveness for many cultures, religions, ideologies, and organizations.

In our transcommunal framework, one does not approach another group without an interactively developing sensitivity and recognition that permission is required to enter, and that such permission may not always be forthcoming. The existence of "structural" similarities and issues among different groups (e.g., "we are all in the same boat together") are not enough. Personal and subjective issues of growing trust, respect, and recognition are also important. Those seeking a cooperative rather than a conflictual approach must be willing to disengage from as much as engage with the many facets of this pluralistically diamonded world.

Such disengagement is especially important if the "outsider," no matter how well intentioned, comes from the dominant section of society. For example, Guillermo Delgado, in his work on Indigenous movements, remarks on how activists from grassroots communities told their urban left sympathizers to help by not helping. He writes, "When popular organizations asked, 'What can we do to help you?' Indigenous communities answered, 'Nothing'" (1994, 8). Similarly, Haunani-Kay Trask expresses wariness of well-meaning, white would-be allies, whose cooperation comes with the baggage of their dominant position that weighs them down, preventing them from having the alertness necessary for working respectfully with the very people to whom they want to offer assistance. Such allies, she argues, "still want control" and as a result can disrupt the development of mutually respectful coalition creation (Trask, 1993, 250).

From the perspective of transcommunal potential for oscillation between engagement/disengagement, under many circumstances "good fences" can indeed "make good neighbors." But fences can have portals that can be opened when needed. Neighbors can and should be able to call upon one another for help and receive it, when needed, based on the relationships of trust and respect that they have already established.

The Haudenosaunee concept that illuminates the importance of clear-cut boundaries and of openness is that which Francis Jennings translates as "woodsedge." In this understanding of working with "outsiders," polite requests for entry must precede any interaction: "Protocol demanded that friendly visitors stop at the wood's edge before entering a village. The concept is so distinct that it is best rendered in English as one word—*woodsedge*. There they shouted to announce themselves, upon which a party came out to escort them into the village. To be at the wood's edge, therefore, was a manner of announcing one's readiness to treat" (Jennings, 1985, 124).

Contained within these images of "good fences" and "woodsedge" is the constant potential for reconstructive engagement of those who are not always in direct contact but who know each other from previous productive encounters. Such engagement effectively, and flexibly, recreates the structures of cooperation that may have lain dormant, on an as-needed basis, with the assent of all involved.

We find similar dynamic principles in African American culture. For example, the creative improviser Leo Smith writes: "The concept that I employ in my music is to consider each performer as a complete unit with each having his or her own center from which each performs independently of any other, and with this respect of autonomy the independent center of the improvisation is continuously changing depending upon the force created by individual centers at any instance. . . . In other words each element is autonomous in its relationship in the improvisation.

Organizationally, this principle of "independent centers" creates what Smith calls "an ensemble of orchestras" that is structurally very much like that we have discussed for the Longhouse. According to Smith, "the forms that I use in my music ... are EeLO'jsZ and AFmie. EeLO'jsZ is an ensemble-orchestra form for improvisors, and simply refers to the grouping together of more than one orchestra, more than one ensemble, or several orchestras with one or more ensembles in such a way as to preserve the autonomy of each improvisor within a group, each group within the orchestra, and each improviser within the unit-total."

On the basis of this approach, Smith proposes the need to go beyond European classical formats to a transcommunal-like set of connections:

> It is high time that we begin to help and set up cultural ties with the other more than three-fourths of these americas (north, central, south) while also seeking other culture that have improvisation as their classical art music (india, pan-islam, the orient, bali and africa) and make lasting cultural commitments with them. For the days are set in time that this vast world of ours can only survive if we, as humans, become earth-beings committed in our cultural and political aspects to a pan world future. (1973, 22–23)

Whether socially, politically, culturally or in some combination, such capabilities for disengagement/reengagement have long-lasting, positive effects for alliance building precisely because the parties involved cement their ties with one another, both individually and communally, when they do come together. So while the push to engage in shared actions can be very practical and task-oriented, it does not result in a "strange bedfellows" approach in which merely pragmatic, tactical issues take precedence over everything else.[3] Those who come together over many such gatherings cannot remain total strangers to one another. Consequently, for the transcommunal activists, such moments of reengagement are also reaffirmations of strong affiliated sensibilities. For example, the gatherings of the entire Haudenosaunee Confederacy around the central fire at Onondaga (and similar gatherings such as those of the Wabanaki Confederacy at their central fire at Canadaigua, Québec) were such moments of reaffirmation as well as problem solving. These transcommunal moments of reengagement speak to the strength of past links and of the future of their continuation. Similarly, a 1998 two-part meeting of Indigenous writers, artists, and activists that I attended in California at the University at Davis and at the Institute for Oaxacan Studies in Mexico in 1998 brought together participants from around the Americas, north and south. All came from distinct settings, but we all established and reestablished relationships that can be called upon in the future, based on increased knowledge and friendship.

The Dangers of Transcommunal Success: From Being Bridges to Becoming Isolates

There are real potential limitations in the very success of transcommunal activists in creating associations of mutual interaction. They can change from being a communication bridge to being isolated. In environments of intense conflict and competition, transcommunalists from different emplacements, some of whose members are normally suspicious of or hostile to other populations, may appear as traitors or at least as suspect. The structural dilemma for transcommunalists is that they must have roots in their main emplacements of affiliation if they are to be effective as bridges. It is this rootedness that gives them the ground from which to reach out to others. Conversely, the reaching out—making transcommunal associations and engaging in transformative dialogue that expands their understandings of those "on the other side"—can also mark them as different from the very community, organization, or system of belief with which they are affiliated.

Community dispute resolution activist Marcia Choo of the Black/Korean Alliance in Los Angeles tells of being criticized both by some in the Korean community for her associations with African Americans and by African Americans because she is Korean (Choo, 1994). As Edward J. W. Park notes, those Korean American activists in Los Angeles who called for alliances with Latinos and African Americans lost some ground after the 1992 upheavals in that city that pitted some in those communities against Koreans. A campaign in the African American community against the rebuilding of Korean-owned liquor stores in the inner city made it possible for some in the Korean community to argue that those calling for Korean Americans to "join Blacks and Latinos to fight white racism" were "simple and idealistic" and out of touch with their community (Park, 1998, 53). Of course, Korean American activists such as Bhong Hwan Kim and Angela Oh, who strongly support multiethnic alliances, do not lose all support. But such criticism indicates the way transcommunal activists can face real dilemmas precisely because they are reaching out to other groups.

In the United States, many efforts to create inter-racial clusters of people often run up against polarized, organized hostility in a wide range of contexts, from prison yards to school yards. In the former Yugoslavia and in Rwanda, those who sought to create links across ethnic/community lines were very much the target of attack from political elites and their paramilitary cadres that sought to benefit from a ferociously genocidal, compartmentalized, nationalistic identity. In an interview that I conducted with Petra Kelly, one of the founders of the German Green Party, she commented with great sadness on the way in which environmental and human rights activists in Yugoslavia, who had worked together, were torn apart by the conflict there. She said: "In Yugoslavia we knew many environmental and human rights groups coming from all different parts of the country. When the civil war broke out, they split. They hated each other, although they had worked together in the underground for 20 years. This is one of the saddest things I can imagine" (Kelly, 1993, 135). Observing similar splits in other parts of Europe, Petra Kelly concluded, "This is something that nobody was prepared for, nobody understood it" (135). In Rwanda, those who were called in the western media "moderate Hutus," and who were also subjected to mass murder alongside the Tutsi community, were targeted by Hutu militias (backed by some western forces) precisely because those "moderates" attempted transcommunal bridging of those groups and tried to help Tutsi people. In such settings, a transcommunal approach not only can be lethally dangerous to its adherents, but it can isolate them from the very communities to which they belong and which they are trying to connect. Even if such transcommunalists remain linked to their communities, political elites with ruthless power at their disposal can make the existence of such in-between activists virtually impossible under some circumstances.

On the other hand, I think of the 1993 Kansas City National Gang Peace Summit in which I participated as a member of the community organization Barrios Unidos. The summit, organized through such groups as the predominately Latino Barrios Unidos and the predominately African American National Urban Peace and Justice Coalition gathered gang members, community activists, and spiritual leaders from Latino, African American, and Indigenous backgrounds at the African American St. Stephen's Baptist Church. All those associated with the summit charted new ground as they crossed over gang, ethnic, and racial lines around the common goal of creating peace on the street. The Kansas City Summit was made possible by interaction that crossed various boundaries of mistrust and miscomprehension. For the several hundred who attended, it was an essential transcommunal moment. Similarly, John Calmore points to the Multi-Cultural Collaborative in Los Angeles that reaches out to a wide variety of populations precisely "because they know that any strategy to transform local neighborhoods must be multiracial and multi-ethnic. To change South-Central or Pico-Union, one cannot just attend to the needs of Blacks and Latinos" (Calmore, 1995, 1233).

Indeed, on the inner-city streets of the United States, I see increasing signs of the pragmatic/visionary impulse of transcommunality among grassroots community activists, many of them young people. For example, one of my students, Luis Muñoz, is a member of the Hip Hop music group Black N Brown, which emphasizes what I would call transcommunal interactions based on visions of social justice and practical openness to all those concerned with that objective. "Goldtoes," who heads this effort, bringing African American/Latino/Pacific Islander young people and others together, says: "Black N Brown.... It's not a color or race trip. We're not prejudice, that's one thing Black N Brown is not, we're not prejudice. I mean you could be a white dude and be Black N Brown and be down with Black N Brown." Importantly, from a transcommunal perspective, Goldtoes sees his organization as "a way of thinking and a mentality" that seeks out interconnections while celebrating difference. The ties that bind the members of Black N Brown are the thick relations of *interpersonal relations* based on *shared practical action*. Goldtoes says: "That's what it means to us, you know Black N Brown is a way of thinking a way of mentality, way of working together no matter what race you are, you feel me.... I'm gonna ride with you. That's what Black N Brown is ... we'll roll until the wheels fall off" (Goldtoes, 1999, 1).

Although the bridging aspect of transcommunality can run the danger of isolating its participants, this mode of action can also lay down a breakthrough pathway that allows pent-up positive energy to be directed toward constructive mutual understanding among previously sealed-off groups. As James Jennings proposes about such urban developments in the United States, the "realization of progressive coalitions" among diverse "communities of color ... could possibly represent the spark and substance of a new movement for social and economic change" (Jennings, 1997, 10).

For a transcommunal constellation of affiliated participants that coexists in a Haudenosaunee-like form–as both an overarching network and autonomous multiple communities and organizations—diversity is not some kind of intrinsic problem. Rather, diversity is an essential part of the solution to the question of how to combine cooperation and pluralism.

6

Roots of Cooperation

TRANSCOMMUNALITY is a practical mode of interaction that crosses and draws from distinctly rooted group locations or "emplacements." Transcommunality draws from the resource of the particularistic affiliations of its interacting participants. Being rooted in shared and tangible everyday actions, sometimes of the most minute kind, transcommunal activists do not depend completely on abstract slogans of unity. Instead, they actualize coordination through direct interpersonal relations in which the reputations of all involved are proven through their own actions. Transcommunality is process—often difficult, slow, and even defeated at certain moments—that constantly creates, and when necessary rebuilds, structures of commonality among diverse peoples. There is no map to El Dorado, to a better world to which every step must lead. Rather, improvement comes through actions that can be quite small, but all of which embody to some extent the ideals of justice and equality in however limited and imperfect a way. In its emphasis on constant dialogue to reaffirm links among diverse peoples, transcommunality is premised on the reality of imperfection. The transcommunalists recognize that humans cannot be ideal and that we are tangles of weaknesses and contradictions, individually and collectively. Indeed, "perfection" and its cousin "purity" are perceived as carrying the seeds of authoritarian dangers. That way lies dogmatism, exclusion, and eventually the excommunication and elimination of those who do not meet impossible standards exactly. Transcommunality offers a way to achieve coherence without the deadening effects of heavy-handed systems of obedience that constrain initiative and freedom in the name of initiative and freedom.

Transcommunal perspectives provide a capacity for an alliance that can be both a single structure and many structures at different moments, under different circumstances, similar to the Haudenosaunee Longhouse with its distinctly autonomous, yet flexibly cooperative, levels of organization. Such transcommunal capabilities are desperately needed to resist the nightmare of being crushed by the dead hand of a corporate world order whose destructive power is accelerated by our fragmentation and lack of constructive interaction.

My friend Guillermo Delgado pointed out to me that the Indigenous Aymara peoples of the Andes use a word that in both its complexity and vision is cousin to transcommunality. The concept *Aruskipasipxajañakasakipunirakispawa* entails the multiple, yet linked requirements "that we communicate with each other / face to face / our feet rooted in the earth / with which we also must communicate / if we are to live." This Andean Indigenous vantage point describes, I believe, an essential element of transcommunality's ability to be both rooted and embracing. It is similar to the system of coordinated autonomy developed by peoples such as the Haudenosaunee, the Wabanaki, and many others.

Hope for victory over the ravages of gigantic centralizing, militaristic systems of economic profit and power requires that we draw from a transcommunal interweaving of the diverse forms taken by the spirit of justice and freedom among the many peoples of the world.

Cummautaunchemókous.
[I have finished with my story.]

Acknowledgments

MY WIFE Delgra's love, insights, and her steadfast faith in me made this book possible.

This work draws in part from my participation in the 1998 Indigenous Intellectual Sovereignties Conference—A Hemispheric Convocation sponsored by Native American Studies at the University of California, Davis, and held consecutively at Davis, and then in Oaxaca, Mexico, at the Instituto Cultural Oaxaca. My special thanks go to Inés Hernández-Avila and Stefano Varese at the University of California, Davis, Native American Studies Department, through whose vision and efforts these important gatherings of Native American scholars, writers, and artists drawn from throughout the western hemisphere took place. The Chicano/Latino Research Center at the University of California, Santa Cruz, directed by Norma Klahn, generously supported my attendance at the Oaxaca portion of this conference, and earlier provided me with a forum for exploring these ideas of transcommunality. Temple University Press editor Micah Kleit's intellectual acuity and scholarly support were indispensable. Troy Duster and an anonymous reader for Temple University Press offered astute observations. Cheryl Van De Veer and Zoe Sodja of the Document Publishing and Editing Center at the University of California, Santa Cruz, provided very helpful assistance.

Close collaboration with Guillermo Delgado-P. (Quechua) at the University of California, Santa Cruz, makes this work possible for me. Shared work over many years with Jeremy Brecher is essential in my thinking. Discussions with Herman Gray, Troy Duster, Hardy T. Frye, and Hiroshi Fukurai over many years have been invaluable. Conversations with Risa D'Angeles and Ali Eppy have helped me develop my focus. My membership in community organizations that are attempting to bring peace to youth who are in gangs has sharpened my awareness of the importance of transcommunal alliances and the significance of respect for making such alliances work. In particular I am indebted to Daniel Nane Alejandrez of the National Coalition of Barrios Unidos as well as Mike Chavez and Lorenzo Abeyta in Watsonville, California. I have been helped by conversations with Khalid Shah of Stop the Violence/Institute the Peace in Inglewood, California.

In developing this work, I have also benefited from participating in numerous seminars and colloquia in a variety of institutions and locations. These include the Fulbright Foundation's Thomas Jefferson Chair of Distinguished Teaching in the Netherlands that I held in American Studies at the University of Utrecht in 1997. Talks that I gave in Utrecht and at the University of Amsterdam, the Hogeshschool of the University of Amsterdam, the University of Leiden, Nijmegan University, and the United States Embassy in the Hague were highly useful, as were the insightful students in my seminars at Utrecht and a lecture in 1999 in the African American Century Series in American Studies/Literature at the University of Leiden. In the Netherlands I owe special thanks to Eduard van der Bilt, Tilly de Groot, Joke Kadux, Jaap Verheul, and the many other Dutch colleagues whose hospitality was so helpful. Also, colloquia at the Centre de recherches et d'études internationales (CERI) in Paris, and the Centre d'Études Canadiennes (CEC), Université de Paris III—Sorbonne Nouvelle were invaluable. I owe special thanks to Denis-Constant Martin of CERI, and to Danièle Stewart and Jean-Michel Lacroix of the Sorbonne.

I benefited from a colloquium that I gave in Japan at Senshu University and meetings with the hospitable Wakayama City Government. Conversations in Japan with Haruhiko Kanegae, Michihiko Noguchi, and my Santa Cruz colleague John Kitsuse were valuable. In New Zealand, Valerie Kuletz helpfully arranged for my participation in productive discussions at a Christchurch University Fulbright-sponsored American Studies Conference. I gained a great deal from discussions at a colloquium organized by Bogumil Jewsiewicki and Jocelyn Létorneau of CÉLAT at l'Université Laval, Québec.

Discussions with Renate Holub and others at the Center for European Studies at the University of California, Berkeley, were also helpful. At the University of California, Santa Cruz, James Clifford and the Center for Cultural Studies provided an important early setting for some of these thoughts, as did Arif Dirlik at Duke University. The Coalition of Black Health Care Professionals in Tallahassee, Florida, provided an important public forum for expression of some of these ideas, as did the Community of Reconciliation Church in Pittsburgh, Pennsylvania; Temple Beth El in Santa Cruz, California; as well as the University of Pittsburgh Theological Seminary and the Maryknoll People to People Peacemaking Conference of 2002. Michael Perstchuk, David Cohen, Kathleen D. Sheeky, and Maureen Burke of the Advocacy Institute in Washington, D.C., continue to provide important settings for the discussion and practice of cooperation and dialogue that has transcommunal implications.

Talking with Mohawk/Mississagua-descent Lynne Williamson and Gerald Taiaiake Alfred (Mohawk) aided my thinking about the Haudenosaunee. Also sustaining was the hospitality of Peter Jemison (Seneca), Director of the Gonondagon Historical Site in New York State, during an inspiring visit that I made to that Seneca location where the Peacemaker met with the Mother of the Nations to begin the founding of the Haudenosaunee. Visits to the former land of my Massachusett Native American ancestors at Punkapoag in the Blue Hills outside of Boston and at the ancient village site of the Quabbin "Rock House" in Massachusetts similarly gave me heart and direction, as did my return to the red clay land of my father's family in Marion, Alabama. Thomas Doughton of the Nipmuck Tribal Council in Worcester, Massachusetts, was helpful in discussions about my family connections there.

Early short versions of portions of this work have appeared in *Z Magazine, Theory and Society, Razateca, Social Justice,* and in the anthology *Places and Politics in an Age of Globalization* (R. Prazniak and A. Dirlik) as well as in the University of California, Santa Cruz, Chicano/Latino Research Center Working Paper Series.

Notes

Epigraphs: Adapted from the Algonkian language used by my Massachusett ancestors. See Roger Williams, *A Key into the Language of America or An Help to the Language of the Natives in That Part of America Called New England* (1643).

The Message of the Peacemaker is adapted from *The White Roots of Peace* by Paul A. W. Wallace.

First Words

1. For another important discussion of rootedness, see Toni Morrison's essay "Rootedness: The Ancestor as Foundation" and G. Alfred's *Heeding the Voices of Our Ancestors.*

2. See for example Guillermo Delgado and Marc Becker, "Latin America: The Internet and Indigenous Texts."

3. See for example Herman Gray, *Watching Race: Television and the Struggle for "Blackness."*

4. For a parallel discussion of global homogenization, see Arif Dirlik, "The Past as Legacy and Project," where he writes that the "assertion of homogenized cultural identities on the one hand celebrates success in the world economy but also, on the other hand, seeks to contain the disintegrative threat of Western commodity culture, the social incoherence brought about by capitalist development, and the cultural confusion brought about by diasporic populations that have called into question the identification of national culture" (1996b, 9).

Chapter One

1. There are many different editions of the *Communist Manifesto.* This citation is from Arthur P. Mendel's edited *Essential Works of Marxism.*

2. For a discussion of globalism, see Jeremy Brecher and Tim Costello, *Global Village or Global Pillage*. Lenin's analysis in *Imperialism, the Highest Stage of Capitalism* remains a vital work for understanding today's global structures. For an analysis of the absorption of significant portions of national middle classes into a global "hyperbourgoisie," see the essay by Denis Duclos, "Naissance de l'hyperbourgoisie."

3. For an important discussion of some of the philosophical issues related to these questions of cooperation, community, and heterogeneity, see Ernest Gellner's *Language and Solitude*.

4. For an important description of pragmatic utopian thinking parallel to my concerns here, see Immanuel Wallerstein's *Utopistics* (1998). Also useful are the essays in the September/October 1998 "Mannier de voir" 41 of *Le Monde Diplomatique*, edited by Ignaciao Ramonet and entitled *Un Autre Monde Est Possible* (Another World Is Possible).

Chapter Two

Epigraph: Cited in Raymond K. Kent, *Early Kingdoms in Madagascar, 1500–1700.*

1. Such confederacies were fluid and their composition could change over time. This is another important transcommunal aspect of such modes of organization.

2. For a description of the Burr family in the context of Massachusetts Native American history, see Thomas L. Doughton, "Unseen Neighbors: Native Americans of Central Massachusetts: A People Who Had 'Vanished.'"

3. For an epic depiction of the cross-currents created by oppression in the Americas, see Eduardo Galeano's trilogy *Memory of Fire*.

4. For discussions of issues related to this sense of the "in-between place," see Jack Forbes, *Africans and Native Americans;* Jean-Loup Amselle, *Logiques métisses;* and James Clifford, *Routes*. For discussion of African Americans and Native Americans in New England, see the following chapters in the book *After King Philip's War*, edited by Colin G. Calloway and Jean M. O'Brien, "'Divorced' from the Land: Resistance and Survival of Indian Women in Eighteenth-Century New England"; Ann Marie Plane and Gregory Button, "The Massachusetts Indian Enfranchisement Act: Ethnic Contest in Historical Context, 1849–1869"; and Thomas L. Doughton, "Unseen Neighbors: Native Americans of Central Massachusetts: A People Who Had 'Vanished.'" Also, Paula Gunn Allen's *Off the Reservation* is an important contribution to the discussion of these dimensions.

Chapter Three

1. This transcommunal view, with its emphasis on participants who interact based on their *clearly defined* fundamental affiliations, stands in contrast to the "blurring of genres" concept pioneered by Clifford Geertz (1983). For anthropological renderings of the way in which fluidly interacting groupings can also be clearly defined rather than having to be blurred, see E. R. Leach, *Political Systems of Highland Burma,* and my book *The Political Black Minister.*

2. For discussion of nonlineal, or circular modes of thought, see the classic Mayan text *Popol Vuh.* There are several translations of this now available. The one I have read is translated by Ralph Nelson. The great Muslim scholar of Moorish Iberia, Ibn Khaldun, offers a nonlineal, cyclical view of history as oscillating tension between the urban and the nomadic in his magnum opus *The Muqaddimah: An Introduction to History* that is an important alternative to Marx and Engels's famous dictum in the *Communist Manifesto* about history being class struggle. Ibn Khaldun's formulation is more explanatory of much of European, Chinese, and Meso-American history than is the class struggle. Also see Fiumara, *The Other Side of Language,* Dorothy Lee's *Freedom and Culture,* and Carlos Fuentes's discussion of a Baroque outlook as "circular and not frontal" (1997, 8). Gilles Deleuze has important insights on this angle of approach in his work *The Fold: Leibniz and the Baroque* (1993b). The fact that some New Age romantics may overdo or mangle the emphasis on Indigenous "circular thinking" should not diminish the importance of this nonlineal/antilineal mode of thought that is found in many different cultures and historical moments around the world.

3. For an important analysis of the significance of listening that parallels many of my concerns, see Fiumara, *The Other Side of Language.*

4. For important discussion of linked autonomy, see Patricia Hill Collins, *Black Feminist Thought.*

5. For a useful discussion of the term *Indigenous* as an aspect of autocreation, see Stefano Varese, ed., *Pueblos Indios* (1996). Franke Wilmer's *The Indigenous Voice in World Politics* (1993) is an important contribution to this area. For a short discussion of this topic, see John Brown Childs and Guillermo Delgado, "On the Idea of Indigenous," in *Current Anthropology* (1999).

6. Indigenous Mapuche activists in Chile have developed the concept of "free determination" as distinct from "self-determination." As I understand it, free determination precedes self-determination, which usually implies national independence. These Mapuche activists argue that it is up to Indigenous peoples to decide what form and degree of "self-determination" vis-à-vis the state should take place. Aucan Huilcaman,

spokesperson of the Mapuche organization "Aukin Wallmapu Ngulam," says of this issue, "Indigenous peoples are fighting for free determination not self-determination. These concepts have different meanings and implications. . . . Indigenous peoples have yet to determine whether we want to develop ourselves within or outside the structures of the so-called nation-states" (1994, 24).

7. As Arif Dirlik observes, "Indigenous claims to identity are very much tied in with a desperate concern for survival; not in a 'metaphorical' but in a very material sense" (1996b, 11).

8. Although it is obviously a quite different phenomenon from that of Indigenous concerns with ancestral/spiritual space, much of African American political thought in the United States is also land oriented, as James Jennings points out in *The Politics of Black Empowerment* when he says, "Black empowerment activism, however, focuses on control of land. . . . It surpasses affirmative action, job discrimination, or school integration as priorities." Moreover, says Jennings, such land-oriented activism is community oriented rather than being aimed to "primarily benefit Black individuals" (1992, 77). For a pivotal analysis of Indigenous land issues and the state in Africa, see M. A. Mohamed Salih, "Indigenous Peoples and the African State."

9. For a sobering analysis of the devastating "radical" consequences of western scientific thought on the environment and Indigenous peoples in the U.S. Southwest, see Valerie Kuletz's *The Tainted Desert*.

10. See Simone Weil's critique of the negative consequences of the French Revolution's dramatic severing of the links to the past in her work *The Need for Roots*.

11. Important discussions of tradition can be found in Robert Warrior (1995) and Paul Gilroy's *Black Atlantic* (1993). Joke Kadux's 1998 discussion of Toni Morrison's work offers important insights on this subject.

12. Rev. James Cone wrestles with similar structural problems in his discussion of the black church and Marxism. Cone notes that "The indifference of socialism toward the black church is mirrored in the indifference of the black church toward socialism." But, says Cone, given the corrosive pressures of capitalism, both of those perspectives should work together. "Perhaps what we need today is to return to that 'good old time religion' of our grandparents and combine it with a marxist critique of society" (1980, 3, 10). Similarly in my work with African American politically active ministers in Buffalo, New York, I found a complex and fluid intermingling of spiritual faith and critiques of capitalism (Childs, 1980).

13. Similarly bell hooks argues that "One of the greatest difficulties the left faces in reaching out to masses of people in America is its profound disrespect of spirituality and religious life" (1998, 43).

14. See also, for example, Ronald Niezen, *Defending the Land*.

15. Frantz Fanon provided a pivotal discussion of Shantytown social/political potential in *The Wretched of the Earth*, although his emphasis on the marxist term "lumpenproletariat" or "underclass" with its "pimps" and "gangsters" misses the more richly textured multidimensionality of these suppressed and beleaguered communities.

16. Antonio Gramsci, one of the most open of Marxist theorists/activists, recognized the need for such inclusionary approaches when he argued that the northern Italian industrial working class would have to incorporate the distinctive situations and outlooks of the southern peasants to make a broadly developed revolutionary organization a reality as in *The Modern Prince*. For my own use of Gramsci's approaches to analyze the United States, see my "Transcommunality: A 21st Century Social Compact for Urban Revitalization in the United States" in *Villes et Politiques Urbaines*. Another example of a nondogmatic and inclusionary Marxist was Ricardo Ramirez, secretary general of a political party organized by the "Guatemalan National Revolutionary Unit." Jorge Castañeda notes, in *Utopia Unarmed*, that Ramirez was especially alert to the ways in which Indigenous peoples had to be accepted as allies on terms that met their own needs. For a further important discussion of such issues in Marxism, see Cornel West, *The Ethical Dimensions of Marxist Thought*.

Chapter Four

1. See for example John Calmore's discussion of multicultural alliances (1995), Piven and Cloward's work on "poor peoples movements" (1979), and David V. Carruthers's "Indigenous Ecology and the Politics of Linkage in Mexican Social Movements" (1996). Also worth examining is John Kuo Wei Tchen's "The Chinatown-Harlem Initiative" (1990). The French underground resistance to Nazi occupation had many of the elements that I discuss under the term *transcommunality*. See for example John F. Sweets, *The Politics of Resistance in France* (1976). The Southwest Network for Economic and Environmental Justice brings together a range of Native American, Mexican American, African American, and Mexican communities in its cross-border work. The Advocacy Institute in Washington, D.C., that works to enhance the capacity of social/economic grassroots organizing is creating a broad range of interactions among community organizers from South Asia and South Africa and Eastern Europe to the United States. For an extended discussion by Robert A. Williams of Haudenosaunee alliances that builds on his 1996 *California Law Review* essay cited in this book, see his *Linking Arms Together: American Indian Treaty Visions of Law and Peace, 1600–1800* (1997).

2. For example, Colin G. Calloway describes the Western Abenaki organization as "fluid and flexible, and bands accommodated both separation and integration" (1990, 10).

3. There is a lively debate on the issue of how and what influence the Haudenosaunee had on the development of U.S. constitutional thought. See also the Mohawk Nation/Akwasasne (undated) pamphlet about the "Great Tree of Peace." For a perspective different from that of the scholars listed here, see Elisabeth Tooker's "The United States Constitution and the Iroquois League" (1988).

4. For an important overview discussion of the relationship of Indigenous organizations to global activism, see Franke Wilmer's *The Indigenous Voice in World Politics*.

5. Hiawatha is not to be confused with the character of Longfellow's poem, "The Song of Hiawatha," which has nothing to do with the Haudenosaunee. Longfellow's poem is based on the epic story of the Algonkian hero Nanabozho. Longfellow dropped that name and inaccurately adopted the name of Hiawatha.

Chapter Five

1. See also Luis Rodriguez's *Always Running: La Vida Loca: Gang Days in L.A.*

2. This classic Haudenosaunee form of flexible organization foreshadows, I believe, Gilles Deleuze's observations on "multiplicity," in which he describes "movements of deterritorialization and processes of reterritorialization" (1993, 32a). A symposium on various modes of knowledge that emphasize such engaged/disengaged flexibility/unity/diversity would be useful.

3. For an example of such a mechanical approach to coalition building in which the emphasis is on trade-offs among different "players," see Gary Marx and Michael Useem, "Majority Involvement in Minority Movements: Civil Rights, Abolition, Untouchability."

References

Adamson, Rebecca. 1996. "The Spirituality of Indigenous Development." *Native Americans: Akwe:kon Journal of Indigenous Issues*, 8(1): 64.

Alfred, Gerald Taiaiake. 1995. *Heeding the Voices of Our Ancestors*. New York: Oxford University Press.

Allen, Paula Gunn. 1998. *Off the Reservation: Reflections on Boundary-Busting, Border-Crossing, Loose Canons*. Boston: Beacon Press.

Alexie, Sherman. 1995. *Reservation Blues*. New York: Warner Books.

Amselle, Jean-Loup. 1990. *Logiques métisses: Anthropologie de l'identité en Afrique et ailleurs*. Paris: Payot.

Angotti, Thomas. 1995. "The Latin American Metropolis and the Growth of Inequality." *NACLA Report on the Americas*, 28(4): 13–18.

Aukin Wallmapu Ngulam/Consejo de Todas las Tierras. *Temuco Wall-Mapuche Declaration on the North American Free Trade Agreement, Indigenous Peoples and Their Rights*, 1994 [235-97 Casilla 448] Temuco, Chile. <http://abyayala.nativeweb.org/cultures/chile/nafta.html>

Bakhtin, Mikhail B. 1993. *Toward a Philosophy of the Act*. Trans. V. Liapunov. Austin: Univ. of Texas Press.

Berlin, Isaiah. 1957. *The Hedgehog and the Fox: An Essay on Tolstoy's View of History*. New York: New American Library.

Bond, Horace Mann. 1972. *Black American Scholars: A Study of Their Origins*. Detroit: Balamp Publishing.

Brasser, T. J. 1978. "Early Indian-European Contacts." In *Handbook of North American Indians*. Ed. Bruce Trigger et al. Washington, DC: Smithsonian Press.

Brecher, Jeremy, and Tim Costello, eds. 1994. *Global Village or Global Pillage*. Boston: South End Press.

Bruchac, Joseph. 1993. *Dawn Land*. Golden, CO: Fulcrum Publishing.

Calloway, Colin G., ed. 1998. *After King Philip's War: Presence and Persistence in Indian New England*. Hanover, NH: Dartmouth College/Univ. Press of New England.

————. 1990. *The Western Abenakis of Vermont, 1600–1800: War, Migration, and the Survival of an Indian People*. Norman: Univ. of Oklahoma Press.

Calmore, John. 1995. "Racialized Space and the Culture of Segregation: 'Hewing a Stone of Hope from a Mountain of Despair.'" *University of Pennsylvania Law Review*, 143: 1233–1273.

Campbell, Maria, and Winona Stevenson. 1998. "Towards a Cree Understanding of Colonialism." Talk given at conference, Indigenous Intellectual Sovereignties: A Hemispheric Convocation, Native American Studies Department, University of California, Davis.

Carruthers, David V. 1996. "Indigenous Ecology and the Politics of Linkage in Mexican Social Movements." CERLAC Working Paper Series, No. 5, York University, Ontario.

Castañeda, Jorge G. 1994. *Utopia Unarmed: The Latin American Left After the Cold War*. New York: Vintage Books.

Cayuqueo, Nilo. 1982. "Interview with Nilo Cayuqueo." Conducted by Zoltan Grossman, trans. Jo Tucker. *Latin American Perspectives*, 9(2): 100–107.

Chase, Steve. 2001. "Quebec City Reflections—A Letter from Quebec." Internet <communique/owner-ecopolitics@efn.org>

Childs, Idella. 1991. "The Lincoln Normal School." In *A History of Perry County, 1814–1877*, by W. Stuart Harris. Marion, AL: W. Stuart Harris.

Childs, John Brown. 1980. *The Political Black Minister: A Study in Afro-American Politics and Religion*. Boston: G. K. Hall.

————. 1989. *Leadership, Conflict, and Cooperation in Afro-American Social Thought*. Philadelphia: Temple Univ. Press.

————. 1994. "The Value of Transcommunal Identity Politics: Transcommunality and the Peace and Justice Gang Truce in Kansas City." *Z Magazine*, 7(7/8): 48–51.

————. 1994. "Field Notes" (unpublished).

————. 1995. Notes on the 1995 National Coalition of Barrios Unidos Youth Peace Summit, Santa Cruz, California (unpublished).

————. 1996. "Peace in the Streets: The New Youth Peace Movement." *Z Magazine*, 9(11): 40–43.

————. 1997. "Transcommunality: A 21st Century Social Compact for Urban Revitalization in the United States." In *Villes et politiques urbaines au Canada et aux États Unis*. Ed. Jean-Michel Lacroix. Paris: Presses de la Sorbonne Nouvelle.

———, and Guillermo Delgado. 1999. "On the Idea of Indigenous." *Current Anthropology*, 40(2): 211–212.

Choo, Marcia. 1994. "Being a Korean-American Activist in Post–Rodney King Los Angeles." Talk given at the Emerging Majority or Warring Minorities Conference, Univ. of California, Santa Cruz.

Christian, Charles M., and Sari J. Bennett. 1995. *Black Saga: The African American Experience*. Boston: Houghton Mifflin.

Churchill, Ward. 1996. *From a Native Son: Selected Essays on Indigenism, 1985–1995*. Boston: South End Press.

Clifford, James. 1997. *Routes: Travel and Translation in the Late Twentieth Century*. Cambridge, MA: Harvard Univ. Press.

Cojean, Annick. 1998. "Vivre et mourir au Nunavut." *Le Monde* (29 August): 13.

Collins, Patricia Hill. 1990. *Black Feminist Thought: Knowledge, Consciousness, and the Politics of Empowerment*. New York: Routledge.

Cone, James. 1980. *The Black Church and Marxism: What Do They Have to Say to Each Other?* New York: Institute for Democratic Socialism, Occasional Paper.

Coon-Come, Matthew. 1991. "Where Can You Buy a River?" *Northeast Indian Quarterly*, 8(4): 6–11.

Corradi, Laura. 1993. "Between Integration and Seclusion: The African-Italian Labor Force." Presented at the Italian Research and Study Group, Univ. of California, Berkeley.

Deleuze, Gilles. 1993a. *The Deleuze Reader*. Ed. Constantin V. Boundas. Minneapolis: Univ. of Minnesota.

———. 1993b. *The Fold: Leibniz and the Baroque*. Trans. Tom Conley. Minneapolis: Univ. of Minnesota.

Delgado, Guillermo. 1994. "Ethnic Politics and the Popular Movements." In *Latin America Faces the 21st Century*. Ed. Susanne Jonas and Edward McCaughan. London: Westview.

———, and Susan O'Donnell. 1995. "Using the Internet to Strengthen the Indigenous Nations of the Americas." *Media Development*, 42(3): 36–39.

———, and Marc Becker. 1998. "Latin America: The Internet and Indigenous Texts." *Cultural Studies Quarterly*, 21(4): 23–28.

Deloria, Vine. 1992. "The Application of the Constitution to American Indians." In *Exiled in the Land of the Free*. Ed. Oren Lyons et al. Santa Fe: Clear Light Publishers.

Dennis, Matthew. 1993. *Cultivating a Landscape of Peace: Iroquois–European Encounters in Seventeenth-Century America*. Ithaca, NY: Cornell Univ. Press.

DePalma, Anthony. 1998. "Throughout the Americas, Natives Invoke the Law of the Land." *New York Times*, 30 August.

Dewey, John. 1927. *The Public and Its Problems*. Denver: Allan Swallow Press.

Dirlik, Arif. 2001. "Place Based Imagination: Globalism and the Politics of Place," In *Places and Politics in an Age of Globalization*. Ed. R Prazniak and A. Dirlik. New York: Rowman and Littlefield.

———. 1996a. "Mao Zedong and Chinese Marxism." In *Marxism Beyond Marxism*. Ed. S. Makdisi, C. Casarino, and R. E. Karl. New York: Routledge.

———. 1996b. "The Past as Legacy and Project: Postcolonial Criticism in the Perspective of Indigenous Historicism." *American Indian Culture and Research Journal*, 20(2): 1–31.

Doughton, Thomas L. 1998. "Unseen Neighbors: Native Americans of Central Massachusetts: A People Who Had 'Vanished.'" In *After King Philip's War: Presence and Persistence in Indian New England*. Ed. Colin G. Calloway. Hanover, NH: Univ. Press of New England.

Duclos, Denis. 1998. "Naissance de l'hyperbourgeoisie." *Le Monde Diplomatique* (August): 16–17.

Fanon, Frantz. 1963. *The Wretched of the Earth*. New York: Grove Press. (Orig. published as *Les damnés de la terre*, 1961, Francois Maspero, Paris, S.A.R.L.).

Fiumara, Gemma Corradi. 1990. *The Other Side of Language: A Philosophy of Listening*. London: Routledge.

Fixico, Donald L. 1998. "Ethics and Responsibilities in Writing American Indian History." In *Natives and Academics: Researching and Writing about American Indians*. Ed. Devon A. Mihesuah. Lincoln: Univ. of Nebraska Press.

Forbes, Jack. 1992. *Columbus and Other Cannibals*. New York: Autonomedia.

———. 1993. *Africans and Native Americans: The Language of Race and the Evolution of Red Black Peoples*. Urbana: Univ. of Illinois Press.

Friedman, Jonathan. 2001. "Indigenous Struggles and the Bourgeoisie." In *Places and Politics in an Age of Globalization*. Ed. R. Prazniak and A. Dirlik. New York: Rowman and Littlefield.

Fuentes, Carlos. 1997. *A New Time for Mexico*. Berkeley: Univ. of California.

Galeano, Eduardo. 1985. *Memory of Fire* (3 vols.). New York: Pantheon.

Geertz, Clifford. 1983. *Local Knowledge: Further Essays in Interpretive Anthropology*. New York: Basic Books.

Gellner, Ernest. 1998. *Language and Solitude: Wittgenstein, Malinowski, and the Hapsburg Dilemma*. New York: Cambridge Univ. Press.

Gilroy, Paul. 1993. *The Black Atlantic: Modernity and Double Consciousness.* Cambridge, MA: Harvard Univ. Press.

Goldtoes. 1999. "Interview with ILLTIP, Black N Brown Entertainment 18 Wit a Bullet." *The ILLTIP,* 28: 1–2.

Gorz, André. 1988. *Metamorphoses du travail, Quête du sens: Critique de la raison économique.* Paris: Editions Galilee.

Gramsci, Antonio. 1992. *The Modern Prince and Other Writings.* New York: International Publishers.

Grand Council of the Cree (of Québec). 1994. *Status and Rights of the James Bay Cree.* Nemaska, Québec.

Gray, Herman. 1995. *Watching Race: Television and the Struggle for "Blackness."* Minneapolis: Univ. of Minnesota Press.

Grinde, Donald, Jr. 1992. "Iroquois Political Theory and the Roots of American Democracy." In *Exiled in the Land of the Free.* Ed. O. Lyons et al. Santa Fe: Clear Light Publishers.

Hamer, Fannie Lou. 1981. "Interview with Fannie Lou Hamer and Ella Jo Baker." *Southern Exposure* (1): 44–48.

Hecht, David, and Maliqalim Simone. 1994. *Invisible Governance: The Art of African Micropolitics.* Brooklyn, NY: Autonomedia.

Hernández-Avila, Inés. 1998. "Meditations on the Spirit." *American Indian Quarterly,* 20(3): 329–352.

Holub, Renate. 1992. *Antonio Gramsci: Beyond Marxism and Postmodernism.* London: Routledge.

hooks, bell. 1989. *Talking Back: Thinking feminist, thinking black.* Boston: South End Press.

———. 1998. "Critical Consciousness for Political Resistance." In *Talking About a Revolution.* Ed. South End Press Collective. Boston: South End Press.

Huilcaman, Aucan. 1994. "Chiapas as Seen from Temuco: Interview with Aucan Huilcaman, Consejo de Todas las Tierras en Chile." *Abya Yala News: Journal of the South and Meso American Indian Information Center,* 8(1/2): 12–14.

———. 1994. "Free Determination and the States: Commentary on Barbados III." *Abya Yala News,* 8(4): 23–24.

Illich, Ivan. 1973. *Tools for Conviviality.* New York: Harper and Row.

Jennings, Francis, et al., eds. 1985. *The History and Culture of Iroquois Diplomacy: An Interdisciplinary Guide to the Treaties of the Six Nations and Their League.* Syracuse, NY: Syracuse Univ. Press.

Jennings, James. 1997. "Introduction: New Challenges for Black Activism in the United States." In *Race and Politics.* Ed. James Jennings. London: Verso.

—————. 1992. *The Politics of Black Empowerment: The Transformation of Black Activism in Urban America*. Detroit: Wayne State Univ. Press.

Johansen, Bruce E. 1982. *Forgotten Founders: How the American Indians Helped Shape Democracy*. Boston: Harvard Common Press.

Kadux, Joke. 1998. "Witnessing the Middle Passage: Trauma and Memory in the Narratives of Olaudah Equiano and Venture Smith and in Toni Morrison's *Beloved*." In *Mapping African America: History, Narrative Formation, and the Production of Knowledge* (pp. 147–161). Ed. Maria Diedrich, Carl Pedersen, and Justine Tally. Hamburg: LIT Verlag.

Kastoryano, Riva. 1996. *La France, L'Allemagne et leurs immigrés: négocier l'identité*. Paris: Armand Colin.

Kelly, Petra. 1993. "A Very Bad Way to Enter the Next Century." In *Global Visions: Beyond the New World Order*. Ed. Jeremy Brecher, John Brown Childs, and Jill Cutler. Boston: South End Press.

Kent, Raymond K. 1970. *Early Kingdoms in Madagascar, 1500–1700*. New York: Holt, Rinehart and Winston.

Khaldun, Ibn. 1989. *The Muqaddimah: An Introduction to History*. Trans. Franz Rosenthal, Ed. N. J. Dawood. Princeton, NJ: Princeton Univ. Press.

King, Martin Luther, Jr. 1967. *Where Do We Go From Here: Chaos or Community?*. New York: Harper and Row.

Kuletz, Valerie L. 1998. *The Tainted Desert: Environmental and Social Ruin in the American West*. New York: Routledge.

Kuo Wei Tchen, John. 1990. "The Chinatown-Harlem Initiative: Building Multicultural Understanding in New York City." In *Building Bridges: The Emerging Grassroots Coalition of Labor and Community*. Ed. Jeremy Brecher and Tim Costello. New York: Monthly Review Press.

LaDuke, Winona. 1991. "Environmental Impacts of Hydro-Development in the James Bay Region." *Northeast Indian Quarterly/AKWE:KON Journal*, 8(4): 16–19.

—————. 1998. "Power Is the Earth." In *Talking About a Revolution*. Ed. South End Press Collective. Boston: South End Press.

Lăm, Maivăn Clech. 1996. "A Resistance Role for Marxism in the Belly of the Beast." In *Marxism Beyond Marxism*. Ed. Sarce Makdisi, Cesare Casarino, and Rebecca E. Karl. New York: Routledge.

Leach, E. R. 1954. *Political Systems of Highland Burma: A Study of Kachin Social Structure*. Boston: Beacon Press.

Lee, Dorothy. 1959. *Freedom and Culture*. Englewood Cliffs, NJ: Prentice-Hall.

Lenin, V. I. 1973. *Imperialism, the Highest Stage of Capitalism*. Beijing: Foreign Language Press. (Orig. published 1917.)

León-Portilla, Miguel. 1993. *La Filosofía Náhuatl: Estudiada En Sus Fuentes.* Mexico, D.F.: Universidad Nacional Autnomoma de Mexico.
———. 1997. *Pueblos Originarios y Globalizacíon.* Mexico, D.F.: El Colegio Nacional.
Lopez, Atencío. 1994. "Interview." *Abya Yala News: Journal of the South and Meso American Information Center,* 8(1/2): 21.
Lyons, Oren. 1992. "The American Indian in the Past." In *Exiled in the Land of the Free: Democracy, Indian Nations, and the U.S. Constitution.* Ed. O. Lyons et al. Santa Fe: Clear Light Publishers.
Martin, Denis-Constant. 1992. *La découverte des cultures politiques.* Paris: Fondation National des Sciences Politiques, Centre d'études et de recherches internationales.
———. 1994. "Introduction. Identités et politique: Récit, mythe, et ideologie." In *Cartes d'identité: Comment dit-on "nous" en politique.* Ed. Denis-Constant Martin. Paris: Presses de la Fondation National des Sciences Politiques.
Marx, Gary, and Michael Useem. 1977. "Majority Involvement in Minority Movements: Civil Rights, Abolition, Untouchability." In *Issues in Race and Ethnic Relations: Theory, Research, Action.* Ed. Jack Rothman. Itasca, IL: F. E. Peacock.
Marx, Karl, and Friedrich Engels. 1963. "The Communist Manifesto." In *Essential Works of Marxism.* Ed. Arthur P. Mendel. New York: Bantam Books.
Mohawk, John. 1986. "Prologue." In *The White Roots of Peace* by Paul A. Wallace. Saranac Lake, NY: Chauncy Press.
———. 1992. "Indians and Democracy: No One Ever Told Us." In *Exiled in the Land of the Free.* Ed. O. Lyons et al. Santa Fe: Clear Light Publishers.
Mohawk Nation/Akwasasne. N.d. *The Great Law of Peace and the Constitution of the United States.* Akwasasne, NY: Tree of Peace Society.
Morgan, Lewis Henry. 1851. *The League of the Ho-di-no-sau-nee, Iroquois.* Rochester, NY: Sage and Brother.
Morrison, Toni. 1984. "Rootedness: The Ancestor as Foundation." In *Black Women Writers, 1950–1980: A Critical Evaluation.* Ed. Mari Evans. Garden City, NY: Doubleday.
Nelson, Ralph, trans. 1977. *Popol Vuh: The Great Mythological Book of the Ancient Maya.* Boston: Houghton Mifflin.
Niezen, Ronald. 1998. *Defending the Land: Sovereignty and Forest Life in James Bay Cree Society.* Toronto: Allyn and Bacon.
O'Brien, Jean M. 1997. "'Divorced' from the Land: Resistance and Survival of Indian Women in Eighteenth-Century New England." In *After*

King Philip's War: Presence and Persistence in Indian New England. Ed. Colin G. Calloway. Hanover, NH: Univ. Press of New England.

Pablo, Gordon. 1992. "The Land Is My Mother." In *A Story to Tell: The Working Lives of Ten Aboriginal Australians*. Ed. Nan Gallagher. Cambridge: Cambridge Univ. Press.

Park, Edward J. W. 1998. "Competing Visions: Political Formation of Korean Americans in Los Angeles, 1992–1997." *Amerasia Journal*, 24(1): 41–57.

Piven, Frances Fox, and Richard A. Cloward. 1979. *Poor People's Movements: Why They Succeed, How They Fail*. New York: Random House.

Plane, Ann Marie, and Gregory Button. 1997. "The Massachusetts Indian Enfranchisement Act: Ethnic Contest in Historical Context, 1849–1869." In *After King Philip's War: Presence and Persistence in Indian New England*. Ed. Collin G. Calloway. Hanover, NH: Univ. Press of New England.

Ramonet, Ignacio, ed. 1998. *Un Autre Monde Est Possible. Mannier de voir, 41/Le Monde Diplomatique*.

Rodriguez, Luis. 1993. *Always Running: La Vida Loca: Gang Days in L.A.* New York: Simon and Schuster.

Salih, M. A. Mohamed. 1993. "Indigenous Peoples and the African State." In *Never Drink from the Same Cup Twice*. Copenhagen: Working Group on Indigenous Peoples and the Centre of Development Research, Univ. of Copenhagen.

Salwen, Bert. 1978. "Indians of Southern New England and Long Island, Early Period." In *Handbook of North American Indians*. Ed. Bruce Trigger et al. Washington, DC: Smithsonian.

Shah, Khalid. 1996. "Stop the Violence/Increase the Peace" (interview by Robin Wright). *Hope Magazine*, 1(1): 36.

Sioui, Georges E. 1992. *For an Amerindian Autohistory: An Essay on the Foundations of a Social Ethic*. Trans. Sheila Fischman. Montreal: McGill Univ. Press.

Smith, Wadada Leo. 1973. *notes (8 pieces) source a new world music: creative music*.

Soyinka, Wole. 1988. *Art, Dialogue, and Outrage: Essays on Literature and Culture*. New York: Pantheon Books.

Sweets, John F. 1976. *The Politics of Resistance in France, 1940–1944*. DeKalb: Northern Illinois Univ. Press.

Tehanetorens. 1976. *Tales of the Iroquois*. Mohawk Nation, Rooseveltown, NY: Akwasasne Notes.

Thancoupie. 1993. "Thankoupie." In *Murawina: An Authentic Aboriginal Message*. Ed. Roberta B. Sykes. Sydney, Australia: Smith and Taylor.

Tocqueville, Alexis de. 1960. *Democracy in America.* New York: Vintage.

Todorov, Tzvetan. 1984. *Mikhail Bakhtin: the Dialogic Principle.* Minneapolis: Univ. of Minnesota Press.

——. 1993. *On Human Diversity: Nationalism, Racism, and Exoticism in French Thought.* Trans. C. Porter. Cambridge, MA: Harvard Univ. Press.

Tokar, Brian. 1995. "Grassroots Victories, Lobbyist Gridlock." *Z Magazine,* 8(2): 47–53.

Tooker, Elisabeth. 1988. "The United States Constitution and the Iroquois League." *Ethnohistory,* 35(4): 305–336.

Trask, Haunani-Kay. 1993. *Notes from a Native Daughter: Colonialism and Sovereignty in Hawai'i.* Monroe, ME: Common Courage Press.

Varese, Stefano. 1982. "Restoring Multiplicity: Indianities and the Civilizing Project in Latin America." Trans. Cesar Terrientes. *Latin American Perspectives,* 9(2): 29–41.

——. 1997. "Identidad y Destierrro: Los Pueblos Indigenas Ante La Globalizacíon," *Revista de Critica Literaria LatinoAmericana,* 2: 19–35.

——, ed. 1996. *Pueblos indios, sobreania y globalismo.* Quito, Ecuador: Abyaala Press.

Wallace, Paul A. 1986. *The White Roots of Peace.* Saranac Lake, NY: Chauncy Press.

Wallerstein, Immanuel. 1998. *Utopistics: Or, Historical Choices of the Twenty-First Century.* New York: New Press.

Warrior, Robert. 1995. *Tribal Secrets: Recovering American Indian Intellectual Traditions.* Minneapolis: Univ. of Minnesota Press.

Weil, Simone. 1952. *The Need for Roots: Prelude to a Declaration of Duties Towards Mankind.* Trans. A. Wills. New York: G. P. Putnam's Sons. (Orig. published as *L'Enracinement: Prélude a une déclaration des devoirs envers l'être humain.* Paris: Editions Gallimard, 1949.)

West, Cornel. 1991. *The Ethical Dimensions of Marxist Thought.* New York: Monthly Review Press.

Williams, Robert A., Jr. 1996. "Linking Arms Together: Multicultural Constitutionalism, a North American Indigenous Vision of Law and Peace." *California Law Review,* July, West Internet Services, pp. 1–195. (Orig. published in the *California Law Review,* July 1994.)

——. 1997. *Linking Arms Together: American Indian Treaty Visions of Law and Peace, 1600–1800.* New York: Oxford.

Williams, Roger. 1936. *A Key into the Language of America or An Help to the Language of the Natives in That Part of America Called New England.* Bedford, MA: Applewood Books. (Orig. published 1643.)

Williamson, Lynne. 1993. "The Great Tree of Peace." In *Global Visions: Beyond the New World Order*. Ed. Jeremy Brecher, John Brown Childs, and Jill Cutler. Boston: South End Press.

———. 1995. Personal Communication.

Wilmer, Franke. 1993. *The Indigenous Voice in World Politics*. Newbury Park, CA: Sage Publications.

Commentaries

John Brown Childs

A Quipu String of Commentaries

Some Reflections

TRANSCOMMUNALITY emphasizes openness to many voices, many places. Consequently, I would undermine the very essence of this concept were I to present it only through my voice. I do not want a monologue about dialogue. So I invited a range of perspectives on this notion of transcommunality to be included as part of the book itself. My aspiration here is to add several different vantage points from thoughtful commentators, all of whom are involved in their own places of social justice creativity. But these commentaries do more than simply add on to the book and to each other. Rather they act more dynamically in the same way as did the supple system of knotted-string recording by the Inca nation, known as the *Quipu*.

The Quipu consisted of cotton threads with many knotted cords of different colors. They were used to keep tallies on the resources of the Inca's vast nation. But as Adrien von Hagen and Craig Morris suggest, "they may also have served as mnemonic aids for remembering oral tradition."[1] Most importantly, the adding of knots of different colors did not simply result in compilations. Rather, as my Andean friend and colleague, the writer/anthropologist Guillermo Delgado, points out, each new knot changes the meaning of the thread. So in addition to accumulation of information, there is also transformation of meaning through the interaction of the different locations.

Of course each of these commentaries adds further information to our discussion of transcommunality. But with a Quipu-like intent, each one, by contributing a distinctive vantage point, also transforms the overall discussion. So it is in the transcommunal spirit of both interaction and transformation, of the Quipu knotted string, that these commentaries are offered here.

Note

1. Craig Morris and Adriana von Hagen. 1998. *The Cities of the Ancient Andes*. London: Thames and Hudson.

Guillermo Delgado-P.

Transcommunality

Beyond Tolerance, for Understanding

> We depend on one another, the living on the living, the living on the dead, and the dead on the living.
>
> —Jesús Urzagasti, *In the Land of Silence* (1987)

"WARRING MINORITIES/EMERGENT MAJORITIES," a multiethnic conference organized by Dana Takagi and John Brown Childs in 1994, met at the University of California, Santa Cruz, during the peak year of neoliberal reforms taking place in the globalized world. The conference can now be remembered as inspiring the meditation and contemplation of the notion of *transcommunality*. Often the term *contemplation* can be interpreted in a passive way, but I would rather like to invoke its *active* connotation, its ability to entice and inspire, to promote mutual understandings from *positions of strength, mediation, and wisdom.*

A year before, in 1993, Jeremy Brecher, John Brown Childs, and Jill Cutler as editors had offered an important compilation of up-to-date essays entitled *Global Visions: Beyond the New World Order.* The text offered readers different perspectives of the notion of "globalization from below," to contrast with "globalization from

Editor's Note: Guillermo Delgado-P.'s name also appears as Guillermo Delgado elsewhere in this book.

the top" (1993, xvi–xxi). Those were the early 1990s. U.S. Marines intervened in Haiti as they had a few years before in Panama. On the first of January 1994, the Zapatistas of southern Chiapas, Mexico, rebelled in what has become a historical watershed. The Zapatistas fulfilled predictions made in the early 1960s when several Indigenous organizations of the Americas called for the decentralized and coordinated unification of "originary peoples" of the Eagle and the Condor, the Jaguar and the Quetzal, after 500 years of marginalization and dis/memberment.

Extending the title of the conference into similar situations of other minorities in the Americas, beyond the U.S. mainstream, I am positive that confidence in peoples' capacity to think, dream, and cross over barriers and borders has been tenacious. Grassroot confidence had hesitated during the Reagan era, sometimes overshadowed by leadership personalities, contrived by nation-state interests, often challenged by transnational corporations, media schemes, and great banking systems. The Santa Cruz conference addressed strategies that would help to enhance alliances among minorities, building on political agency beyond constraints imposed by interethnic fear, racism, or misunderstanding. It called for the multicultural displacement of the classic U.S. black and white divide, a narrative that continues to feed the diachronic imagery of official U.S. history and much journalism. It was at this conference that I heard the public coinage of the concept of *transcommunality* for the first time.

The merging of minority-majority dialogue that I observed at Santa Cruz elicited the need to coordinate action, often for self-defense, within the "entrails of the monster," as evoked by Cuban liberationist José Martí at the outset of the twentieth century. Activists and scholars attending the conference valued the need to be culturally transgressive, or better yet, culturally political. Against the backdrop of imperialist (and neocolonial) realignments, these voices, leading their respective communities, rose from the depths of ignored, invisible, or denied histories, to testify about the sizzling element of the melting pot. (Américo Paredes said decades ago that in the United States, "more than a melting-pot we had a sizzling fry-pan.") An eloquent rethinking of such a position that reaches out in a transcommunal way has been articulated by Cherríe Moraga in her 1993 text "Queer Aztlán: The Re-formation of the Chicano Tribe." Such a piece responds to the concern for understanding sharper articulations of solidarity of peoples' movements.

Several who attended the gathering were seeking to reestablish *transcommunal cadres* of Asian Americans, Afro-Americans, Chicano/Chicana, Latino/Latina Americans, and Native Americans. All were crossing borders to confront the Republican administration and its offspring, globalization, and neoliberalism. Still, after Republican administrations, current forces of globalization can be interpreted as renewed attempts at erasing cultural particularities, biodiversity, and Indigenous rights to self-determination. The homogenizing forces that provoke the direct and indirect disavowal of Indigenous and other sociocultural forms of being, thinking, and "protecting what is ours"—which Native American activists hemispherically agree upon—need our full attention in order that we might strategize effective oppositional responses and viable political alliances. Such opposition has been as persistent and varied as have nation-state programs of genocide, dispossession, and assimilation. Oppositional struggles persevere against the relentlessness of the allegedly new transnational corporate power.

I understand transcommunality as having heuristic and political dimensions. It illustrates the possible agency of concrete communities and social movements for social justice and social change. It provides a solid foundation on which to build alliances drawing on cultural specificity or self-knowledge and the politics of self-respect. Seeking to solve actual human strife, transcommunality embodies the predisposition of people to bear specific cultural histories, gender or sex identities, class origins, and ethnic backgrounds by going beyond constraints imposed by such specific histories. Such constraints hinder our ability to interact within what Childs calls *the ethics of respect*. In several ways, transcommunality rejects ethnic nationalisms that flourished after the 1960s. The transcommunal conversation means that rather than only *tolerating* each other, we procure *understanding* of the minority, historic-specific Other. I have thought about how *culture* could be constraining, but I have come to understand, as Gramsci had previously stated, that culture—now appropriately de-essentialized—could also act as a springboard to encourage and to trigger counter-hegemonic alliances in a transcommunal way. This, I take it, is John Brown Childs's main contribution. In a sense, the concept of transcommunality is directly linked to, and a sharper rethinking of, an early text entitled "From the 1960s into the Future" (Childs, 1989, 123–148).

I would like to reflect further on this particular concept, since concepts tend to be overlooked in the field of international and interethnic relations. This neglect is related to previous emphasis on "realist" paradigms; as a consequence, recent forms of peace-seeking strategies based on the innovative projection of concepts—such as transcommunality—are disregarded. The concept, nevertheless, can be considered as the result of concrete, situated engagement and should be seen as an important contribution of an organic intellectual.

I would like to think that transcommunality is a reply to indiscriminate, aimless violence in U.S. inner cities that are devoid of constructive projects, self-defensive, and territorialized—all well documented in Childs's "Barrio, Ghetto, or 'Hood Warfare"—as such violence has been racialized. This inner-city violence coincided with a noticeable period of change in the economic system in the United States (Childs, 1994, 49–51). Such change was known as the Republican Revolution. Reaganomics, neoliberalism, and globalization prompted strategies of self-defense amidst the U.S. urban poor in response to the Republicans' dismantling of the welfare state. Childs documented the impact as it seeped onto dejected individuals and communities.

As I situate myself in the California of the late 1980s, the following scenario appears. In the background there is Reagan-Bush and the infamous governor Pete Wilson; Republicans are ready to dismantle previous "gains" obtained by "minorities." "Hispanics" in particular lost bilingual education and Affirmative Action in California. It is also the time of *utopias* made obsolete, but where militaristic prowess could be shown, as in Iraq. Naturally, the picture is that God is on the side of the United States, protecting it (along with the "American way of life") against the evil empire of Hussein. As an awkward reflection, the left is dispersed, inhabiting its own ontological crisis, trying to reestablish a counter-hegemonic project against the "End of History" choir, but without much luck. After all, 1989 marked the collapse of the Soviet Union and the fall of the Berlin Wall, and messianically, Francis Fukuyama chanted a requiem for socialism and "Hosanna!" to the triumph of capitalism.

In 1994, inhabiting the entrails, one could be digested and excreted by capitalism gone globalized. However, the implied triumph—we know now—has been cosmetic, anonymous, and constrained to the few Silicon Valleys replicated as satellites around the world. The Janus's other face is poverty, wars, deforestation, and radical displacement. These have been persistent tropes throughout the twentieth century that especially worsened toward the end of the millennium, castigating specific peoples, specific minorities.

Prof. Hardy Frye, a former civil rights fieldworker for the Student Nonviolent Coordinating Committee (SNCC), was a very active participant at the multiethnic dialogue at UCSC. He raised several questions regarding the notion of race and politics. My own paper illustrated the idea that, as an activist and supporter of Indigenous causes, I was also seeking to establish not only inter-ethnic communication, but also intra-Indigenous dialogue to oppose racism from a decolonized perspective. I took the concept of *decolonization* as it had been retrieved by the international Indigenous movement and had been discussed in several intra- and inter-Indigenous meetings throughout the Americas. Briefly, according to Satya P. Mohanty, *decolonization* is "the process of unlearning historically determined habits of privilege and privation, of ruling and dependency—such a difficult intellectual matter that we cannot acknowledge our past or present location and simply get on with the business" (1995, 108). My point was that there is a need to *decolonize* history relentlessly. I was inspired by this term used for the first time by Silvia Rivera Cusicanqui in a seminal article, *"El Potencial Epistemológico y Teórico de la Historia Oral: De la Lógica Instrumental a la Descolonización de la Historia"* (1988).

From the hemispheric perspective of Indigenous activism, Indigenous peoples of the Condor came to understand the impact of colonialism across the Americas on the Indigenous peoples of the Eagle, the Jaguar, the Quetzal. The communication process of alliance building and revisionism are all needed to carry out the praxis of *decolonization*. Decolonizing is today an ongoing process that may never be fully completed, since new colonizers in different attires continue to arise. Yet this project serves to reinforce notions of individual and communal liberation, based on ancient wisdom, re/invented traditions, rearticulated identities and political philosophies, as the continuous challenge we pose for ourselves and to civil society in general.

Within U.S. society there exists strong determinants to demonstrate that, after all, democracy has not been a perfect system; better yes, but not perfect. Richard Rorty thinks that "democracy is still in the making—*la democracia todavía está en construcción*" (Courtoisie, 2000, 4). Leftovers of structural discrimination inhabit the minds of people who culturally reproduce a terrible distinction based mostly on constructions of race. In such a context within the United States, Latin Americans are lumped together, essentialized, regardless of regional, national, or individual identities and histories. On the other hand, racism that is also rampant in Latin American societies, rooted in historical legacies of Spanish and Luso origin, recreating a notion of intra-ethnic racism among Hispanic-rooted populations within the United States, dangerously reconstitute racial hierarchies. According to Steve Martinot, who wrote a sharp introduction to a forgotten work of Albert Memmi, "The structure of racism has four moments: First, there is an insistence on difference, whether 'real or imaginary.' It can be somatic, cultural, religious, etc.; what counts is the discernment of its existence, rather than its nature or content. Racism will add what content it needs for its purposes. The second aspect is that a negative valuation is imposed upon those seen as differing, implying (by the act of imposition) a positive valuation for those imposing it. Third, this differential valuation which renders the difference unignorable, is generalized to an entire group, which is then deprecated in turn. And fourth, the negative valuation imposed upon that group becomes the legitimization and justification for hostility and aggression" (Memmi, 2000, xvi–xvii). If you noticed, the world events of the 1980s and 1990s have all been mediated by race, ethnicity, or gender issues, including the Zapatista rebellion.

Despite the fact that several notions of assimilation or social integration have been sponsored by the U.S. government as its main tenet of nation-state consolidation (the melting pot), a tremendous racial anguish (the sizzling frying pan) bursts into flames from time to time; it is tangible in everyday forms of confrontation. Racial divides run deep and throughout the ethos of Anglo-European culture, especially on white / black dyadic oppositions; yet other ethnicities within that picture are strategically ignored and are not taken into account in the actual polyadic complexity. A few of them have just statistical presence, and others qualify to be invisible. So it should not be any surprise to read articles with such titles as "Invisible Men," "Invisible Indians," "Borderlands," "From Different Shores." Given this reality, it was simply great to see at Santa Cruz so many leaders having a great multicultural dialogue over what to do next—precisely against the backdrop of invisibility and often mutual ignorance of each other.

The conference, housed at Oakes College on the UCSC campus, honored multiculturality as a socioanthropological—I mean, *human*—reality that contributed in reproducing the well-being of the whole society, against the will of a few purists, racists, classists, homophobes, and misogynists. Multiculturality at this point meant leaving behind anachronistic expressions of unidirectional *nationalism* and *class* as sole agglutinative determinants to trigger social mobilizations; instead, it proposed the understanding of ethnic, class, and gender historical processes and dimensions that, without prevalence, focused on transcommunal arrangements. Still and all, "peoples—if they are so—form communities on the way," observed Mexico City chronicler Carlos Monsiváis after the 1985 major earthquake that made visible entire communities of people that surpassed the government's ability to manipulate or control (1987, 79).

Naturally, the multicultural picture was also complicated by our own capacity to *understand* (rather than simply to tolerate) the contributions of feminist and postcolonial theoreticians. To *tolerate* is associated with the notion of *"laisser faire, laisser aller;* hold a loose rein, give rope enough, give free rein to." I see the term implying colonial prejudice, authority over the unruly. Naturally, there are situations when *toleration* associated with "lenity, mildness, gentleness, indulgence, mercy, clemency, etc.," can be enacted, but note its subservient implication.

It may serve us to remember that in April 1992, the so-called "L.A. Riots"—triggered after the acquittal of white police officers accused of beating to the ground Afro-American motorist Rodney King—shook American democracy by implementing military occupation of the L.A. area, which progressive newspapers entitled "Foreign Policy at Home." Chicano/Mexicano/Central American East L.A. had a potential political ally from South Central. A problem interpreted as white/black became a bit more complicated. The newspaper headings "Foreign Policy at Home" referred to the ancient federal strategy to militarize conflictive zones, à la Panama in 1989, with the difference that, this time, it was not a "banana republic" but Los Angeles, California. Demographically speaking, neighborhoods had changed, and their new profile was immediately related to earlier 1980s U.S. interventionist policy in Central America that prompted emigration. The Sanctuary Movement, in response, received and processed the persecuted victims of Central American civil war. The trend was further complicated by NAFTA's infamous maquiladoras, postmodern colonial sweatshops with very modern forms of labor exploitation, especially in rural California, along the U.S.-Mexico border, and in Central American countries. What happened? Precise strategies of labor feminization created a painful picture of workers losing their basic human rights.

At the Santa Cruz conference, activists and scholars testified to the concrete experience of a considerable portion of the population rooted in the politically weakened U.S. working class. They showed that vulnerable ethnicities were afflicted by the brunt of global reforms, the transformation and reconversion of the economic spectrum, the migration of entire industries to Mexico and other developing countries, and the feminization of labor. Population displacement during the late-twentieth century went along with greater transformation in land use, industrial reconversion, and continuous processes of depeasantization and deforestation around the world. It meant the historical expulsion of populations that accommodated (anthropologists call it "adaptation") via migrations, grafting themselves to the dominant system of core world areas. What we often fail to explain is that those great waves of displacement respond to geopolitical re/arrangements often provoked by core countries. A few examples constitute the results of the previous East/West divide well expressed during the height of the Cold War. The "third world" became "developing countries"—a euphemism to hide persistent inequalities and create the illusion of modernization. Muhammad Yunus, a winner of the Nobel Prize in Economics, poignantly illustrated this issue in his book *Banker to the Poor* (1999).

The next great wave of displacements has been expressed in the imposition of neoliberalism and globalization. However, both can be interpreted as capitalistic repositioning rather than focusing on better forms of wealth redistribution. To see the effects closer to home, the new "benefits" of the North American Free Trade Agreement signed between Canada, the United States, and Mexico prompted capital movement but not labor. It indirectly accompanied the overconsumption and oversupply of drugs that directly affected the so-called "minority" neighborhoods in the United States.

In Latin America, the receding strength of the Cold War military mentality gave way to a new process of "redemocratization," as if democracy had been a truly working system there. The 1990s registered staggered social movements of women, Indigenous peoples, rural inhabitants, environmentalists, gays, industrial workers, teachers, and retired men and women—with their struggles over water, housing, employment, better wages, social services, territories, and against racism, xenophobia, domestic violence, and racial and gender discrimination. Expelling transnational corporations with great records of pollution, and sharper communal activities of self-defense never seen before occurred relentlessly. Community activists gave meaning to the notion of *transcommunality*, because they were operating from newly thought positions in which class, gender, and ethnicity mixed with no obstacles.

Globalization and cultural homogenization triggered forms of *transcommunality*, of *decentralized coordination* of social movements that paralleled the failure of political parties that could no longer be seen as privileged, nor sole mediators (or manipulators) of civil society. Concrete adoptions of the notion of transcommunality can clearly be seen in the practices of the independent Mexican Indigenous National Congress (Congreso Nacional Indígena, CNI) that according to Eugenio Bermejillo has served as "a national referent in order to produce consensus and to summarize future activities. Representatives of member organizations determined that rather than an organization it should be a space for encounters. . . . We are a network when separated, and when together an assembly" (2000, 3). The 1990s have been the "communications" decade as well, and despite uneasy access to interactive computer technologies and communications by civil societies (in the peripheries) it—*mutatis mutandis*—served to facilitate the circulation of important information, proving that civil society enabled itself to reach a world audience.

Up to this point, however, transcommunality has been thought of as a strategy that entails face-to-face dynamics, since it proposes to enhance the coming together of concrete communities and to cure the excesses of mutual ignorance. We must take the notion of *community* in a postmodern sense; rather than being fixed or territorialized, the postmodern community is made up against the backdrop of deterritorialization. It is the community that chooses to be one, not the traditional fixed community of the first part of the twentieth century, nor the historically territorialized community such as a tribe of the Amazonian Basin still united via complex kinship systems (unless Texaco has already taken over their territory).

An important point to stress here is that Childs's transcommunality is inspired by the Haudenosaunee (Iroquois) strategy, a detail that speaks to the positionality of the author. Childs comes to acknowledge that previous human behaviors of peace building can still lend themselves as alternatives to current peoples in conflict. The fact that colonialism undermined viable forms of community building and conflict resolution does not hinder the ability of rooted individuals to inspire themselves through the practices and legacies of previous ancestors. In this sense, Childs is involved in the task of decolonizing, by bringing back disregarded notions that contributed to peace making long before U.S. democracy. Anthropologist Jack Weatherford discusses Native American contributions that inspired the U.S. Constitution in his book *Indian Givers: How the Indians of the Americas Transformed the World* (1988). Of course, there is no reason to believe that if Native American thought inspired good deeds then, it has the power to do the same nowadays. The issue needs to be confronted from the perspective of decolonization, from the perspective of western democratic limitations and imperfections.

We must remember that full democracy is an ideal, and that the great social mobilization of the preacher Martin Luther King Jr. denounced democratic flaws in the 1960s. Up to that point it was generally despicable to claim democracy against perverse discriminatory practices in the name of democracy. Let us leave such a detail to the stupor of the centuries. Here, Childs needs to be seen, as several women and men of his generation, amidst the young Afro-Americans and their allies who marched throughout the Deep South with their SNCC "One Man, One Vote" black and white background button. Yet one might ask almost fifty years later, "How are things in the Deep South?" A statement by Amy Bach can be noted here: "Selma, Alabama, a touchstone in the civil rights movement, is frozen in a way that confounds onlookers. Despite the fact that blacks are now the majority of registered voters, they have been unable to unseat the very man who, as mayor in 1965, played a crucial role in keeping blacks away from the polls, making Selma known internationally as Hate City, USA. It turns out that equal access to the vote is no match for what critics charge is a well-oiled voter-fraud machine" (Bach, 2000, 7, 30). We should read this as an example of the perversities of democracy. (Interestingly, Bach's article spells out little-known interstices of democratic ethics in the United States, anticipating the Gore-Bush post-presidential-election legalistic maneuvering.)

One recollects now, as a long gone dream, authors, poets, and texts read that, I am sure, invigorated the Civil Rights marches. Certainly, activists then, beyond Marx and Weber, have been inspired by Marcuse, who was very present, as was Dietrich Bonhoeffer, Martin Buber, Althusser, Sartre, and Simone de Beauvoir. Franz Fanon, Albert Memmi, Samir Amin, Bruno Bettelheim, Heidegger, Levi-Strauss, Julius Nyerere, and Paulo Freire offered substantial thinking. Other authors read as in other latitudes of the world were Piaget, B. F. Skinner, Susan Sontag, Tom Bottomore, Vine Deloria, Gary Snyder, the Beat Poets, Reyes Tijerina and "El Movimiento Chicano de Crystal City," the *Theologians of Liberation*, Gustavo Gutiérrez, Hans Küng, Harvey Cox, the Berrigan brothers, and "the Catonsville Nine" serving time for having burned draft cards, saving U.S. lives from Vietnam's carnage.

On another field of struggles were the Latin American writers of the Boom Generation, E. F. Schumacher of *Small Is Beautiful*, Cardoso and Faletto's *Dependency Theory*, the resonant conversation Malcolm X and Fidel held at Harlem's Theresa Hotel on Fidel's first visit to the United States as a dignitary (September 19, 1960), and the Black Panthers with radical politics inspired by other methodologies in the struggle for power. Echoes of the U.S. struggles were heard in Latin America; after all, "modernization theory" (Gegeo and Watson-Gegeo, 2000) à la Rostow was also a main course in our syllabi.

I remember Angela Davis, Allende's guest in 1971, addressing a large, packed auditorium of students at the Universidad de Chile, in Santiago, speaking as a recently released political prisoner and providing the audience with an evaluation of U.S. radical politics, against Kennedy's "Alliance for Failure" (as Jack's "foreign policy" was rebaptized by the student movement there). The year before, Regis Debray of *Revolution dans la Revolution* had been liberated from a Bolivian military jail, after serving a couple of years for his participation in Ché's failed guerrilla war, and still persecuted were the student movement leaders of Mexico's 68, exiled in Allende's Chile.

All of these situations could now be seen as early manifestations of Childs's notion of transcommunality at work. Such dynamism can now be thought of in relation to the overreaction of Latin American military dictatorships that induced an out of proportion tragedy in the name of "restoring order" during the 1970s and 1980s. The active support of the U.S. government cannot be forgotten. One thinks, one sees.

In any case, transcommunality is about concrete issues and real people with tangible problems, viable proposals, and unequivocal solutions. There cannot be transcommunality if one is not situated, positioned, rooted in a particular history, within the context of community that wants to be community, or community that has become community. There cannot be community within the context of colonialism or neocolonialism, of racism, homophobia, or misogyny. Transcommunal practitioners need to decolonize, they cannot just tolerate, nor patronize, but need to go beyond, they need to understand and to forge, as if hammering metal, transcommunal alliances. Consulting a thesaurus, and coming back to my earlier thoughts, I examined the epistemic distinction between *tolerance* and *understanding*. Transcommunality goes beyond liberal tolerance. Transcommunality is about understanding, and respect.

Note

Acknowledgments: The author is grateful for comments and editorial suggestions and would like to thank Norma Klahn, Macarena Gómez-Barris, and Mónica X. Delgado. As former co-director of the Chicano/ Latino Research Center at UCSC, Professor Klahn encouraged the formation of the Inter-Ethnic Research Cluster, space originally inspired by Professor Childs's conceptual contribution.

Bibliography

Bach, Amy. 2000. "Selma Is Still Selma." *The Nation,* 271(8): 6–7.

Bermejillo, Eugenio. 2000. "Congreso Nacional Indígena: Muchos Ríos que Cruzar Todavía." *Ojarasca/La Jornada* (Mexico), Lunes 11 de Septiembre.

Brecher, Jeremy, John Brown Childs, and Jill Cutler, eds. 1993. *Global Visions. Beyond the New World Order.* Boston: South End Press.

Childs, John Brown. 1989. *Leadership, Conflict, and Cooperation in Afro-American Social Thought.* Philadelphia: Temple University Press, ch. 5.

———. 1994. "The Value of Transcommunal Identity Politics: Transcommunality and the Peace and Justice Gang Truce in Kansas City." *Z Magazine,* 7(7/8): 48–51.

Courtoisie, Agustín. 2000. "El Estado de las Cosas. Cómo Hacer más Util a la Izquierda." *La Jornada Semanal* (Mexico), 20 August, 4.

Debray, Regis. 1965. *¿Revolución en la Revolución?* Lima: Ediciones de Cultura General.

Delgado, Guillermo. 1994. "Ethnic Politics and the Popular Movement." In *Latin America Faces the Twenty-First Century* (pp. 77–88). Ed. Susanne Jonas and Edward J. McCaughan. Boulder: Westview Press.

Frye, Hardy T. 1980. *Black Parties and Political Power: A Case Study.* Boston: G. K. Hall.

Gegeo, David Welchman, and Karen Watson-Gegeo. 2000. "Whose Knowledge? The Collision of Indigenous and Introduced Knowledge Systems in Solomon Community Development" (ms).

Harries-Jones, Peter. 1998. "From Cultural Translator to Advocate: Changing Circles of Interpretation." In *Advocacy and Anthropology: First Encounters* (pp. 224–248). Ed. Robert Paine. St. John: Institute for Social Research, Memorial University of Newfoundland.

Harrison, Faye V. 1989. "The Persistent Power of 'Race' in the Cultural and Political Economy of Racism." *Annual Review of Anthropology,* 24: 47–74.

Memmi, Albert. 2000. *Racism*. Trans. and Intro. Steve Martinot. Minneapolis: University of Minnesota Press.

Monsivais, Carlos. 1987. *Cronicas de una sociedad que se Organiza*. Mexico: Editorial ERA.

Mohanty, Satya P. 1995. "Colonial Legacies, Multicultural Futures: Relativism, Objectivity and the Challenge of Otherness." *PMLA*, 110(1): 108–118.

Moraga, Cherríe. 1993. "Queer Aztlán: The Re-formation of the Chicano Tribe." *The Last Generation: Prose and Poetry* (pp. 145–174). Boston: South End Press.

Rivera Cusicanqui, Silvia. 1988. "El Potencial Epistemológico y Teórico de la Historia Oral: De la Lógica Instrumental a la Descolonización de la Historia." *Temas Sociales*, Universidad Mayor de San Andrés (La Paz), 11: 49–64.

Weatherford, Jack. 1988. *Indian Givers: How the Indians of the Americas Transformed the World*. New York: Crown.

Yunus, Mohammed. 1999. *Banker to the Poor: Micro-Lending and the Battle against World Poverty*. New York: Public Affairs.

Arif Dirlik

Places and Transcommunality

A Comment on John Brown Childs's Idea of the Transcommunal

JOHN BROWN CHILDS'S case for transcommunality is significant most importantly for its courage to hope. Hope in a better future does not come easily these days when what remains of the political left despairs of the relevance to a changed world of the solutions it once espoused, and its putatively radical successors wallow variously in self-inflicted if not self-serving agonies of identity, or in the euphoria of corporate-sponsored sensory overload ("tittytainment," according to that coiner of puerile slogans, Zbigniew Brzezinsky), neither of which allows for anything beyond an eternal, and eternally fractious, present. Idealism and utopianism are the undesirables of the age, viewed with cynical disdain by sophisticated cultural theorists when they are not actually blamed for the ills of past efforts to change the world, as is the case most notably with subjects of former communist regimes. There is no apparent end to the revival, under the guise of cultural diversity, of the most reactionary practices masquerading as expressions of alternative cultural visions.

Under the circumstances, it seems especially risky to espouse a vision that claims the legacy of left radicalism. Yet transcommunality appears in Childs's presentation as such a vision—one that

118

seeks to redirect radical left practice in response to present challenges, but also calls for as a precondition a reevaluation of long-standing leftist assumptions with the help of inspiration drawn from indigenous pasts conventionally ignored, or even disdained, by leftists. What Childs has to offer is not a blueprint for the future drawn from the past, as in traditionalist and right-wing revivalisms that refuse to recognize their own historicity, and reject in the name of cultural autonomy the aspirations born of the experience and promise of modernity. On the other hand, his insistence on the inescapable historicity of social practices, and the indispensable transformative vision that must inform all radical practice, distinguishes what he has to say from liberal or New Age appropriations of indigenism. For Childs, if I read him correctly, indigenous practices of transcommunality serve most importantly as an inspiration for going about radical practice differently than in the past: not repudiating fundamental questions of material circumstances and needs, but redirecting attention away from a persistent economism to the conjuncture between the material, the social, and the cultural to rethink political practice. What he has to offer is not a solution, but a new beginning to solutions yet to be imagined, and a few considerations that may help us along the way. This is what a transformative, nondogmatic radicalism is all about.

The source of the inspiration is interesting, and also has much to tell us about our times. If the fall of socialist regimes, the revelations of their misdeeds, and the social and political transformations that have accompanied the global victory of capital have discredited, rendered irrelevant, or called into question earlier left solutions, they have also made it possible to ask hard questions about a socialist legacy that was in many ways informed by the same assumptions about the world as the capitalism that it challenged. The "politics of conversion" in the subtitle of Childs's work refers to a socialism that proposed identical paths for all into the future, and presupposed homogenized constituencies, mostly around the paradigm of the laborer under capitalism (the proletariat), in order to realize such a future. It also shared in the developmentalist assumptions—an unquestioning faith in the necessity of a technologically advanced economy for human salvation—of a capitalism of which it was a progeny. To be sure, leftists of all stripes, from Marxists to anarchists, have been driven by an urge to place real, living people at the center of questions pertaining to the economy and society, but it is hardly deniable that socialisms in practice aspired to development with even greater faith than under capitalism, and engaged through the image of the proletariat in even more egregious abstractions of living people than the capitalism they opposed.

It is fashionable these days to repudiate socialist histories as deviations of one kind or another, which serves to justify the invasion of the globe by the forces of capital. Such repudiations, most notably by postsocialist regimes, ignore not only that there were good historical reasons for socialist revolutions, but more importantly that it might have been impossible to gauge the effects of socialism without first going through it. Most importantly, they ignore the extent to which the ills of socialism may have been the products of those economistic assumptions that socialism shared with capitalism, which a bureaucratized path to development rendered into an instrument of social homogenization and repression, in the process obstructing the very development to which it aspired. As remaining socialist states such as China seek to remake themselves by abandoning the revolutionary vision that brought them to power, all that remains of socialism is state-led national development. The ills that were particular products of socialist regimes may be a thing of the past, but the ills which they sought to overcome are still with us. The fall of socialisms as we have known them makes it possible to ask once again if the best way to overcome the ills of capitalism is by replicating its assumptions about human salvation.

The latest phase in the globalization of capital, ironically, has served not to unify humanity in a march toward an identical, or even a common, future, but on the contrary has resulted in the further fracturing of societies worldwide along lines of religion, nation, and ethnicity. This very fracturing allows for challenges to conceptualizations of the future in terms of models derived from the advanced capitalist societies of Europe, North America, and East Asia (divisions among which are also expressive of such fracturing). The challenge to Eurocentrism must be welcomed, but with an appreciation of its contradictory consequences. The cultural reassertion around the world of social practices once thought to be remnants of the past is not an unmixed blessing. In many cases, it issues in the revival of retrograde and repressive social practices in the name of cultural diversity. But it may also serve as an inspiration for reconsidering the whole project of modernity, and the oppositional practices informed not by the negativities of contemporary intellectual life, but by the search for practices that may help recapture the vision of human liberation that is also a fundamental aspect of modernity.

Indigenous practices are especially important to this end.[1] To be sure, indigenous claims to identity may be as open to reification and abuse as any other. On the other hand, conceived historically with due recognition of the need to respond to changing social circumstances, and the new social challenges they bring, indigenism may have a fundamental contribution to make to a contemporary radical discourse on economic and political transformation. We may recall here that within a United States context, some of the earliest challenges to the developmentalism built into socialism came from radical Amerindian scholars who were products of the radical ferment of the 1960s, and sympathetic to its social goals.[2] Indigenous insistence that the relationship of humans to nature is fundamental to any consideration of social change has acquired wide currency in radical thinking since then; ecological concerns have become central to radical consciousness. This is also a predicament, however, as the absorption of indigenous ideas into a diffuse radicalism may also take the critical edge off a critique that is driven not merely by a vague concern for nature, but is informed by a conviction that a harmonious relationship with the environment is possible only with social arrangements that give priority to everyday human needs and welfare. The indigenous critique of developmentalism is not just another reminder for including ecological concerns in radical agenda; it is

radically social in its implications, and forces a reconsideration of
the dimensions and modes of radical practice.

No less important is the indigenous challenge to ideas of political sovereignty based on the nation form. Arguments for national
sovereignty ignore that the nation-state itself is a product of colonialism, both in its replacement of more localized sovereignties
by the sovereignty of the nation and its homogenizing cultural
policies that erase local diversities. In no case is the colonial nature
of the nation-state more evident than with indigenous peoples
whose ways of life have been totally marginalized if not actually
eradicated by nationalist political and cultural homogenization.
The restoration of indigenous sovereignty, as indigenous scholars
argue, is a precondition for any meaningful end to colonialism. On
the other hand, if indigenous forms of organization in the past
inspired political forms such as federalism in the United States,
those forms may be more relevant than ever at a time when the
nation form is under attack from the inside and the outside, and
its future status less certain than ever.[3]

Indigenism, Childs reminds us, represents more than just
another expression of identity politics that calls into question cultural and political boundaries. It is not to be contained within a
liberal multiculturalism to which one form of resistance is much
the same as another in a quest for a new politics of which diversity is the goal—and the ultimate political horizon. Indigenous
practices, and the very meaning of indigenism, are subject to the
ideological pressures of the age, and are by no means immune to
the threat of fragmentation internally, which makes it necessary
to distinguish a radical transformative indigenism from its accom-
modationist forms. The possibility of indigenous self-expression
presently may owe much to globalist ideologies that call into question earlier ideas of sovereignty, but indigenism in its very insistence on the groundedness of everyday life ultimately presents a
radical challenge to a developmentalism that nourishes off-ground
cultural and institutional arrangements.

If we may no longer recapture an innocently holistic way of
conceiving life in which the economic, the social, the cultural,

and the political are indistinguishably blended together, we may at the very least insist on conjoining the various spheres of life in arrangements that take different forms in accordance with the diverse needs of different places. What indigenism is about, ultimately, is a radical reconceptualization of cultural and political space from the bottom up.

Although one would scarcely guess it from the record of socialist regimes in power, the creation of democratic spaces from below has been a crucial component of most radical projects associated with socialism, including Marxism. While dismissed as utopian (or, alternatively, backward) in the tradition of "scientific socialism," insistence on the importance of local control over local economic and political resources has refused to disappear. Socialist states such as China, products of guerrilla revolution, did indeed struggle with the problem, but to no avail in a hostile environment that inevitably reinforced considerations of national power in socialisms that were already marked by an urge to national liberation from colonial or imperial oppression and exploitation. It is important to revive this alternative tradition once again. State socialism may have had a progressive part to play within the historical circumstances that gave rise to it, but at this particular historical juncture, there are at least three important reasons that a radical agenda should turn to local control over local economic and political resources in order to achieve more egalitarian and democratic ways of living, mindful of the ecological conditions of human existence.

First is the necessity of abandoning the illusion that these progressive goals can be achieved through the agency of the state. It is not that state action is irrelevant, but rather that the role the state has to play needs to be considered historically: state-centered policies that are progressive at one historical juncture may inhibit further progress at another. Where the socialist experience is concerned, it seems apparent that while socialist states did achieve certain ends for their constituencies, the achievements came at the very cost of the professed ideals of equality and democracy. Even in less bureaucratized states, progressive measures may prove in the end to be meaningless unless they allow for local diversity, and are internalized locally.

A second illusion that needs to be abandoned is that somehow an abstraction that goes by the name of socialism may replace another abstraction that goes by the name of capitalism to remake society anew globally. As it becomes increasingly difficult to locate a center to capitalism, it becomes even more difficult to imagine that such a center may be captured in the name of socialism—which seems to hold as much for individual nation-states as it does for that totality called capital. It is not that totalities need not be accounted for; what needs to be recognized is that the totalities themselves are fractious and contradictory, and they do not allow for the identification of "centers" that may be captured for the revolution in the manner in which, say, V. I. Lenin envisaged it. One of the most contradictory consequences of the contemporary globalization of capital is the simultaneous decentering of capital (to be distinguished from the continued centrality politically and militarily of certain states), and the production of new localisms. Any sense of totality needs to be accompanied by this sense of fracturing and the generation of new diversities. Radical agenda must in turn respond to such diversity and abandon developmental and social teleologies.[4] The recent preoccupation in radical circles with the global and the local is indicative that this awareness is already quite prevalent, although it seems in general to lead to a sense of helplessness, rather than to its articulation to the alternative socialist tradition discussed above.

Finally, to the extent that there is visible radical activity in our day, it takes the form of place-based or community-based social movements, the "new social movements," that nourish off diverse radical traditions (including homespun traditions of protest against injustice) but share common goals of survival and control over everyday life. From the United States to Latin America, Europe, Africa, and Asia there has been a proliferation of localized movements against global capital, against the alliance between states and capital, and against the policies of supranational institutions such as the World Bank and the International

Monetary Fund that make no allowance for local needs and circumstances. Rather than dismiss these movements as expressions
of backwardness, or mourn their proliferation as signs of the
breakdown of socialism, radicals need to rethink inherited ideas
of socialism to account for these new movements from the bottom up.

To be sure, not all such movements are necessarily progressive,
or benign. Community itself appears more often than not as a
location for inequalities and oppressions inherited from the past,
which need to be overcome in the process of the struggle for life
against the ravages of states and capital. It is for this reason that
I myself prefer "place-based" over community in describing this
mode of politics: place-based in the sense of grounded but with
open boundaries both within (among the constituencies of the
place) and in the relationship to the outside.[5] Places, if they are
to serve as the locations for progressive rather than regressive politics, need to allow for negotiations of such inherited inequalities
and oppressions (whether of class, gender, race, ethnicity, religion, etc.), as well as enter alliance with other places that share
their goals.

Simply to be against capital and the state is not sufficient; it is
also necessary in the process to generate new, more democratic
and egalitarian ways of living. It is equally necessary to recognize
that the very diversity of places calls for diverse resolutions of
these problems in different places. The abandonment of the illusions of past socialisms only reveals the complexity and difficulties of social change to progressive ends.

Perhaps the most intractable difficulty, often pointed out by
left theorists who prefer more conventional left politics, is the
helplessness of places against the control of spaces by capital,
states, and even diasporic ethnicities. In other words, if places are
to be able to fulfill any progressive role, they need to be able to
project themselves into the spaces of power without losing their
own grounded diversities. This may be the most important challenge to radical politics in our day. Supra-place organizations (from
labor to gender to radical associations all the way to the more

progressive and less-government controlled NGOs) may be essential to connecting places in alliances which may counteract the power of globalizing forces that erase places or manipulate them against one another. In order to achieve this end, however, such supra-place organizations need to be able to reorient themselves from the centers of power to the needs of the powerless, and be more mindful of place-based needs against corporate identities of one kind or another. We need to remember, as numbers of writers have pointed out, that even capital and states need places for their operations, and their personnel, too, live in places.

On the other hand, what today passes for radicalism has become an obstacle to the radical reconceptualization of politics that a place-based imagination requires. I am referring here to the preoccupation with identity politics that has been a prominent feature of "radical" intellectual life in the United States over the past decade. While the question of cultural identity is by no means a trivial one, *where* identities confront one another and seek for the resolution of difference is equally important. In its attachment to globalist ideologies, as is the case with many contemporary discussions of identity, identity politics is biased toward the reification of off-ground "diasporic" identities that contribute further to divisions between the constituencies of places who otherwise have to live and deal with one another. The diasporization of identity is not only divisive at the level of the local, but it also conceals unequal relations of power among the constituents of diasporas, and it is open to all manner of self-serving manipulation.

The grounding of identities at the level of everyday life may be a precondition to resolving the many conflicts over identity, especially ethnic and racial identity; otherwise they may contribute to perpetuating the very divisions and oppressions that they seek to overcome. Whether self-assumed or imposed from the outside, moreover, a sense of cultural, class, or gender identity may be a necessary condition of countering the oppressive practices that are the legacies of the past. The problem with cultural politics presently is not its insistence on the need to account for the recognition of diverse identities, but in rendering diversity into an end in itself, which also makes possible its appropriation for liberal and even managerial ends that leave intact existing arrangements of power.[6]

From a radical perspective, however, the ultimate goal of identity politics is not to establish boundaries to identity, which only further contributes to setting people against one another on the basis of some identity or other, but to enable them to live together with all their differences—which presupposes some sense of the historicity of identity. If identities are products of histories, they are also subject to change with changing historical circumstances. It may be important, therefore, to speak less of identities, as if they were carved in stone, and speak more of identifications, with some sense of human agency in self-definition, and the definition of relations to others. This, too, may well be achieved best at the level of concrete everyday social relationships.

The idea of transcommunality may be pertinent to resolving questions raised by relationships within as well as between places. The way I read it, *transcommunal* carries a deconstructive sense similar to what Edward Said calls "contrapuntal"—a decoding of a text, a culture, or whatever with the aid of its acknowledged or suppressed Other, while recognizing the integrity (and even the boundaries) of both.[7] Childs's goal, however, is also fundamentally reconstructive; it goes beyond the reading of texts or cultures to find grounds for common action to resolve concrete problems of everyday life. While he stresses the ethical bases of transcommunality, we may note that transcommunality is also quite relevant as a principle of flexible associations that allows for diversity even as it promotes alliances for the common good.

I do not mean to imply in suggesting this that the epistemological or the ethical dimension is subsidiary. If transcommunality as an organizational principle is to be viable, it will take a fundamental reorientation of our thinking on what are progressive ends, and what may be the best means to achieve them. It calls for educational work at the most fundamental level, but educational work that addresses questions of basic human needs and not corporate needs, or the needs of corporate identities. Such educational work, if it is to be effective, cannot be satisfied with abstract formulations but, as Childs points out, must be informed by the concrete practices in the context of which people may learn to live with one another in different ways.

Notes

Acknowledgments: I am grateful to Henry Giroux and Roxann Prazniak for their support, as well as comments which helped me enunciate more clearly the arguments in this paper.

1. It is not my intention, in discussing indigenism as a radical option here, to assimilate indigenism to general problems of radicalism as one more radical paradigm, erasing in the process the specific meaning it has for indigenous peoples themselves. Nevertheless, I believe it is important that indigenous peoples, and indigenous paradigms, be brought into the dialogue on social change not as "resources" but as subjects of their own fates.

2. Ward Churchill, ed., *Marxism and Native Americans* (Boston: South End Press, 1982).

3. Franke Wilmer, *The Indigenous Voice in World Politics* (Newbury Park, CA: Sage Publications, 1993).

4. For further discussion of this problem, the reader may be referred to Arif Dirlik, *After the Revolution: Waking to Global Capitalism* (New Hampshire: University Press of New England for Wesleyan University Press, 1994).

5. For further discussion, see Arif Dirlik, "Place-Based Imagination: Globalism and the Politics of Place," *Review,* 22(2) (Spring 1999).

6. For a discussion of this problem, see Henry A. Giroux, "Rethinking Cultural Politics: Challenging Political Dogmatism from Right to Left." I am grateful to Henry Giroux for sharing this unpublished paper with me.

7. Said has discussed "contrapuntal" in a number of places. For one discussion, see the preface to *Culture and Imperialism* (New York: Knopf, 1994).

Stefano Varese

Language of Space

The Territorial Roots of the Indigenous Community in Relation to Transcommunality

JOHN BROWN CHILDS'S stimulating notion of trans-communality raises some old sociological questions regarding the definition and scope of community, as well as more recent discussions on the function of location/placement in the social construction of ethnic identity. The classic sociological distinction put forward by F. Tönnies (1955/1887, cited in Jary and Jary 1991) between *Gemeinschaft* (the community of close, intimate relationships, where kinship, a bound and shared territory, and a common culture dominate the social relations) and *Gesellschaft* (translated in English as "society," where relationships are impersonal, contractual, transitory, and calculative rather than affective) has been enriched by contemporary British anthropologist Peter Worsley, who has emphasized locality (geographical expression) as a constitutive condition of any definitional undertaking. Even for those contemporary communities (whose members are scattered around the world) and are defined as a type of relationship where communality is expressed as *a sense of shared identity* rather than a localized social system, the question of locality and spatial location of "community members" may rise time and again as an organizational and political challenge (the Jewish community comes to mind) (Worsley et al. 1987, 238–245).

The preeminent role of space in communal definition is particularly true in the case of the indigenous people of Latin America. For the forty or so million indigenous people (Psacharopoulos and Patrinos 1994; Varese 1991) belonging to more than four hundred ethnolinguistic groups, living in thousands of rural communities spread throughout all sorts of geographical and environmental zones, issues of territory, land, resources, nature, and the world are intrinsically tied to the cultural conception and social practice of community. The community is in the first place the village, the geographical space where one was born or where one's parents and ancestors were born and are buried. This communal space with names, stories, history, cosmological references is where the individual and collective identity is constructed in a tight web of meanings expressed in a specific ethnic language or in a local variety of the national language. It is essential to recognize that for indigenous people, the territorial, spatial, locational, and land issues remain at the core of any discussion about meanings of community, ethnicity and politics of cultural identity, cultural reproduction, and autonomy. Consequently, I am addressing my commentaries to the centrality of the notions and practices of space jurisdiction and cultural jurisdiction in indigenous communities as well as the related issues of intellectual sovereignty and epistemological autonomy which are a set of tightly interwoven questions (Varese 1999).

Recently the question of Latin American indigenous people's land/territory has been revisited by anthropologists (Díaz Polanco 1991; Hale 1994, 1995; Kearney 1991, 1996; Kearney and Varese 1995) with a broader more ethnopolitical approach and a less peasant productivist focus, which has been the dominant mode of study of Latin American indigenous communities since the founding analyses of Marx (1963/1852), V. I. Lenin (1956/1899), A. V. Chayanov (1986), J. C. Mariátegui (1976/1928), T. Shanin (1990), and the analytical school initiated by E. Wolf (1959, 1966). During at least the last eight decades, indigenous people of Latin America have been treated by social scientists as peasants, that is to say, they have been put symbolically in the proverbial "sack of potatoes" of Karl Marx's *Eighteenth Brumaire of Louis Bonaparte* (1963 / 1852) and have become thus prey of convoluted debates between economic theorists and anthropologists, revolutionaries, and developmentalists. Questions about the cultural and economic autonomy of peasantry, the independent nature of their mode of production, their crucial or marginal role in peripheral capitalism, and the immanent or transitional character of their historical presence have obscured other important cultural and political characteristics of the indigenous people, such as their "long historical duration" (in a Braudelian sense) as "autonomous" ethnic entities which have survived and reproduced themselves during millennia throughout different larger social formations (precolonial and colonial states, and contemporary republican nation-states of all political coloring).

It is well known that the extreme civilizational and ethnic diversity of precolonial Native America was reduced by European colonialism to the homogenized and generic subalternity of "indios" for purposes of labor control and ideological and political domination. The process produced ruralization, campesinización / peasantization of the Indians but also proletarization (through labor in mining, "obrajes" or sweatshops, haciendas, and plantations), and the concurrent phenomenon of Indian urbanization. These new multiple indigenous ethnoses that reconfigured themselves throughout the last five centuries of colonial and neocolonial occupation (and that we could define as permanent processes of ethnogenesis) have a series of cultural and social characteristics that require more than limited, if not simplistic, economic analyses framed in terms of Euroamerican and Eurocentric perspectives and interests.

It is obvious, for instance, that the Formalist-Substantivist debate of the early 1960s about precapitalist societies, the Neoclassical-Marxist ongoing dispute about third world rural development / revolution, and even the more updated contributions of the "moral economy" à la James Scott (1976, 1985) and the "rational peasant" à la Samuel Popkin (1979) are all analytical approaches that privilege a fundamentally western (and philosophically Enlightened) conception of individual social life and economy: "value" as determined by labor and exchange is at the ethical center of life in civilized society.[1] The axis around which the whole society rotates is production of value for exchange. The language of this system is the language of individualism, and increasingly the language of profit; its *ethos*, its moral code is, since Max Weber told us in 1905, the spirit of capitalism (Weber, 1958). The cultural language of this system is also spatially disembodied; it is valid and performable anywhere, in any deterritorialized space. Increasingly the space of the "exchange value" is uprooted, ungrounded, ethereal, or "cyberial" as Arturo Escobar (1995) would say. Indigenous communities and people scrutinized with this cultural lens make very little sense. In fact this type of analysis constitutes a splendid instrument for increasing the frustration of economists, social scientists, and institutions involved in indigenous people's development.

An indigenous epistemological and axiological approach to the relation between individual and society uses instead, to paraphrase Lakota scholar Elisabeth Cook-Lynn, the "language of place": a language embedded in the locality, in the concrete space where culture is grounded and reproduced in a familiar landscape where naming of things, space, objects, plants, animals, living people, and the dead, the underworld and the celestial infinity evoke the total cosmic web as an awesome and mysterious social and divine construction. This is why a paradigmatic shift that accentuates "topos" rather then "logos" is needed to understand indigenous people. This is also why I believe that the beauty of our particular discipline, our intellectual endeavor, is that it does not solve all mysteries: it announces them.

The indigenous cultural language is constructed around a few principles and a cultural logic or a cultural topology that privileges diversity and heterogeneity over homogeneity, eclecticism over dogma, multiplicity over bipolarity. As I write these lines I can feel the reaction of an intellectual audience that is ready to dis-

qualify these ideas as "romanticism," "idealization of the indigenous people," or simply "populist idealism" and "political and economic *narodnism*" (in the old Leninist language). *Déjenme curarme
en salud*, as they say in Mexico, "Let me heal myself while I am
still healthy," and let me discuss with some details the historical
formation of what I believe are the central components of the
indigenous people's civilizational projects.

One initial central idea that needs to be clarified is that *globalization* is not a new political, economic, and cultural phenomenon,
but rather a five-century-old arrangement of the world imposed
by Europe and Euroamerica upon the multiplicity of local social
and cultural expressions as a permanent attempt to configure and
reconfigure people and resources into an acceptable and naturalized order of things easily exploitable. A corollary is that the analytical frame for understanding the local people of this continent,
the indigenous people in all their various localized/communal/
territorial expressions that since the sixteenth century have suc-
cumbed under Euroamerican expansionism, must be a global and
a hemispheric one. The local (each indigenous people, culture,
ethnohistorical formation) acquires full meaning as long as it is
perceived as dialectically constructed within the structure and
configuration of colonial and neocolonial power, which since its
inception manifested itself as a program of global domination. As
a consequence, while the theoretical need for a *global approach* to
the study of indigenous people has its foundations in the logic of
the political economy of power (fundamentally the understanding of the role played by indigenous people's labor, culture, science, and technologies in the monumental accumulation of wealth
and power of the Euroamerican elites), the need for a *hemispheric
approach* is based on the recognition that the Native people of the
Americas in all their cultural diversity share and are part of a common and unique civilization. The most obvious analogy that can
be made to illustrate this statement is one drawn out of the cultural history of Europe and the Mediterranean area where many
local cultures developed historically within one civilizational
matrix (Amin 1989). In the Americas, as in the Mediterranean,

many peoples and many cultures shared one civilizational unity grounded in millennia of codevelopment.

I would like to expand on this idea of unity and plurality, commonality and diversity among indigenous people by providing some observations with a few strokes of a broad ethnohistorical brush. While *polyculture* (the practice of biodiversity in agricultural production) seems to be found prevalently in the tropical and subtropical regions of the world, it is among the indigenous people of the Americas of different and varied ecosystems that this technology has reached an astounding level of refinement. The Andean and Amazonian *chacra* and *conuco*, the Mesoamerican *milpa*, and the "three sisters" or "sacred triad" of eastern and central North America and the Southwest constitute some of the expressions of a common indigenous conception, throughout thousands of miles and hundreds if not thousands of ethnic groups and cultures. This conception holds that concentrating, nourishing, and developing diversity in the reduced space of human agricultural intervention as well as in the larger space of economic activity of the entire group is the most appropriate way of dealing with land, water, animal, botanical, and resources conservation, and in general with the preservation of the environment and the nurturing of nature.

Clearly Native American agricultural biodiversity and environmental management are millennial practices and sciences that resulted from early intentional and planned domestication of plants such as corn, beans, squash, chiles, potato, manihot, sweet potato, amaranth, peanuts, coca, tomato, avocado, tobacco, and thousands of other cultigens and semidomesticated plants. What needs to be pointed out is that the extreme variety of indigenous cultigens and semidomesticated plants is matched by an equally diverse and multiple use of the environment and a systematic cultural preoccupation for maintaining and increasing the diversity of the biosphere. Polyculture and the intentional maintenance of biodiversity are historical realities, but also metaphors of the indigenous people's cultural gravitation toward diversity rather than homogeneity, eclecticism rather than dogma.

Polyculture, the nurturing of biodiversity, and the multiple use of the environment seem to constitute the crucial conception of what has been called by James Scott (1976) the "moral economy" of peasants/indigenous people. This axial cultural notion, which operates along the "principle of diversity," accompanies and shapes the whole cosmology of innumerable Amerindian societies that place at the center of the universe not the man (the anthropocentric, patriarchal, dominant character of both the sacred and secular history of Euroamerica), but rather diversity itself, expressed in the multiplicity of deities with their polymorphic characteristics and at times contradictory functions. The ancient Mesoamerican Quetzalcoatl is serpent, bird, and human at the same time. He is historical cultural hero on his way back to repossess the stolen Indian world, and he is Morning Star. He is also the fragile and vulnerable humanistic holy principle that privileges the sacrifice to the gods of jades and butterflies instead of human offerings. He certainly does not stand at the center of the Mesoamerican Indian cosmologies, because there is no center but rather an intricate polyphony of symbols and values, a "spiritual polyculture," a "sacred *milpa*," a "holy *chacra*," an infinite domain for the encounter and interaction of diversity.

Today for the Mixe-Popoluca Indians of the southern Mexican state of Veracruz, the tender sprouts of corn and beans planted together with squash in the *milpa* (that chaotic polyculture despised and misunderstood by modern agronomists) carry the same name during the early period of their germination. They are, at their initial stage of growth, the symbol and image of the archetypal twins sacrificed at the beginning of times by their grandmother for the good of humanity. Each year, each growing season, each corn and bean in each *milpa* is a sacrament of memory and hope, and a tribute to diversity.

The biblical and Judeo-Christian foundations of the anthropocentric Mediterranean and Euroamerican worldview, which establishes a confrontational relation between humans and nature, men and animals, forests, mountains, jungles, and deserts, have been analyzed thoroughly by recent studies (for example, Amin 1989; Sale 1991). This representation of the world and the resulting human positioning in it demands the homogenization of the surroundings and of nature in order to control, subjugate, and exploit both. Even Marxism, as the secular revolutionary version of the Judeo-Christian utopian thought, pays homage to this dichotomous view of the world, where humans are separated from the rest of nature and struggling to control it. Recently James C. Scott (1998) has explored extensively the cultural obsession of homogenization in societies ruled by elite classes engaged in state-building projects. The simplification, and thus the legibility and possibility of administrative manipulation, of nature and society is a *sine qua non* condition of every political system that aims at centralization and concentration of power and the concomitant subjugation of local autonomy and epistemological sovereignty. Precolonial indigenous states such the Mexica-Tenochtla, the Mixtecs, the Zapotecs, the Maya, or the Inca, just to mention the most renowned, do not show indications of having had interest in homogenizing the conquered natural and social space. In fact, it has been well documented that precolonial indigenous tributary states practiced a sort of cultural, ideological, and spiritual inclusive eclecticism that contributed to the constant growth and increasing complexity of their multicultural societies (Clendinnen 1995; Murra 1978).

In contrast to Euroamerican anthropocentrism, the indigenous people of the Americas for millennia seem to have constructed cosmoscentric and polycentric cosmologies based on the logic of diversity and the logic of reciprocity. In their diverse cosmos, no center is privileged, no singularity is hegemonic. A world that is constantly enriched by the interaction of each of its elements, even those that are antithetical, requires a moral code (a customary code of behavior) based on the logic of reciprocity. Whatever is taken has to be returned in similar and comparable "value." Whatever I receive (good, gift, service, resource) I will have to reciprocate at some point with similar and comparable value. What I take from earth has to be returned; what I give to earth or to the gods or my human counterparts will be given back to me. Sociologist of religion G. Van Der Leeuw (1955) synthesized splendidly many decades ago this civilizational logic with the Latin formula *Do ut possis dare,* "I give so that you can give."

It would be simplistic and reductionist to argue that this whole millennial civilizational proposition of the indigenous people of the Americas could be condensed in the descriptive equation that these are "agricentric societies" which have historically favored agricultural development at the expense of other areas of social and cultural growth. I am suggesting, instead, that both *the principle of diversity* and *the principle of reciprocity* have been and are present in the economic, social, political, and cultural life of indigenous societies that have established their ethnic distinctiveness on gathering, hunting, and fishing activities, or in more recent colonial and neocolonial times in a "mixed" economy that has combined wage labor, petty mercantile activities, and sub-subsistence horticulture. At the end of thousands of years of evolvement and their incorporation into social and cultural formations that advance opposite values, the majority of indigenous people of the Americas who have not been totally destroyed by the dominant national societies (and their capitalist *weltanschauung*) are still struggling to live their social lives guided by these principles.

Obviously, for contemporary indigenous people, life in the midst of a permanent contradiction between the "culture of use value," guided by the logic of diversity and reciprocity, and the "culture of exchange value," guided by the logic of homogenization and individualistic profit, is fraught with tremendous ambiguities and conflicts. This tension between two logics, two sets of principles, which can be summarized as *culture of economy of use* and *culture of economy of profit,* characterizes the social, economic, and cultural life of the great majority of indigenous people and communities of Latin America. The acrid polemics that for decades have torn apart Substantivists and Formalists, Marxists and Neoclassical economists, and that are now confronting the

Mayan Zapatistas of Chiapas with neoliberal bureaucrats turned into aspirant bankers, reveal at a magnified scale the degree of penetration of capitalist *weltanschauung* into every interstice of the world's societies.

Let me bring in an example that is becoming increasingly familiar in vast areas of the United States, where there are currently thousands of indigenous migrants from Latin America and especially from Mexico. For transnational Indian migrants that are coming from Mexico to the United States, the issue of "communal citizenship" is of vital importance. Indian migrants can spend many years as farm workers or cooks in California and keep their social position within their home community in Mexico as long as they contribute annually to the communal well-being by participating in the *ceremonies of reciprocity. Reciprocity* may consist in performing different annual social and political tasks, sponsoring one of the patron saint fiestas, participating routinely in communal public service, or carrying out civic responsibilities within the organization of the community. The community member is not paid for these activities; on the contrary, each activity and commitment may cost a small fortune to the community member. Why does a Mixtec or Chinantec or Zapotec living in California feel obliged to return to his or her community in the southern state of Oaxaca to perform an onerous, burdensome, and expensive duty? What is at issue here is the moral strength of the collective demand of being an active participant in the life of one's own community. Indian communal citizenship has to be renewed and nurtured by its carrier through a series of ritualized acts and social functions that are based on the logic of reciprocity. Each member of the indigenous community is aware of the linking that exists within all its members and wants to make sure that everyone else recognizes his or her contributions to the well-being of the collective body. Here the logic of reciprocity overrules the opposite logic of individualism and accumulation/profit that leads and regulates social life outside the indigenous community.

In some previous work I tried to define the intricate links that exist between culture and production, and I argued that in the case of indigenous people it is important to look at "decisions about production ... [and about] consumption, ideas about both moments of a social reproduction and decisions, and fundamental definitions concerning surplus. For every people and every historical moment have defined surplus differently, assigning to it a qualitatively different use, which at the end has also defined, through its uniqueness, the group and its civilization" (Varese 1985). There are, however, some central questions that require further analysis: How much of these indigenous civilizational principles and logic are still present in contemporary indigenous peoples? How has the expansion of capitalist economy and worldview affected the various indigenous people? Can we naively assume the existence of numerous indigenous people-communities relatively unadulterated by the opposite logic of individualism, profit, commoditization, and primacy of "exchange value" over "use value"?

Let us assume the hypothesis that the thousands of indigenous communities of Latin America (more than forty million indigenous people and hundreds of ethnolinguistic groups) can be divided into the following schematic typology:

1. Agrarian-peasant communities of Mesoamerica, Central America, and the Andes (increasingly relying on external wage labor and circular migration). In this category we find a whole range of levels of subsistence economies, from sub-subsistence to a few cases of affluent subsistence.
2. Indigenous communities of horticulturists of the lowlands of South America and Central America (who rely still very much on hunting and gathering and an historically dynamic involvement in the local labor and commodity market). Again, here we find a whole range of levels of subsistence economies, from sub-subsistence to a few cases of affluent subsistence.
3. Proletarianized rural and urban indigenous people who rely mostly on wage labor at the level of subemployment and/or temporary employment (with incomes that are complemented by cyclical returns to the community and the practice of some agricultural activity).

Clearly a class analysis must be introduced in this typology to dis-
close the presence, in most of the indigenous ethnic people, of a
small elite of intelligentsia and professionals, a petty bourgeoisie
linked in most cases to nation-state bureaucracy and services, and
in some cases of a flourishing bourgeoisie (some clear examples
are to be found among the Isthmus Zapotecs of Mexico, and the
Guajiro of Venezuela).

How did the process of transformation of the indigenous people take place during the last few centuries? How are the transformations produced today by the globalization and the induced
transnational migration and diaspora affecting the indigenous
people's relation to their territory, their homeland? Obviously
these are questions that would require much more space and time
than I have in this opportunity. I postulate, nevertheless, that a historical analysis within Ferdinand Braudel's perspective of the
"Longue Durée" (Long Duration) is absolutely indispensable if we
are to understand not the "eventful history" but the more permanent cultural and social characteristics of indigenous societies.

As we consider indigenous people, we are looking at millennia
of accumulated history, trends, and cultural characteristics that
have survived and adapted to many radical social and economic
changes through precolonial time, centuries of colonialism-impe-
rialism (which produced fragmented mosaics of territorialized
"Indian community," early Indian diasporas, and the Indian proletariat), more than one century of nationalism (which accentu-
ated the expansion and penetration of the capitalist market in indigenous territories), and finally a few decades of transnationalism
and globalization (which are inducing Indian neodiasporas, transnational migration, and processes of cyclical deterritorialization).

In this schematic chronology, it is important to emphasize that
the formative period of pre-Colombian, pre-European, preinva-
sion, preconquest or "independent indigenous evolvement" was
a period of construction of polycentric cosmology as well as polycentric social practices that Eurocentrism would later call poly-
theism and misinterpret by confusing diversity with chaos and
disorder. This is the complex of biocultural diversity that has been

attributed by anthropologists to early indigenous social formation of hunters and gatherers, horticulturists, and agrarian societies which evolved in the tropics. Is biodiversity an exclusive function of the tropics? It is evident that there is more biodiversity in
subtropical and tropical zones; however, even in temperate cli-
mates and subarctic regions, biodiversity seems to be the central
characteristic of indigenous people's culture.

As discussed previously, *reciprocity* is the associated and homol-
ogous social and cultural principle of biodiversity—a principle
that supports the whole logic of social interaction as well as the
whole moral of cosmic transactions, those arrangements that take
place between humans and the rest of the tangible and intangi-
ble universe. American Indian languages are repositories of these
intellectual and practical constructions, and hundreds of terms can
be found in Amerindian semantic fields that refer to reciprocal
social and cosmic transactions. The Zapotec *guzún y guelaguetza*,
the Nahuatl *tequistl, tequio*, the Quechua *mit'a, ayni*, the Ashaninka
ayumparii are only some examples of terms that refer to elaborate
cultural institutions of diversity and reciprocity. Even in historical societies that were organized hierarchically in social classes,
like those of Mesoamerica and Andes, the logic of reciprocity was
at the basis of every exchange of goods, services, labor, tributes,
gifts. The tributary system was based on the principle of reciprocity, which could be symmetrical, asymmetrical, or differed.

In any case, *complementarity* is the logical and practical concurrent principle of diversity and reciprocity that allowed, for instance,
the Andean peoples to build the elaborate and monumental agro-
ecological system based on the combined vertical use of different
ecosystems or "ecological floors" distributed at different altitudes
of the Andes (Murra 1978; Dollfus 1981). In the case of the Amazon region, a similar principle made it possible for indigenous people to establish a macrosystem of horizontal complementarity in
a large geographical area in which scarce and scattered resources
such as salt, stone axes, or the hunting poison "curare" could be
circulated and exchanged by larger numbers of people separated
by thousand of miles (Varese 1983). Mesoamerica expressed the

same principles of reciprocity, diversity, and complementarity through the "solar market system," which articulates the people of numerous and diverse villages and regions in periodical encounters for the exchange of goods, ideas, ceremonies, and culture (Wolf 1959).

Until a few decades ago, the Campa-Ashaninka of Peru's upper Amazon, who live in hamlets scattered throughout a vast territory of tropical rain forest, used to achieve and maintain social and cultural cohesion by performing a cyclical, ritual, panethnic encounter called *parawa*. In this large gathering, hundreds of Ashaninka would meet to celebrate and renovate their common ancestry, their kinship and community ties, their collective identity, and the complex web of debts and credits, of gifts and services, which bonds every Ashaninka adult male in a tense relation of reciprocal complementarity with numerous and distant members of his people. In a manner similar to the nineteenth-century Sundance ceremony of the Plain Indians (Albers and Kay 1987), the Ashaninka used this opportunity to renegotiate their collective identity, reconfigure spatial and social boundaries, establish alliances, reclaim new and old debts, and assert the validity of this social arrangement while assuring, expanding, and developing diversity.[2] I use this ethnographic case as an example, among possibly hundreds of them, to highlight the permanence and continuity of the principles that I characterize as constitutive of the indigenous people of the Americas. More than forty years ago Eric Wolf argued that in Mesoamerica there is a further correspondence between biocultural diversity and multilinguism; he pointed out that the presence of many areas of development, maintenance, and coexistence of different languages in regions, communities, villages, and families is an indication of the ability of indigenous cultural formations to deal with diversity also at the conceptual and ideological level (Wolf 1959). I have argued the same for the case of the pre-Andean Amazon region (Varese 1983).

At the end of this long and winding itinerary through the indigenous notions and practices of territorial/spatial community—

which seem to be so distant from John Brown Childs's idea of *emplacement* and its spatial fluidity—I find myself coinciding, however, with his position. Why? Because cosmoscentrism, spatial jurisdiction, diversity, polyculturalism, the principles of diversity, reciprocity, and complementarity are all components of a symbolic capital that may or may not still hold the material ground, the territorial foundation of the origins, but that nevertheless constitutes the imaginary cultural space—the semantics of indigenous space—on which the whole network of relationships between humans and between the humans and the universe is based. In this sense, contemporary indigenous diasporas (an elegant formula for naming the continuing and unfinished colonial ethnocide) are all grounded in the concrete territory / space of their specific ethnic origin, which every member of the community can claim as his or her own, and in its symbolic representations as "sites" of shared cultural values that can be carried around in journeys of migrations, exile, and deportation or in pilgrimages toward autonomy and self-determination as the old Native American sacred bundles or the Mesoamerican *petacas parlantes* or *cruz parlante* or the Andean sacred cloths or maybe simply as the inalienable memory of a possible future of sovereignty.

Notes

1. This is the line of thought established by Adam Smith's *An Inquiry into the Nature and Causes of the Wealth of Nations* and followed by Karl Marx's *Capital*.

2. See *La Sal de los Cerros* (Varese, 1967). More than thirty years ago, when I was doing my research among the Campa-Ashaninka, I did not pay much attention to the stories I heard about the *parawa* ceremony. In my juvenile ignorance I relegated them to a field note booklet filled with what I considered, at that time, exotic but useless information. Today as I review my old field notes for an updated English translation of the book, I discover with dismay my arrogance and the missed opportunities.

References

Albers, Patricia, and Jeanne Kay. 1987. "Sharing the Land: A Study in American Indian Territoriality." In *A Cultural Geography of North*

American Indians. Ed. Thomas E. Ross and Tyrel G. Moore. Boulder: Westview Press.

Amin, Samir. 1989. *Eurocentrism.* New York: Monthly Review Press.

Chayanov, A. V. 1986. *The Theory of the Peasant Economy.* Madison: University of Wisconsin Press.

Clendinnen, Inga. 1995. *Aztecs: An Interpretation.* New York: Cambridge University Press.

Díaz Polanco, Héctor. 1991. *La Autonomía de los Pueblos Indígenas.* Mexico: Siglo XXI Editores.

Dollfus, Olivier. 1981. *El reto del espacio andino.* Lima: Instituto de Estudios Peruanos.

Escobar, Arturo. 1995. *Encountering Development: The Making and Unmaking of the Third World.* Princeton, NJ: Princeton University Press.

Hale, Charles R. 1994. *Resistance and Contradiction: Miskitu Indians and the Nicaraguan State, 1894–1987.* Stanford, CA: Stanford University Press.

Hale, Charles R. 1995. "De la militancia indígena a la conciencia multiétnica: Los desafios de la autonomía en la Costa Atlántica de Nicaragua." In *Etnicidad y Derechos Indígenas.* Ed. S. Varese. Quito: Ediciones Abyayala.

Jary, David, and Julia Jary. 1991. *The Harper Collins Dictionary of Sociology.* New York: Harper Perennial.

Kearney, Michael. 1991. "Border and Boundaries of State and Self at the End of the Empire." *Journal of Historical Sociology,* 4(1): 52–74.

———. 1996. *Reconceptualizing the Peasantry.* Boulder: Westview Press.

Kearney, Michael, and Stefano Varese. 1995. "Latin America's Indigenous Peoples Today: Changing Identities and Forms of Resistance in Global Context." In *Capital, Power and Inequality in Latin America.* Ed. Sandor Halebsky and Richard L. Harris. Boulder: Westview Press.

Lenin, V. I. 1956/1899. *The Development of Capitalism in Russia: The Process of Formation of a Home Market for Large-Scale Industry.* Moscow: Foreign Languages Publishing House.

Mariatequi, Jose Carlos. 1976 (1928). *La Polemica del indigenismo.* Lima: Mosca Zul Editores.

Marx, Karl. 1963/1852. *The Eighteenth Brumaire of Louis Bonaparte.* New York: International Publishers.

Murra, John V. 1978. *Formaciones Económicas y Politicas del Mundo Andino.* Lima: Instituto de Estudios Peruanos.

Popkin, Samuel. 1979. *The Rational Peasant: The Political Economy of Rural Society in Vietnam.* Berkeley: University of California Press.

Psacharopoulos, George, and Harry Anthony Patrinos, eds. 1994. *Indigenous People and Poverty in Latin America: An Empirical Analysis.* Washington, DC: World Bank.

Sale, Kirkpatrick. 1991. *The Conquest of Paradise: Christopher Columbus and the Colombian Legacy.* New York: Penguin.

Scott, James. 1976. *The Moral Economy of the Peasants: Rebellion and Subsistence in Southeast Asia.* New Haven: Yale University Press.

———. 1985. *Weapons of the Weak: Everyday Forms of Peasant Resistance.* New Haven: Yale University Press.

Scott, James C. 1998. *Seeing like a State: How Certain Schemes to Improve Human Condition Have Failed.* New Haven: Yale University Press.

Shanin, Theodor, ed. 1990. *Defining Peasants: Essays Concerning Rural Societies.* Oxford: Basil Blackwell.

Tönnies, F. 1955/1887. *Community and Society.* London: Routledge.

Van Der Leeuw, G. 1955. *La religion dans son essence et ses manifestations.* Paris: Payot.

Varese, Stefano. 1973. *La Sal de los Cerros: una Aproximacion al mundo Campa.* 2nd ed. Lima: Retablo de Pael Ediciones.

———. 1983. "Los Grupos Etno-Lingüísticos de la Selva Andina." In *América Latina an sus Lenguas Indigenas.* Ed. B. Pottier. Caracas, Venezuela: Montes Avila Editores.

———. 1985. "Cultural Development in Ethnic Groups: Anthropological Explorations in Education." *International Social Science Journal,* UNESCO, 37: 201–216.

———. 1991. "Think Locally, Act Globally." *NACLA Report on the Americas,* 25(3): 13–17.

———. 1999. "Local Epistemologies in the Age of Globalization." American Anthropological Association, 98th Annual Meeting, Society for Latin American Anthropology Session: Reconceptualizing the Americas.

Weber, Max. 1958. *The Protestant Ethic and the Spirit of Capitalism.* Trans.: Talcott Parsons. New York: Charles Scribner's Sons.

Wolf, Eric R. 1959. *Sons of the Shaking Earth.* Chicago: University of Chicago Press.

———. 1966. *Peasants.* Englewood Cliffs, NJ: Prentice-Hall.

Worsley, Peter, et al. 1987. *The New Introducing Sociology.* New York: Penguin.

Renate Holub

Transcommunality in a Global World

Communicative Action

DRAWING FROM the social philosophies of the Amerindians in general, and the Haudenosaunee of Northern America in particular, John Brown Childs develops what he calls "transcommunal" approaches to global struggles for freedom and justice. Intrinsic to these approaches are communicative actions. These are actions preceded by communication between individuals and groups and communication that results in purposive action. Hereby Childs counters the inward-focused identity politics of the multiculturalisms that dominated academic and juridical debates here in the United States for several decades. Identity politics, as Childs says in his introduction in this book, can "cut off its participants from contact with others in the name of racial, ethnic, or ideological claims of purity." Rather, Childs, with his transcommunalism, seeks to establish bridges, not only between differently traditioned groups, but also between differently traditioned individuals. Communication begins between individuals. Key elements of this communication are shared assumptions about respectful speech and listening, and the idea that words are nothing without deeds, and that deeds are task focused. This outlook has parallels to the notion of a "communicative action" as the central piece of the political theory of the western philoso-

146

pher Juergen Habermas (1982). Habermas, like Childs, develops his political program in the name of freedom, dignity, and justice. But the transcommunal project that Childs envisions offers a move beyond western modes of thought.

For Habermas, the political and social inadequacies in modern democracies, produced by the functionalist rationality of consumer capitalism, are continuously challenged by the actions of free citizens in their life worlds, who freely associate in the public sphere to discuss inadequacies and maldistribution of public goods against the background of shared ethical values. When people engage in dialogue with each other, the most rational argument will produce consensus among the participants precisely because the most rational argument is the most rational in terms of distributive justice. The rationalization of modern society envisaged by Max Weber (1958, 175–183), to whom Habermas pays conceptual tribute, still affords citizens the space of a public sphere from which and in which they counter the operations of instrumental reason. Their collective interventions reenchant, however sporadically, a disenchanting world.

Habermas's program for social justice has the coherence, simplicity, and elegance of a mathematical model. Its call to a nonnegotiable universality of the human condition as inalienable autonomy, dignity, and freedom carries the clarity and distinctness of the great minds of the western ethical tradition. It universalizes human rights. Yet precisely because Habermas partakes of the western tradition, his project of "communicative action" can only offer to the critical cultural organizers in other global regions a message of solidarity, but not a universalizable process and a practice of social justice. Here Marx's critique of Feuerbach, his "Thesis Number Three," is still relevant in its focus on human action in relationship to context. Marx writes that the materialist doctrine that men/women are products of circumstances and upbringing, and that, therefore, changed women/men are products of other circumstances and changed upbringing, forgets that it is men who change circumstances and that it is essential to educate the educator himself (Marx, 1978, 144).

Importantly, the circumstances from which Habermas derives his principle for change and the changes that he wishes to put into practice are not tied to globality but to the ways in which western modernity is linked to processes of globalization. That modernity consists of specific features, while lacking features that other modernities command. Habermas's modernity pertains, for instance, to the rise of the western nation-state, the formation of European and western institutions of political and social life, the transition from industrial capitalism to finance and consumerist capitalism, the development of colonialism and postcolonialism, and the evolution of particular types of citizens, particular types of political actions, and particular types of civil societies. Most importantly, western modernity also pertains to forms of secularization that in the cultural structures of everyday life successfully amalgamate particular types of religious and spiritual traditions, and social and political norms tied to these traditions, with the production and organization of knowledge. In other words, western knowledge regimes and political propositions are not dissociable from the cultural practices and norms of western secularity. Notably, this persistent recourse to secularisms unintentionally displays its rootedness in and continuous interaction with particular types of religious traditions in the very processes of secularization. These religious-cultural traditions are foremost Christian traditions: Protestantism and Catholicism alike.

It is not the point here to delve into the religious nature of the western project. Much more to the point is to state that a relationship between the secular project and particular forms of religiosity and spirituality exists. Ernest Gellner grasps this dimension when he proposes in his *Postmodernism, Reason, and Religion* (1992) that Enlightenment rationalism, by upholding the notion of a unique truth, is one of the ways to approach the question of faith. Not insignificantly, the cover of Gellner's book evokes Islamicity, which in our contemporary media world easily symbolizes Muslim fundamentalism. But the sense of a Unique Truth lends itself to fundamentalist positions, including those of European Enlightenment rationalism. In theory and in practice, this rationalism is a scientific backdrop to colonialism, imperialism, and economic productivism alike, and has not always managed to stay out of the orbit of ideological fundamentalists.

Many global intellectual elites of previous generations—W.E.B. Du Bois, Girindrasekhar Bose, Frantz Fanon, Octavio Paz—eminently apprehended the fundamentalist dimension of the western project, which, in the name of western rationality, poised itself to deny universality, human rights, dignity, and freedom to subjects of nonwestern worlds (Fanon, 1963, 1967; Nandy, 1995; Paz, 1995). Global intellectuals of our contemporary worlds—writers, filmmakers, cultural organizers, and organizers of knowledge—with clarity and distinction create images, categories, conceptualities, and measurements that assess the circumstances not of the western subject, but of their own lives (for example, see Grovogui, 1996; Appadurai, 1996; Shayegan, 1997; Jameson and Miyoshi, 1998; Tomlinson, 1999; Lechner and Boli, 2000). Among them I especially count the economic philosopher Amartya Sen (1992), and among them stands foremost John Brown Childs.

In Habermas's defense, one may argue that the problematic nature of the history of western universality should not distract us from the future-oriented normativity and intentionality inscribed in his communicative action model: images of a global citizenry, moving in a global public sphere, engaged in the democratic regulation of the access to the control of resources and allocation. Pointing to the universal implications of Habermas's normativity and intentionality falls short of explanation, however. For what needs to be explained are not the universal implications of Habermas's theory, or his genuine wish for a universal critical citizenry, but the systemic connectedness of Habermas's specific critical citizens to the operators of consumerist capitalism in a networked, informational, and global economy. In other words, Habermas, on the basis of his communicative action model, continues to envision and work for a global public sphere of critical citizens—the lack of a significant public sphere in the European Union and the world at large is the topic of his writings over the past decade. But he and his followers close their eyes to two facts. First, they ignore that the "critical citizen" whom they uphold is a citizen not of "the world" but of the western democracies. Such a citizen enjoys access not only to high levels of educational and economic opportunities but also to significant political participation in the complex structure of western civil societies. The material circumstances of that citizen are not comparable to those of the majority of global citizens. Secondly, the Habermasians close their eyes to the fact that a global public sphere does indeed already exist.

The challenge for global critical intellectuals is not to merely point to the connectedness of the "western citizen" to the global civil society, however. This initiative would merely reiterate an academically most pervasive negative project, which, under the rubric of "postcolonial discourse" or "postmodern critique," keeps pointing the finger at the complicity of western intellectuality in the processes of globalization. The challenge is rather to develop systematic connections and build bridges with counter-consumerist capitalist forces, and practices, all over the world. John Brown Childs's notion of transcommunality, of an ethics of respect, functions as a central conceptual instrument to developing such systematic connections in a meaningful way. Transcommunality is a refusal to develop a model of social justice, respect, and dignity that ignores the human dimension of Marxian "circumstances," namely our personal rootedness in or inner connectedness to places, cultures, and times. Countless theoretical attempts throughout the twentieth century—such as phenomenology, existentialism, linguistics, and the best of feminist theory—illustrate that *experiences,* and the way they are remembered, involve more than body and mind. They involve places where the body has been and has never been, and where the body is: locations and memories of locations that structure the extent of the material, symbolic, and spiritual well-being of the individual, that determine his or her quality of life. *Domina abstracta* and *Homo abstractus* do not exist.

It is to the extraordinary credit of John Brown Childs that he keeps reminding us of this simple social fact, of the complex synthesis of memory and belonging that are crucial to our strengths, and it is in his spirit that I for the remainder of this essay would like to analyze—however tentatively—conditions for global social justice in a globalized world. Against the background of the Gramscian concepts of hegemony, intellectuals, historic bloc, and civil society, I will first sketch the outlines of the global civil society as it currently exists and in which we as citizens in centers of global capitalism—as taxpayers, bank account holders, credit card holders, and pension plan holders, etc.—all partake. Moral values do not exempt us from financial complicity. I will conclude, against the background of John Brown Childs's theory of trans-communality, by exploring the informational, global, and net-worked possibilities the new economy offers to a politics of transcommunal social justice, dignity, and respect.

Global Civil Society, Hegemony, and the Question of Intellectuals

A global civil society already exists. It is not the public sphere of citizens controlling the distribution of public goods. It is a public sphere of international citizens privately controlling the distri-bution of public goods. The actors predominantly inhabiting it are not critical citizens of cosmopolitan persuasions rooted in an eighteenth-century universalism of human rights. Rather, the pre-dominant actors of the global public sphere are the organizers and agents of the ideology of consumer capitalism. These range, on the one hand, from the consumerist elites of the merchants and the media to the globalized politicians, professionals, and state bureaucracies, and, on the other hand, from the executives and local affiliates of the transnational capitalist class to the regulators of the transnational corporations. As Peter Gowan details in *The Global Gamble: Washington's Faustian Bid for World Dominance* (1999), since 1989 the United States has used international sys-tems of sovereign states as a mechanism of global hegemony. Economic statecraft, market management, and information man-agement constitute a repertoire of instruments on which state executives rely in their foreign policy-making processes, which are closed to public scrutiny. Recent major trends in the capitalist centers speak to the production of this hegemony. These pertain to transformations in both the domestic and external environments. *Neoliberalism* and *globalization* are the key terms describing these trends that since 1989 have become more rationalized and generalized via multilateral organizations and agreements. Such organizations and agreements benefit primarily the United States, while risks and costs are carried by other states.

As capitalist centers influence individual state policies, the transnationalization and expansion of U.S. economic and political influence provide an opening for U.S. financial operators and U.S. financial markets and U.S. transnational corporations. Even if one were to disagree with Gowan's formidable assessment of the "Faustian bid," recent citizen mobilization efforts, such as the demonstrations against the World Trade Organization in Seattle in December 1999, attest to the fact that critical minds do recognize and object to the dictate, role, and function of the International Monetary Fund, the World Bank, and the G-7 countries in the expansion of the practice and ideology of consumer capitalism into all corners of the world and the human, ecological, and social costs these expansions entail.

On a global scale, "communicative actions" do exist among the first order of organic intellectuals of consumer capitalism—the economic and political elites. They exist as well among the second and third orders of intellectuals as part of networks, organizations, and associations—financial, economic, informational, and network operators, organizers, managers, and distributors. In a complex structure of knowledge, information, and network interconnectedness, consumerist capitalism reproduces itself along an axis of forces which Antonio Gramsci's concept of a "historic bloc" (1971) helps us to grasp. Today, a historic bloc exists between states and economic elites on the one hand, and between U.S.-economic elites and non-U.S. economic elites on the other hand. The latter reside in the dominant network cities, in parts of Frankfurt, New York, London, and Singapore for one, and in parts of Paris, Bangkok, Tokyo, and Seoul for another, a phenomenon which Manuel Castells already by 1989 called "the informational city." As in Gramsci's discussion of the historic bloc and hegemony (1971), the historic bloc of consumer capitalism produces consent to the status quo or its hegemony via a set of institutional apparatuses. These apparatuses pertain not only to economic, financial, and political elites but to cultural elites as well.

Gramsci's analysis of the historic bloc of the Italy of his era is relevant to understanding today's global-reach of cultural elites. Crucial to the production of hegemony under the historic bloc of consumer capitalism are the cultural institutions and their agents, the new international information orders of consumerist elites. Benjamin Barber's *Jihad vs. McWorld* (1995) documents in detail the extent of the sale of consumerist status symbols and values, produced and distributed under the direction of Hollywood. The agents of the new international information orders constitute a broad class of material, symbolic, and virtual commodity producers: advertisers, artists, photographers, film producers, fashion designers, commodity distributors, and so on. That class also consists of the consumers of the status and values of their commodities: the symbolic reproducers of capitalist consumerism, whose consumerist habits turn them into powerful symbolic participants in the communicative actions of the global public sphere. For communication—as feminists, liberational theologists, and colonial independence fighters have repeatedly addressed—transcends the realm of utterance, shapes, colors, gestures, symbols, and silences, that in presence and absence, speak. One of the most powerful texts in this respect remains Frantz Fanon's *Black Skin, White Masks* (1967).

Differential Pragmatics

There is no doubt that the new economy of globalization is regulated by the centers of capitalism. There is equally no doubt that the centers of capitalist power reproduce themselves via the production of hegemony nested in the various orders, institutions, and practices of the international capitalist consumerist class.

Internal and external transformations of the environment of western core countries have shaped this class and have also contributed to the weakening of their civil societies or public spheres, understood in Habermasian terms. Under the impact of neoliberalism, the citizenry—including its leading intellectuals—no longer primarily insist on the accountability of their governments. In fact, there are significant contractions in the state's legitimacy.

It should be noted, though, that as the public spheres of sovereign states recede under the impact of the expansionary dynamics of the new information orders of global civil society, patterns of new information technological practices and network regimes emerge. These participate not only or necessarily in the production of hegemony. The globalization of cultures has been propelled by the historic bloc of media barons, big business, and executive offices, as well as by material and financial consumers who represent their greatest support. Cultural colonization has extended—with the exception of fundamentalist Muslim states—to almost all global regions in the form of Coca Cola, Jeans, Rock music, and Marlboro. Yet cultural imperialists, as a legacy of post-colonialism, with their agents, institutions, and operations, are not the only players that mark globalization. Precisely because globalization also means taking part in networks and information, the globalization of cultures produces its own cultures of globalization. All of these newly emerging cultures are informational and networked. For this reason, they are not simply potentially global, but global in actuality, in real and virtual time.

Surely, the know-how of where to place the nuts and bolts of the network and information technology derives from the leading western economies. But the know-how as to how to play with them does not. A variety of global media centers have leapfrogged into a sphere of influence, status, and power. Mexico, Hong Kong, Egypt, Brazil, and India—and perhaps Iran as of late—have demonstrated with their vast output of media productions that interest in western cultural goods, symbols, and values sharply declines when media centers in their regions respond to the needs of their regions, when they produce symbols, values, and mean-

ings rooted in their local cultures. In those global regions where
TV cultures flourish, they flourish because of their local contents,
not because of Hollywood. This is but one example of the multiple counter-hegemonies that daily emerge in a networked, informational, and global world.

Surely, as in the old economy, actors stage the stakes. No play
takes place without the actors, including those who think they
merely watch. It is difficult to predict to what extent the Internet
will enable the transcommunal practices promoted by John Brown
Childs. What is less difficult to see is that it can. The critical public sphere of the global age has emerged. The north not only
informs itself about the south; the north has become part of the
south. This has become one of the grounds from which we can
practice, in John Brown Childs's sense, our ethics of respect.

Works Cited

Appadurai, Arjun. 1996. *Modernity at Large: Cultural Dimensions of Globalization*. Minneapolis: University of Minnesota Press.

Barber, Benjamin. 1995. *Jihad vs. McWorld*. New York: Times Books.

Castells, Manuel. 1989. *The Informational City: Information Technology,
Economic Restructuring, and the Urban-Regional Process*. Oxford: Blackwell.

Fanon, Frantz. 1963. *The Wretched of the Earth*. New York: Grove Press.

———. 1967. *Black Skin, White Masks*. Trans. Charles L. Markmann. New
York: Grove Press.

Gellner, Ernest. 1992. *Postmodernism, Reason, and Religion*. London: Routledge.

Gowan, Peter. 1999. *The Global Gamble: Washington's Faustian Bid for
World Dominance*. New York: Verso.

Gramsci, Antonio. 1971. *Selections from the Prison Notebooks*. Ed. and trans.
Quintin Hoare and Geoffrey Nowell Smith. New York: International
Publishers.

Grovogui, Siba N'Zatioula. *Sovereigns, Quasi Sovereigns, and Africans: Race
and Self-Determination in International Law*. Minneapolis: University of
Minnesota Press.

Habermas, Juergen. 1982. *Theorie des kommunikativen Handeln, Bd 1,
Handlungsrationalitaet und gesellschaftliche Rationalisierung*. Frankfurt:
Suhrkamp.

156   **Commentaries**

Jameson, Fredric, and Masao Miyoshi, eds. 1998. *The Cultures of Globalization*. Durham, NC: Duke University Press.

Lechner, Frank J., and John Boli, eds. 2000. *The Globalization Reader.* Malden, MA: Blackwell.

Marx, Karl. 1978. "Theses on Feuerbach." In *The Marx-Engels Reader,* 2nd ed. Ed. Robert C. Tucker. New York: Norton.

Nandy, Ashis. 1995. *The Savage Freud and Other Essays on Possible and Retrievable Selves.* Princeton, NJ: Princeton University Press.

Paz, Octavio. 1995. *In Light of India.* Trans. Eliot Weinberger. San Diego: Harcourt, Brace.

Sen, Amartya. 1992. *Inequality Reexamined.* Cambridge, MA: Harvard University Press.

Shayegan, Dariush. 1997. *Cultural Schizophrenia: Islamic Societies Confronting the West.* Syracuse, NY: Syracuse University Press.

Tomlinson, John. 1999. *Globalization and Culture.* Chicago: University of Chicago Press.

Weber, Max. 1958. *The Protestant Ethic and the Spirit of Capitalism.* Trans.: Talcott Parsons. New York: Charles Scribner's Sons.

Jeremy Brecher

Transcommunality as a Foundation for Globalization from Below

JOHN BROWN CHILDS's short but deep reflections on "transcommunality," and the web of approaches he articulates for realizing it, in many ways prefigure the worldwide movement that has arisen to challenge globalization. They also provide profound guidance for directions that the movement needs to take. As John Childs writes, "Today, huge and growing systems of economic domination continue their profit-driven bulldozer crush across the world. . . . [I]ncreasing numbers of people are relegated to disease-ridden, paramilitary-controlled backwaters of the free-market mainstream." That "globalization from above," however, is now being countered by what has been called "globalization from below." The 1999 "Battle of Seattle" that brought the World Trade Organization meeting to a halt marked the coming out party for an emerging global movement that challenges globalization from above. It has been followed by similar international demonstrations from Okinawa to Bangkok and from Prague to Quebec City.

Globalization from below has emerged, not from a plan or ideology, but from the kind of reaching out to each other of very different groups affected by common problems that John Brown

Childs describes as the root of transcommunality. Environmentalists identified globalization as a source of acid rain and global warming and saw global corporations and the World Bank sponsoring the destruction of local environments around the world. Poor people's movements in the third world and their supporters around the globe saw neoliberalism, international financial capital, and structural adjustment as key causes of global poverty. Advocates for small farmers in both developed and developing nations identified new trade agreements as a means to destroy family farming in the interests of agribusiness. Indigenous activists saw global corporations destroying their communities and environments from the Arctic to the Amazon. Labor movements realized that international capital mobility was leading not to mutual benefit for workers but to competitive wage-cutting. Women's movements identified workers exploited in the global sweatshop as predominantly women and structural adjustment as an attack on public programs that women particularly need. Consumer movements identified neoliberalism and new trade agreements as attacks on high national standards for food and product safety. College students became outraged that products bearing their schools' logos were being made by children and women forced to work sixty or more hours per week for less than a living wage. Many more groups could be added to this list.

From diverse origins and through varied itineraries, these movements now find themselves starting to converge. Many of their participants are beginning to recognize their commonalities and to envision themselves as constructing a common movement. In many though not all ways, their efforts use the methods and fit the patterns of transcommunality.

This convergence is occurring because globalization is creating common interests that transcend both national and interest-group boundaries. As author and activist Vandana Shiva wrote in the wake of the Battle of Seattle, "When labour joins hands with environmentalists, when farmers from the North and farmers from the South make a common commitment to say 'no' to genetically engineered crops, they are not acting as special interests. They are defending the common interests and common rights of all people, everywhere. The divide and rule policy, which has attempted to pit consumers against farmers, the North against the South, labour against environmentalist has failed."[1]

This convergence of the many different groups that challenge globalization is initially often negative. They face the same global corporations, international institutions, and market-driven race to the bottom. But there is also a growing positive convergence around common values of democracy, environmental protection, community, economic justice, equality, and human solidarity. Participants in this convergence have varied goals, but the unifying goal is to bring about sufficient democratic control over states, markets, and corporations to permit people and planet to survive and begin to shape a viable future. This is a necessary condition for participants' diverse other goals.

Globalization from below is certainly a movement with contradictions. Its participants have many conflicting interests. It includes many groups that previously defined themselves in part via negative reference to each other. It includes both rigidly institutionalized and wildly unstructured elements. But globalization from below is developing in ways that help it cope with this diversity— ways that are very much in accord with ideas of transcommunality. The movement has embraced diversity as one of its central values, and asserts that cooperation need not presuppose uniformity.

Globalization from below's emerging organizational form also reflects aspects of transcommunality. At its core lie what political scientists Margaret Keck and Kathryn Sikkink call "advocacy networks." They define networks as "forms of organization characterized by voluntary, reciprocal and horizontal patterns of communication and exchange."[2] These networks include non-governmental organizations (NGOs), local social movements, foundations, the media, churches, trade unions, consumer organizations, intellectuals, parts of regional and international intergovernmental organizations, and parts of the executive and parliamentary branches of government. Not all of these groups have the deep rootedness in specific communities of many of the groups discussed in John Brown Childs's *Transcommunality*, but they face a similar need to cooperate despite differences.

Such networks exchange information and support a dense nexus of communication among participants. They also develop a common language and frame issues for participants and the public. Networks have become the main vehicle through which the campaigns of globalization from below have been organized. They function differently in campaigns than either conventional organizations or coalitions. There may be a lead organization and perhaps a formal coalition of supporters, but in practice, most transnational campaigns emerge from planning within networks and are conducted by them, often across formal organizational lines. They are marked by what might be called cross-organization team leadership.

Network participants can be highly diverse and may disagree on many matters, as long as they accept the network's defining frame of the issues that it addresses. Individuals can participate in networks directly, whether or not they are formally affiliated through organizations. Segments of organizations can participate in them, and in the actions they launch, while other segments remain aloof. A somewhat similar structure has developed for coordinating mass action at international demonstrations like the Battle of Seattle. Participants organize into affinity groups. They make their own decisions about how to act, but they coordinate through meetings of a spokescouncil of affinity group representatives.

Protests like the Battle of Seattle have reframed the debate on globalization, put its advocates on the defensive, and forced changes in the rhetoric if not the actions of world leaders and global institutions. But they have also raised the question of whether this is more than a movement of "meeting-stalkers."[3] Such confrontations are only the tip of the globalization from below iceberg, however. The far greater part of its activity consists of local, grassroots action and linking of mutual support, locally and globally, much in the manner of transcommunality.

To take one example among hundreds: In the late 1990s, under heavy pressure from the World Bank, the Bolivian government

sold off the public water system of its third largest city, Cochabamba, to a subsidiary of the San Francisco–based Bechtel Cor-
poration, which promptly doubled the price of water for people's
homes. Early in 2000, the people of Cochabamba rebelled, shut-
ting down the city with general strikes and blockades. The government declared a state of siege and a young protester was shot
and killed. Word spread from the remote Bolivian highlands to the
outside world via the Internet. Hundreds of e-mail messages
poured into Bechtel from all over the world, demanding that it
leave Cochabamba. In the midst of local and global protests, the
Bolivian government, which had said that Bechtel must not leave,
suddenly reversed itself and signed an accord accepting every
demand of the protesters. Meanwhile, a local protest leader was
smuggled out of hiding to Washington, D.C., where he addressed
the large April 16, 2000, international rally against the IMF and
World Bank.

The social composition of the movement for globalization
from below is rapidly changing. The NGOs that spearheaded
transnational response to global issues in the 1980s and 1990s
often did so from a rather narrow social base. They represented
not so much globalization from below as globalization from the
middle: middle-class and even elite groups in the north trying to
act on behalf of the global poor and humanity as a whole. Initially,
most U.S. participants in the movement for globalization from
below were drawn from the "new social movements" of the 1970s
and 1980s, such as the environmental, human rights, peace, and
antinuclear movements. Participants in these movements were
overwhelmingly drawn from the middle class.

The emerging movement that became so visible at the Battle
of Seattle is far broader and more diverse. Nonetheless, it is far
from incorporating or leading all of the movements for social
change locally or globally—nor should it aspire to. Still less does
it embody the billions of people who are affected by globalization and are responding to it in ways (from fundamentalist religion to immigration) that do not fit the pattern of social protest
movements.

Transcommunality offers important wisdom for globalization from below in addressing this situation. Those who currently form the movement could easily become closed off to these emerging forces or mistakenly try to establish hegemony over them. To avoid these pitfalls, they need to recognize that a wide range of social groups are being affected in a variety of ways by globalization from above. Such groups will inevitably develop their own responses and follow their own itineraries. They are unlikely to be subsumed under the movement in its current form.

For example, considerable concern has been expressed in the United States about the relatively modest participation by African Americans in the antiglobalization demonstrations in Seattle and Washington, D.C. In considering this question, the first thing to recognize is that African Americans have their own traditions of internationalism stretching back a century and a half to the struggle against slavery and through the anti-apartheid movement. The second is that African Americans have their own reasons to be concerned about the impact of globalization from above. As National Urban League President Hugh Price put it, "The manufacturing jobs that once enabled blue collar workers to purchase their own homes and occasional new cars have all but vanished from the inner city," and while racism is still widespread, "the global realignment of work and wealth is, if anything, the bigger culprit."[4]

The black community in the United States has in fact been making its own response to globalization. For example, African Americans played a leading role in opposing the "NAFTA for Africa" trade bill and in supporting Representative Jesse Jackson Jr.'s alternative "Hope for Africa" legislation. It also played a major role in the Jubilee 2000 campaign for debt relief. It would be patronizing to assume that the African American community's response to globalization is merely a question of whether or not black people show up at events like the Seattle protests and participate on terms set by other groups.

Recognizing such activities as independent forms of resistance to globalization from above does not mean that the advocates of globalization from below should stand aloof from them. I'd suggest that those active in the current movement should, in the spirit of transcommunality, apply the following guidelines:

- Pursue ongoing dialogue and common ground with groups affected by globalization from above that are not yet part of the movement for globalization from below.
- Recognize that social movements, like the societies from which they grow, are marked by the prevailing inequalities based on race, class, gender, nationality, ethnicity, and other social divides. This requires appropriate forms of compensation, such as directing resources toward groups that need greater resources in order to participate, and affirmative action regarding the role of such groups in movement leadership.
- Encourage independent development of responses to globalization by impoverished and oppressed groups, without presuming that they should be subsumed under the organizational forms of the present movement.
- Provide materials and solidarity without seeking hegemony.
- Keep the movement open to new input and further evolution as new groups begin to relate to it.
- Identify and seek to correct the cultural barriers to equal participation in the movement.
- Accept as legitimate the strategy of tensions through which poor and oppressed groups make demands on other movements for incorporation of their concerns.

John Brown Childs's *Transcommunality* has a great deal to offer as an organizational theory, manual, and inspiration for globalization from below. Many of its themes—such as the mutual dependence of diversity and cooperation, the need for concrete action to address common needs in spite of differences, and the strength of organization based on autonomy and the active, ongoing construction of unity—are already reflected in many ways in that movement. But *Transcommunality* provides a coherent overall perspective, lessons from past experience, and practical guidelines for interaction that will benefit the movement immensely. I hope and expect it will become a foundation document for globalization from below.

Notes

Acknowledgments: This piece draws on *Globalization from Below* by Jeremy Brecher, Tim Costello, and Brendan Smith (Cambridge, MA: South End Press, 2000). My thanks to Tim Costello and Brendan Smith, with whom many of these ideas were worked out.

1. Vandana Shiva, "The Historic Significance of Seattle," 10 December 1999, MAI-NOT Listserve, Public Citizen Global Trade Watch.

2. Margaret E. Keck and Kathryn Sikkink, *Activists beyond Borders: Advocacy Networks in International Politics* (Ithaca, NY: Cornell University Press, 1998), 8.

3. The phrase comes from Naomi Klein, "The Vision Thing," *The Nation*, 10 July 2000.

4. Hugh B. Price, president and CEO, National Urban League, keynote address to National Urban League Convention, Indianapolis, IN, 24 July 1994.

Hayden White

On Transcommunality and Models of Community

WE LIVE in an age of postcommunality. Does anyone believe in the possibility of genuine community anymore? As we all know, the very concept of community is a product of nostalgic reflection on the disappearance of small-scale social formations—the world of agrarian production, the village, peasant life with its extended family structures, face-to-face exchange systems, and customary linkages destroyed by capitalism, industrialization, urbanization, and transnational economies. Today, the ideal of community exists if at all as a rallying cry for groups threatened by assimilation to the exigencies of a transnational market geared to consumerism. In the brave new world of commodity production, exchange, and consumption as a good in itself, community is defined by what one possesses and consumes, not by what one believes and has faith in, or what one has inherited from one's ancestors.

This condition is reflected in the creation of the "youth market," which is targeted as a "community" of pure consumers, a community that defines its life goals more in terms of the commodities to which one has access than to the values that one honors. The youth of every society want to look, think, and act like the media models that represent what a good life in modernity ought to be. These models celebrate change according to fashion, a "look" rather than a "substance," being "up to date" rather than celebrating "the ways of the fathers." If custom, convention, and tradition are celebrated at all, it is in the production of pseudo-ethnicities and fake historicities—such as the "Venetian" casinos of Las Vegas and the "small town" locales of the Disney worlds that offer "tours" of exotic places that no longer exist "in reality."

It was instructive, therefore, to read John Brown Childs's inspiring effort to get beyond the harsh dichotomies that typically hamstring our efforts even to think about, much less achieve, community under the conditions of modernity. We live in a time when global social technologies threaten every attempt to create and sustain community at the level of "everyday" life. Childs's manifesto is refreshingly new also in its efforts to get beyond the conventional distinction between "community" and "society." He asks, how is community possible in an age in which every "social" force seems to militate against it? Thus, in place of another defense of "community" against the "social" forces that conduce to homogenization and undermine thereby any basis for effective political action at the local level, Childs attempts to envision another kind of communality that might promote an effective form of coalition politics at the local level. This is given in his equation of "Heterogeneity + Cooperation" with "Resistance and Freedom," an equation which he uses to characterize the ideal of transcommunality.

Childs likens the ideal social formation to a "mosaic" of communities, each informed by an ideal of respect for other communities and mediated by principles of friendship, cooperation, and alliance, rather than those of suspicion, enmity, and violence. These principles provide the difference between his *transcommunality* and the *communitarian* ideologies of modern fascist regimes based on the principle of racial purity and programs of "ethnic cleansing" of the kind met with in contemporary Serbia—and not only there. But I would like to suggest that rather than the mosaic model, his description of his ideal might profit from employment of the contemporary theory of the "fractum."

Traditional conceptions of the community were based on a mosaic model in which each tile has a regularity and isomorphism that make it a formal replication of every other tile in the whole. This mosaic model is too mechanical to take account of the differences between communities that lead them to resist being defined as interchangeable parts of a larger structure. A "fractum" considered as a building-block of a structure of differentiated parts allows the theorization of the irregular spaces between the parts. These "spaces in between"—the gaps, dissonances, open territories, blanks—constitute the areas of conflict, indeterminacy, and undecidability of any structural whole defined, as Childs wishes to do, by heterogeneity. These are the spaces of possible conflict, where turf may become disputed and contested, and which lead to conflict, not between a community and the larger social structure that encompasses it, but among communities themselves. It is within these spaces—in the border territories—that new rules of civility, of the kind proposed by Childs, have to be worked out. But one must take account of these spaces if one wishes to propose principles for integrating them into transcommunalities.

Now, civility is a concept that pertains not only to the rules governing relations among the members of a given community, but also to the rules for dealing with strangers, visitors, guests, and other travelers who come from abroad. Traditional societies are marked by such rules, which dictate the treatment of heralds, emissaries, messengers, and guests who may have wandered inadvertently into a restricted territory. These rules of civility in the treatment of strangers were as rigorous and inviolable as the rules of war or trade or intergroup marriage for purposes of alliance. But such rules are utterly lacking in modern societies, which typically conceive of *diplomacy* as "war by other means" and *travel* as "tourism" in which the aim is less to visit another culture than to view it from the comfort of an air-conditioned bus.

Childs's project presupposes the ideal of maintaining the integrity of different communities against the threat of homogenization posed by modern and modernizing societies. But his description of those traditional communities that succeeded in the effort of forming alliances and peaceful relations with others contiguous with themselves also stresses the mechanisms, rituals, and rules by which these communities might approach one another peacefully before reverting to hostile actions and violence. He speaks of "woodsedge" as a traditional concept used to define the places between different territories or spaces marked out as belonging to specific groups. But modern territories are marked by a multitude of overlapping "jurisdictions" which define woodsedge in utterly different terms and make the definition of "spaces in between" impossible to determine. Thus, even if there are rules of civility for dealing with strangers in a given community, these may conflict with the rules honored by other constituencies claiming jurisdiction over the same territory. An inner-city gang may claim jurisdiction over its turf, but it has to contend with the police, fire departments, and medical services for control of this space. So the stranger is put in the position of those tourists who wander outside the safe areas of a city into "war zones," where travel is governed by rules of war rather than of hospitality. In this sense, it is impossible to associate a given "community" with a given space or place, as is typically done in "traditional" communities. So in many respects, the notion of a mosaic as a model for defining spatial relationships between contiguous communities is misleading as a guide for ways to mediate relations among them.

What is needed, then, I would suggest, is a theorization of the undefined spaces where no rules of civility can be said to apply in the treatment of strangers. This would be one advantage of a fractal model for describing the relations among different communities. But the model would have to be elaborated both horizontally and vertically: describing ".stacked" or "imbricated" relationships among communities occupying the same or overlapping spaces, and describing relationships of planar contiguity. Further, it would have to imagine a modern equivalent of the traditionalist notion of "hospitality." You can cross many borders at the same time without knowing it, because everywhere is a place of multiple jurisdictions. "Woodsedge" is too simple a model for defining modern territorialities. Unlike mosaics, fracta are disjoined one from another. Is it possible to conceptualize a transcommunality that can reach across fractalized communal spaces?

Would this be an idle, merely theoretical exercise, without any practical consequences or utility for understanding the "real world" of intercommunity relationships? It might well be, but I submit that it has benefits not possessed by both the mosaic model and the once prominent salad bowl model for describing relationships among different ethnic communities in the United States occupying the same social structure. Indeed, Childs, in his criticism of the Marxist model of class conflict and the utilitarian model of "free market activity," suggests as much. In both of these models, the pertinent relationships presumed to exist among contiguous social groups do not allow for mixtures, hybrids, and undefined and undefinable social zones between downturns in the economy on the failure of consumers to "spend enough."

A fractal model would allow us to avoid the errors consequent on the presumption that communities possess a "proper" space and a "proper" profile that are isomorphic to the spaces of the other communities surrounding them. It would lead to the effort to identify the circumambient "unoccupied" or "essentially contestable" spaces around, above, and below them. The fractal model would allow us to view communities in terms of their class, ethnic, and cultural identities without presuming that they were organic unities, lacking internal conflicts, and fully conscious of their "essential" natures. I fear that in Childs's characterizations of certain of the traditional communities he has identified as possible models for theorizing transcommunalist relations, he has sometimes idealized them. It may well be that communities with well-defined caste functions possess this commendable sense of self-identity. But it is certainly not true of modern and modernizing communities, which are as heterogeneous in their internal structures as they are different from other communities in their totalities.

Nonetheless, Childs describes traditional communities that possessed well-defined rules of civility for dealing with strangers that our modern communities do not possess. This is a promising avenue to follow in our efforts to determine how community is possible in the modern world. Very little is constant and continuous in communities subjected to the pressures of the modern market economy and the media. What is needed is a dynamical as well as a structural model for their characterization. Childs admirably presents many of the principles governing intra- and intergroup dynamics in traditional communities. Moreover, he has extended his analysis of these phenomena to a number of modern local communities reacting to the pressures of modernization. But I have to admit that I find lacking any sustained consideration of what modern communities, living under the pressures of modern society, might contrive by way of rules of civility for negotiating a modern transcommunality. I do not think that invocation of an "ethics of mutual respect" is sufficient. For it is precisely the basis for "respect" that the commodification of society and culture has destroyed. In a world in which everything has only exchange value and in which the very notion of the substantive value of a thing has no meaning, what is there to respect in anything?

It is not even that one could argue for an ethics of respect on pragmatic grounds, as leading to peace and freedom rather than to war and oppression. For capitalist societies are committed to unlimited production and competition among producers, rather than peace and freedom—if freedom means even relative autonomy from the lure of consumerism. So if diplomacy is war by other means, so too is economic competition. In this state of total war, the claims of communities are heard only when they can be of use in competition. When asked to define the difference between a dialect and a "true" language, linguists are fond of saying that a dialect is a language without an army. In the modern world, "community" stands in relation to "society" as "dialect" stands in relation to "language." Communities are societies without an army, and without much else to help them in the work of self-making and self-preservation.

What are the realistic hopes or even the possibilities of "community" in our time? I confess that I am not optimistic. The forces of homogenization possess means and weapons that communities based on custom, convention, and tradition have small chances of countering. An alliance of communities such as that proposed by

John Brown Childs is certainly the only hope any given community has of sustaining its integrity against these forces. But the enormity of the task of saving community in our time certainly justifies the question being raised again regarding the "value" of community itself.

I do not think that the argument of "variety" of cultural forms as a good in itself can carry much weight with the capitalist apparatus. Efficiency and prediction (of markets above all) favors a smoothing out of all substantive variety. There exists today even a "culture industry" intent upon substituting "changes in fashion" for "cultural variety." The "heritage industry" in many modern societies commodifies traditions in the way that the Catholic Church once manufactured holy relics for sale to the faithful. We have to be careful that in our desire for an authentic community, we do not mistake the manufactures of the culture industry for the authentic article.

But do we (or "they") need the authentic article? It was once thought that a fake relic could be as efficacious as an authentic one if it had been revered as such for a sufficiently long time by the pious faithful. Should we not be as satisfied with the "community effect" as we would wish to be by the "effect of community" if our aim is communal solidarity rather than social dissolution? Is not fake community as beneficial as authentic community for a group's well-being?

How can the ideal of cultural variety, which has hitherto underwritten the value assigned to communities, withstand the forces of homogenization? In those parts of the world not yet "modernized," the only effective counterforces have been religious—as in Islam. Is it possible to sustain a *community*, much less a transcommunal supercommunity, without the moral resistance to every *society* that the traditional religions have inspired? I do not think so. But religions that have inspired resistance to the homogenizing effects of modernization have also featured dogmatic faith, priestly hierarchies, and authoritarian leadership as the price of that power of resistance. This is no doubt why John Brown Childs has gone to other traditions of community—those of Native

Americans, liberated American slaves, and other communities of oppression—to inspire his vision of a more humane, if less modern, future transcommunality.

It would be tactless and beside the point to criticize this vision for its idealism. Visions—as against points of view—are supposed to be idealistic. But perhaps we need to revise our notions about the realism that presumes to indict as merely idealistic those visions of community which are meant to provide a basis for criticizing "the way things are." The very notion of community is an ideal concept. It has never been achieved except for extraordinary moments and under exceptional conditions in the history of "society." Community has always been a dream, or more specifically a wish-fulfillment fantasy set up against the lived conditions of division and oppression of one group by another under the conditions of "society." Every successful revolution in modern times has exploited the appeal of this fantasy to advance the interests of an oppressed group against the oppressive policies of its dominators. These revolutions have always resulted in the installation of a new system of oppression in the place of the deposed one. This is because the revolutionaries have been incapable of conceiving community as anything other than a condition of their own liberation. The liberation of others different from themselves never crossed their minds. This is why the American Constitution was written to preserve "the rights of men" where "men" did not include women, slaves, the poor, or anyone else who did not have an interest in separation from the British oppressor.

The fantasy of community has to be reconceptualized to include everyone occupying a given space and condition of historical existence. The relevant space and condition is now the globe, which is to say, the "nonspace" of world politics, economy, and sociality. Whether this space can be imagined as a "communal" space rather than merely "social" is the question that confronts us at this time. It falls to such visionaries as Childs to convince us that such a space is imaginable, and whether it can be imagined as habitable by peoples who possess notions of civility that allow them to inhabit it as friends rather than as enemies.

Andrea Smith

Pragmatic Solidarity and Transcommunality

JOHN BROWN CHILDS'S articulation of transcommunality in many ways echoes for me Bernice Johnson Reagon's discussion of coalition politics: "You don't go into coalition because you just like it. The only reason you would consider trying to team up with someone who could possibly kill you, is because that's the only way you can figure you can stay alive" (Reagon, 356–357). What both writers suggest is that the politics of solidarity must be based to a large extent on pragmatic rather than ideological grounds. To develop effective movements for social change, we have to forego the "politics of purity" to develop a movement based on strategic political alliances. Many groups on the left or identity-based movements have often refused to ally themselves with groups that do not share their identity or the proper political ideology. This isolationist tendency then undermines the ability of progressive organizations/communities to develop a mass movement for social change. In light of the economic power welded by multinational capitalism, the only thing those committed to social change could potentially have on their side is numbers of people all fighting for social justice.

To develop a mass movement that could change the current state of affairs, it is necessary to realize that the majority of the world's population (even white, middle-class men) ultimately do

not benefit in the long term from the current social/economic/
political arrangements. Most people do not have control over their
lives; they live at the whim of decision makers in the corporate
world whom they cannot even identify. The key to developing a
mass movement is to convince people to exchange the pursuit of
their short-term interests (such as the maintenance of their white-
skinned economic status, or gender privileges) for the pursuit of
their long-term interest in creating a world based on social equality and justice for all.

But how can this goal be accomplished? As Childs and Reagon
inform us, we cannot effectively mobilize people if we expect
them to always or even most of the time agree with us, like us,
or share our perspective on the world. I have been an activist in a
variety of issues for over ten years now. I was the co-founder of
the Chicago chapter of Women of All Red Nations (an American
Indian women's organization). In addition, I have been and continue to be involved in many coalition efforts with other communities of color around such issues as environmental justice,
reproductive rights, prison abolition, and sexual/domestic violence. In working with other women of color in particular, I found
that women of color organizing efforts often break down because
there is an assumption among the participants that other women
of color will by definition like them, support them, or share their
struggles. In fact, however, communities of color have generally
bought into the same stereotypes about other communities of
color that white people have. There is no necessary allegiance
between women of color; alliances must be forged.

As Childs argues, alliances are most effectively created through
practical action. Or as one activist told me, "We act our way into
a different way of thinking; we don't think our way into a different way of acting." I have been to more women of color gatherings that I can count where attempts to create alliances were made
through social gatherings, "sharing our stories," discussion groups,
etc., but without any action component. In my experience, not
one of these attempts was ever successful. They did not work
because women of color have no real reason to trust each other;

only when women of color find that they can work together successfully on a project that betters or at least attempts to better all of their lives do they develop the basis for trust. Gatherings, discussion groups, sharing of stories, etc., all have their place, but they are most effective when they are done in conjunction with a practical plan of action.

While we should not make hasty assumptions about who our friends are, we should also not be quick to presume who our enemies are. I believe we need to be more creative in considering whom we might develop alliances with. I have noticed among the religious right the effective coalitions that have been built between the Christian right and the Moonies. Christian evangelicals/fundamentalists generally think the Moonies are headed for eternal damnation, but they have still managed to develop political alliances with them to further mutual goals. However, on the left there is a reluctance to think beyond very narrow parameters about which communities are acceptable to build alliances with.

As one Native activist once said to me, "When you have an us vs. them mentality, you united them against you." I have learned that your enemies today could be your friends tomorrow. An example of this phenomenon can be found in the Chippewa spearfishing struggles of the 1980s. When the Wisconsin courts recognized the treaty-protected rights of the Chippewa to hunt, fish, and gather on ceded territory in northern Wisconsin, a flurry of anti-Indian organizing began among the whites in the area. Whenever the Chippewa attempted to spear fish, they would be surrounded by angry white mobs threatening them and yelling racial epithets such as "Save a fish; spear a pregnant squaw." The whites' rationale was that the Chippewa would take all the fish, even though 97 percent of the fish was actually taken by white sports fishers. In order to deescalate the confrontation, a nonviolent witnessing program was formed, of which I was a part. We would go to the boat gatherings and stand in solidarity with the Chippewa to ensure their safety.

Now in this situation, it is easy to see the white people in these mobs as "the enemy" of Indian people. However, that was not the approach of the nonviolent witness program. The Chippewa and their allies recognized that a far greater threat was companies such as Exxon that wished to mine the area, as well as paper mill companies that were polluting the area. In fact, many activists began to suspect that these companies were funding the local hate groups. Exxon, for instance, prior to the spearfishing struggles, had attempted to locate a mine in upper Wisconsin but were defeated by a united Indian and non-Indian front against them. They withdrew from the area, only to return after this united front had been dissolved by the tensions over spearfishing. Thus, the activists reasoned, the individuals in these mobs could be potential allies of Indian people. Ultimately they would be hurt by these mining efforts as much as Indian people, since their economy is based primarily on tourism. The treaty rights were one of the few tools available to stop the companies because their mining ventures would violate the Chippewa's treaty-protected right to hunt, fish, and gather, so it was actually in the best interest of the local whites to support Indian treaty rights.

Consequently, the nonviolent witness program, while denouncing the racism of the white mobs, attempted to organize in such a way that would not paint them as the "real enemy" or cause permanent alienation from them. The treaty rights activists took great pains to attempt to educate them that Indian treaty rights were a solution to the problems local white people were facing, not the problem itself. As it happens, their organizing strategy proved to be correct. When the mining companies did come in, the foundation had been built to begin developing alliances between Indians and non-Indians in the area. These alliances proved so powerful as to force a pro-mining governor into passing an anti-mining moratorium in the state, and to drive one mining company, Rio Algom, out of the state.

If we think more creatively about our alliances, we may find that there are more people who might be on our side than we previously imagined. We may not be able to develop permanent alliances with them; we may have to be careful about how these alliances are shaped. Nevertheless, these strategic alliances, even if they are short lived, may be critical in furthering our social justice goals, and also give us the opportunity to develop relationships that one day may become more permanent.

One reason many progressives are hesitant to broaden their alliances is that they are fearful of co-optation. They are afraid that if they ally themselves with those who are politically "impure," then this impurity will taint their own politics. This fear is not unreasonable, as political co-optation often seems to be more the rule than the exception. That is why, as Childs tell us, a politics of transcommunality is rooted in a strong sense of racial/political/social identity. As Reagon argues: "You don't get fed a lot in a coalition. In a coalition you have to give, and it's different from your home. You can't stay there all the time. You go to the coalition for a few hours and then you go back and take your battle wherever it is, and then you go back and coalesce some more" (Reagon, 359). It is through the maintenance of strong communities and identities that individuals are empowered to work in solidarity with others.

Some sectors of the left blame people of color, and by extension, Native communities, for fracturing the left—people of color are viewed as hopelessly mired in identity politics with little ability to critique and organize around the economic and political structures. Todd Gitlin, for example, complains that racial identity politics are divisive to "real" movements for social change because they supposedly splinter oppositional forces. In addition, identity politics, the argument often goes, ignore capitalist domination and are concerned primarily with issues of cultural representation. As Gitlin states: "It is the identity obsessions, all of them, each fueling the others, that give the question of multiculturalism its charge and its venom" (1995, 227).

There is no doubt that a very narrowly defined identity politics can suffer from all these problems, and that some people do fall into these traps. However, Lisa Lowe's "Work, Immigration, Gender: New Subjects of Cultural Politics" provides an alternative framework for analyzing the significance of identity politics, even as she critiques them. In her discussion of Asian workers, she argues that racism and sexism are not epiphenominal super-structures to the larger structure of capitalism, but constitute it. Contrary to popular notions that capitalism exercises its power through homogenization, she argues that it does so through het-erogenization. The reason stems from the contradiction between capital and nation-state imperatives. Capital, she argues, is uncon-cerned with the identities of its labor. The nation-state, by con-trast, desires a unified culture that participates in the public sphere, and it seeks to maintain a citizenry bound by race, culture, and language. This contradiction is resolved when, through race and gender stratification and legal exclusions, certain sectors of the population, such as Asian immigrants, are both excluded from the citizenry and relegated to the lowest-paying and most exploited jobs. Lowe states:

> Both the racialized gendered character of Asian immigrant labor within the emergence of U.S. capitalism and U.S. colonial modes of development and exploitation in Asia provide the basis for understanding that U.S. capital has historically accumulated and profited through the differentiation of labor rather than through its homogenization; in the global expansion of the capitalist mode, the racial and gendered character of labor has been further exag-gerated, refined, and built into the regime itself. (Lowe, 159)

An analysis of how gender and race stratification constitute capitalism is critical to a formulation of resistant strategies. First, Lowe notes that the racialization and feminization of the prole-tariat also produce sites of contradiction that can form as bases of resistance. She argues, for instance, that these dynamics have displaced traditional patriarchies and lead to a reformulation of categories of race, class, and gender. These reformulations then can serve as sites of opposition to capitalism.

In addition, because women of color are situated in multiple axes of capitalist power—gender, race, and class—it is apparent that an oppositional strategy that attends to only one contradic-tion is inadequate. By relegating race and gender politics to mere "identity politics," we lose sight of how capitalism exerts power through race and gender stratification. "The isolation of one axis of power, such as the exploitation of labor under capitalism, masks the historical processes through which capitalism has emerged in conjunction with, and been made more efficient by, other systems of discrimination and subordination—patriarchy, racism and colonialism" (163).

Like Childs, Lowe is critical of race or gender politics that depends on notions of essentialized, singular, and stable identities. These kinds of politics ignore exclusions and hierarchies within identities, such as sexism within nationalist movements. Yet, like Childs, while contesting the "racial or ethnic" subject, she does not dismiss the importance of identity politics. Rather, she argues for politics based on shifting and multiple strategic alliances based on multiple and unclosed identities. She argues that "the cultural productions of racialized women seek to articulate multiple, non-equivalent, but linked determinations without assuming their containment within the horizon of an absolute totality and its presumption of a singular subject" (363).

However, these politics of identity are informed by economic and political realities. Thus, they are not merely about cultural representation but are also about challenging forces of capitalism. For example, an effective strategy based on identity would not only call attention to the marginalization of Asian and Latina immigrant women, but also to how their exclusions serve to maintain capitalist hegemony. Lowe's politics seem to rest less on a call for a unified party that seeks to seize political and economic control, but more on a confluence of oppositional forces that challenge social relations in all their diversity.

Viewed in this manner, identity politics becomes less about who is more oppressed, and more about understanding how all peoples fit into the larger picture of capitalism and conceiving of how they might be able to work together in the interest of social transformation. Because capitalism shapes identity, perhaps through identity we can understand how capitalism can also be resisted.

Similarly, while Kimberlé Crenshaw notes that the troubling of stable identity formations is also critical to political strategy, she argues against the vulgar construction strain within cultural studies which tends to altogether dismiss the importance of racial/ethnic identity. Crenshaw states: "To say that a category such as race or gender is socially constructed is not to say that category has no significance in our world" (375). She notes that social constructionism is helpful in showing how naturalized categories exclude and exercise power against excluded groups. Yet these categories are still performative and help shape those who are defined by these categories. In other words, as long as many in society define an individual as "Indian," this category will shape her subjectivity, even if she is not comfortable with that identity. As long as the categories race, gender, and sexuality continue to shape institutional structures, oppositional politics on the basis of these identities are critical. Consequently, as Crenshaw notes, "a strong case can be made that the most critical resistance strategy for disempowered groups is to occupy and defend a politics of social location rather than to vacate it and destroy it" (375).

This issue is of particular importance to Native people who, within postcolonial and poststructuralist thought, are often informed that "nationalism" is an inappropriate goal for their political struggles in a postmodern world. All nationalist struggles are seen as necessarily destined to follow the same trajectory as the nationalist conflicts in the former Yugoslavia. However, for nations that are still being actively colonized, the admonition to go "beyond nationalism" by those who are benefiting from living on Indian land seems a little too convenient.

At the same time, however, I would not argue that Native sovereignty struggles are beyond critique. As Childs notes, there is often a tendency in Indian organizing to eschew any alliances with non-Indian leftist organizations. One primary reason is the dismissive way Indian people are treated by these organizations. Yet Native peoples or their admirers often present themselves as having all the answers and not needing the political, social, or economic analyses of anyone who is not Indian.

Native peoples are often positioned as the mascots of various movements, such as the environmental movement—the ancient, all-wise, all-knowing people who hold the key to ending all social ills. One example of this mentality is Ward Churchill, who argues that restoring Indian land rights would necessarily end sexism, classism, environmental destruction, and homophobia in the United States. "So, not only is it perfectly reasonable to assert that a restoration of Indian control over unceded lands within the U.S. would do nothing to perpetuate such problems as sexism and classism, but the reconstitution of indigenous societies this would entail stands to free the affected portions of North America from such maladies altogether" (Churchill, 422). This kind of reasoning assumes that Native people somehow remain untainted by the structures of sexism, classism, and other forms of oppression imposed upon them by European colonization. But because they have been tremendously impacted by these structures, Native peoples stand to benefit from contributions of activists and theorists who have addressed the politics of gender, class, race, etc., even if they are not Indian.

I remember one gathering in which an activist stated about the economy, "We're not going to do things the capitalist way or the socialist way; we're going to do things the Indian way." The "Indian way" of structuring the economy, however, is rarely articulated with any depth; nor is there discussion about how Indian people will be able to do things "the Indian way" in light of the onslaught of multinational capitalism. Roberto Mendoza (Muscogee) argues that Native peoples who adopt this approach "do not really address the question of power. How can small communities tied in a thousand ways to the capitalist market system break out without a thorough social, economic and political revolution within the whole country?" (8). He also terms those who refuse to consider any Marxist analyses as "fundamentalists," and states, "I feel that dialogue and struggle with Left forces are necessary rather than rejection and isolation" (39). It is critical that Native people vigilantly protect their interests, given the tendency for other progressive movements to either ignore or even actively work against the welfare of Native communities. But at the same time, we also have to work with anyone who might be able to help us, because there is no way for tribal communities to isolate them-selves in what Childs refers to as this homogenizing world.

Childs discusses at length the positive possibilities for uniting leftist analysis with indigenous struggles for sovereignty. In addi-tion, it is also useful to consider how Indian cultural/spiritual identities directly impact capitalist operations.

Unemployment rates for Native people are about 50 percent in cities and 85 percent on reservations. It would not make sense for Native activism to center itself around struggles involving the working class, since most Native people are often not working in the formal economy. Rather, the intervention they can make into the capitalist system is based on land. Over 60 percent of the energy resources in the United States is on indigenous lands; 100 percent of uranium mining takes place on or near Indian land. Thus, the protection of indigenous lands fundamentally challenges capital-ist systems of production in this country and elsewhere around the world.

Thus, when Native people fight for sacred sites or for their land bases, they are not just fighting for cultural preservation. Because Native cultures are land based, it is impossible to preserve them without fundamentally challenging corporate hegemony. This fact is particularly evident in the Senate testimony offered by Scott M. Matheson on behalf of various mining associations during the hearings for the Native American Free Exercise of Religion Act. He argued: "much of the country's natural resources are located on federal land. For example, federal lands contain 85 percent of the nation's crude oil, 40 percent of the natural gas, 40 percent of the uranium, 85 percent of the coal reserves. . . . Thus it is obvi-ous that S.2250, by creating a Native American veto over federal land use decisions, will . . . severely interfere with the orderly use and development of the country's natural resources" (Smith, 8). Corporations are fully cognizant that preserving land-based Indian spiritual practices fundamentally interferes with their capitalist operations.

Childs points to the example of the Iroquois confederacy as a possible model for a politics of transcommunality. He argues that it is important to see Native people as having something to say about the world, rather than as irrelevant to the contemporary situation. I agree that it is very important to look at what Native communities have to offer the broader society. However, I have also noticed a tendency to proffer indigenous models without sufficiently contextualizing them. For instance, prison reformers often look to Native traditional forms of justice as alternatives to incarceration. However, the models that are cited are often based on the past rather than on the present-day situation. In reality, it is often difficult to translate these models even just within Native communities. For instance, many tribes used banishment rather than incarceration as a punishment for serious crimes. However, prior to colonization, banishment was essentially a death sentence. Banishment today does not have the same impact when one can simply go live in another community. I'm not arguing that these models have no relevance, but rather, it is a struggle to translate these traditions to fit today's world.

Native people do have much to teach everyone. In particular, the nation status of indigenous communities often affords them the opportunity to develop more fully elaborated community-based models for change than can be found in other communities in the country. However, if we are to take indigenous models seriously, then we must discuss them in all their complexities, honoring the intense struggles Native people face in making these traditions workable today.

Bibliography

Churchill, Ward. 1993. *Struggle for the Land: Indigenous Resistance to Genocide, Ecocide and Expropriation in Contemporary North America*. Monore, ME: Common Courage Press.

Crenshaw, Kimberlé. 1996. "The Intersection of Race and Gender." In *Critical Race Theory*. Ed. Kimberlé Crenshaw, Neil Gotanda, Gary Peller, and Kendall Thomas. New York: New Press.

Gitlin, Todd. 1995. *The Twilight of Common Dreams: Why America Is Wracked by Culture Wars*. New York: Henry Holt and Company.

Lowe, Lisa. 1996. *Immigrant Acts*. Chapel Hill, NC: Duke University Press.

Mendoza, Roberto. 1984. *Look! A Nation Is Coming!* Philadelphia: National Organization for an American Revolution.

Reagon, Bernice Johnson. 1983. "Coalition Politics: Turning the Century." In *Home Girls: A Black Feminist Anthology* (pp. 356–369). Ed. Barbara Smith. New York: Kitchen Table Press.

Smith, Andrea. 1998. *Sacred Sites, Sacred Rites*. New York: National Council of Churches.

David Welchman Gegeo

Inclusive Difference

Transcommunality and the
Hope for a Just World

RECENTLY I was invited to give the keynote address at a conference held at a major U.S. university. Organized around the subjects of diaspora, globalization, and identity in the Pacific Islands, the conference attracted a sizable gathering of indigenous and other interested scholars, professionals, and graduate students from the Pacific, Latin America, and the United States. Among the different issues I addressed in my keynote speech was the current rising tide of interethnic militancy in the Pacific Islands. Although the problem is just now being experienced, the underlying causes are long standing and deeply rooted in globalization and colonization. However, in spite of this western origin, as far as leadership, organization, and the modes of reasoning and thinking can be ascertained, the interethnic conflicts are epistemically hybrids. That is, the knowledge base from which ideas are conceived, woven into plans, and then carried out as structured militia activities is a reconstructed eclectic embodiment of both introduced and indigenous ways of knowing, doing, and being. The issue of epistemic hybridity did seem like possible ground for jumpstarting the peace process, but it was never fully acknowledged or explored by the peace negotiators. Instead, seemingly

185

bent on the promise of their own professional expertise to effec-
tuate a positive outcome, the peace negotiators relied exclusively
on conflict resolution strategies imported from the metropolis,
especially England, Australia, and New Zealand.

While it cannot be established that the dismissal of epistemic
heterogeneity had any connection, the peace negotiation process
was haunted by failure every step of the way. Not only did the
peace talks fail in ending violence, but they also exacerbated the
problem because the conflict resolution strategies imported from
overseas caused greater rifts between the rival militia groups and
the different national and international peace monitoring organizations. The militia groups, for example, complained that the
imported strategies of conflict resolution were foreign and would
not serve the issues for which they were seeking redress. The end
result is, as exemplified by Solomon Islands and Fiji cases, total
chaos, politically, economically, and otherwise.

In light of this, I reiterated, as a matter for discussion in the conference, the idea that it might help if the peace negotiators were
to also include in their repertoire, conflict resolution strategies
that are indigenous to the cultures of the different ethnic groups
in conflict. After I had finished giving my keynote address, a fellow Pacific Islander scholar challenged my suggestion and argued
that the incorporation of any ideas from Pacific Island traditional
cultures in resolving the current interethnic crisis was doomed to
fail. No reasons were given as to why this would be the case.
Moreover, the person argued that the consultation of traditional
culture in such crises would be tantamount to dignifying the primordial past when frequent tribal warfare, rigid sexism, suspicion, and paganism defined social ontology in the islands.

I was taken aback by the challenge because, firstly, it was an
apparent misinterpretation of a simple suggestion that was not an
ideological assertion. Secondly—and more seriously perhaps—it
epitomized the binary or oppositional mode of thinking and reasoning that is rather pervasive in the way in which we human
beings describe and explain social reality and which we seem to
have great difficulty purging from ourselves. Perhaps as the result

of our sociocultural/political and epistemic socialization, most of us seem to be locked in the binarism that if something is not on the left, it must be on the right, and if it is not on the right, then it must be on the left. Similarly, if something is part of traditional culture, it can be applied only with suspicion to the present or future.

We seem unable to readily acknowledge the simple fact that nothing exists in total isolation of other forms of existence. For example, in our ontological schema of things, the concept of a right position or direction exists only because the concept of a left position or direction also exists, and vice versa. Moreover, both the right and left exist only because there is also a center that, functioning as a kind of social fulcrum, connects and holds them together in balance and in place.

The same epistemic vacuity is also apparent in vertical or hierarchical thinking and reasoning where entities (people, objects, ideologies, etc.) situated at the top are generally accorded greater social merit and importance than those situated at the bottom. A manager, therefore, is generally seen as being more important than an office clerk, even though each exists in the work context only as the result of the existence of the other. The ontological balancing through interdependence and coexistence is no less true in human social formations than in other forms of social existence.

I do not seek to defend or prescribe the legitimacy of a centrist approach to solving social problems but rather to further substantiate the argument already advanced by some that, as governments, communities, and individuals around the world are being challenged ever more constantly and strongly by intensifying social inequality, the narrow and unilinear mode of thinking and reasoning to which we are accustomed in dealing with social problems is increasingly becoming wanting. There is, thus, an urgent need to develop new theories and models of conflict resolution and community building that are not only more effective and expeditious, but also epistemically and culturally more inclusive. John Brown Childs offers just such an alternative model in this book.

As a model and theory, transcommunality is illuminating and intrinsically transformative. As such it holds real promise and hope for building communities and interpersonal relationships that are less racialized and less ethnicitized, and more equitable and mutually more trusting. Transcommunality is founded on a vision that will make multiculturalists, multivocalists, and adherents of similar multi perspectives very uncomfortable. This is because the vision is intrinsically a critical praxis (i.e., mode of critical thinking, reflecting, and doing) that first deconstructs and then transcends the assimilationist framework of multiculturalism and other similar theories and models purported to be concerned with diversity. There are several ways in which transcommunality splits from assimilationist theories and models.

Fundamentally, according to Childs, transcommunalists strongly adhere to an orientation that respects and honors autonomy and diversity. On the surface, this does sound similar to the orientation of multiculturalists and other assimilationist groups. The difference, however, lies (or eventually emerges) in the long-term practical objectives or outcomes. In multiculturalism, for example, it is questionable that the call for the recognition of diversity is really for the purpose of conserving it. This fact is self-evident in the various attempts made thus far—from rewriting literacy to redesigning school curricula—where the tendency has been more toward de-diversification—that is, the "melting pot syndrome"—rather than toward honoring the integrity and the conservation of heterogeneity (Childs 1998, 1994; Hall 1995).

In sharp contrast, Childs argues that when transcommunalists speak of the respect for and need to perpetuate or uphold heterogeneity, they envision a very different kind of social formation. It is a social formation characterized by the unfractured coexistence of heterogeneous groups who, despite their diverse histories, worldviews, and practical orientations, are nonetheless bridged or interconnected in their interpersonal relationships with one another. Whenever this bridging or interconnecting occurs, it does so unconditionally because of mutual trust and respect among and between people. That is, whenever the need arises, people will unconditionally engage in the social activism of community building and the bridging of diverse interpersonal relationships because it is the right and human thing to do—right and human in the sense of promoting governance for the benefit of self, community, and society. Childs states, in his book's introduction, the intrinsic vision of transcommunality:

> By *transcommunality* I mean the constructive and developmental interaction occurring among distinct autonomy-oriented communities and organizations, each with its own particular history, outlook, and agenda. This interaction, developed through interpersonal relations of people engaged in common tasks, is producing working groups of activists whose roots are in communities and organizations, but who also form bridges among diverse peoples as they address substantial, albeit often varied corrosive dilemmas—from economic crisis to environmental degradation, from Indigenous land rights to the organizing of workers across national borders.

In further explaining mutual trust and respect among communities and the resulting unconditional bridging that facilitates heterogeneous coexistence, Childs says:

> Transcommunalists do not employ a "melting pot approach" in which particular community and organizational allegiance is obliterated in order for cooperation to occur. On the contrary, transcommunal activists are effective at bridging diverse community and organizational positions precisely because they emerge from and work within distinctive communal and organizational settings. Rather than being an abstract call for "unity," transcommunality relies on concrete interpersonal ties growing out of what I refer to as *shared practical action* from diverse participants. From such practical action flows increasing communication, mutual respect, and understanding.

Although Childs conceives of transcommunality as a model for dealing with social problems of the metropolis, especially in the United States, it also has applicability for third world countries. For example, it addresses one of the fundamental causes of continuous interethnic violence in third world countries in the globalization struggle and the whole modernization paradigm in general.

Globalists and modernists argue that one of the reasons third world countries are haunted by irredeemable poverty, low education rates, and chronic political and economic instability is because of sociocultural and linguistic heterogeneity. These problematic conditions, globalists and modernists are quick to point out, will cease to exist and a higher standard of living will be enjoyed by third world peoples if chronic heterogeneity is obliterated and in its place some kind of universal monolithic culture and language are established (Dunning and Hamdani 1997).

However, when critically examined in the light of the vision of transcommunality, there is preponderant evidence showing that the root cause of the problematic conditions is not heterogeneity but escalating de-diversification or homogeneity. In the Solomon Islands, rising interethnic violence and accompanying political and economic instability are caused not by heterogeneity but escalating homogeneity. It will help to briefly describe the Solomon Islands situation in order to show the connection between interethnic violence and degenerating heterogeneity as argued by transcommunalists.

The Solomon Islands is a thousand-mile-long archipelago of small islands located northeast of Australia in the South Pacific. Before and during a good part of Anglo-European contact that began in 1568, the indigenous people lived independently and self-sufficiently—though by no means always in total harmony—speaking seventy to eighty different languages and adhering to different sociocultural practices accordingly. At the height of the globalization of British imperialism, in 1893 the islands were forcibly brought together under a haphazardly devised central government and were declared a British protectorate. Because they were a colony, the rule of law and order in the Solomon Islands was dictated from England with the indigenous people having no say in it, and they had no say in virtually everything that was done under the rubrics of so-called modernization.

While acts of social resistance by the indigenous people were a commonplace, the novelty and attractiveness of things Anglo-European (e.g., cash, tinned food, tobacco, yardage, iron and steel tools) generally had the social effect of bandaging or camouflaging the inhumanity of colonization. With modernization progressing at snail-pace and social ontology still being defined by sociocultural heterogeneity, there was relative calm among the different ethnic groups. For much of the past century this situation was characteristic of much life in the islands. However, the decades following World War II (which had a major impact on the Pacific region) witnessed an escalation in the modernization process in the Solomon Islands, which placed societal heterogeneity at great risk of being displaced and replaced by homogeneity. Among the more physical aspects of this developmental velocity was the building of a national infrastructure (e.g., improved shipping, the establishment of a national airline, and roads) to facilitate the easy movement of people and goods and services, all in the name of sociocultural/political homogenization, otherwise famously called nation building.

The problem of degenerating societal heterogeneity would probably have been easier to bear if its root cause, escalating homogeneity, was embracing and inclusive—that is, if the Solomon Islands was being rebuilt into a single nation out of the multiplicity of indigenous cultures already in existence. This, of course, did not happen. Instead, the indigenous cultures were increasingly suppressed by Anglo-European cultures, especially British, through the social mechanisms of Christian missionization, Anglo-European education, transnational corporatism, and a colonial system of government. Escalating societal homogeneity was more dramatically established when the centers of modernization (businesses, etc.) were centrally located on only one or two islands, a feature of the modernization process obviously designed to suit the convenience and advancement of the colonialists rather than the indigenous people. The effect of this centralization was to pull large numbers of immigrants to these few centers in search of employment, with the resulting formation of an urbanized, homogenized culture that stood hierarchically above diverse rural cultures.

Since November 1998, the Solomon Islands has been experiencing deadly interethnic violence that has brought the whole country to a virtual standstill, morally, politically, and economically. One of the principal complaints raised by the ethnic group that first started the violence involves the unequal distribution of resources and services. The group complains that, despite their being the landowners and owners of the resources on which the Solomon Islands national economy is built, and the hosts of the national capital, developmentally they feel they have been receiving a smaller portion of the national wealth than other ethnic groups. The group also complains that migrant ethnic groups living on their island as the result of urbanization do not respect the local indigenous cultures.

The issue of unequal distribution of resources is, of course, a historically familiar complaint, one that will no doubt continue to command the scholarly attention of academics and scholars for years to come, as it has done in years past. Of course, the crimes of any system, political or otherwise, that out of full consciousness upholds social inequality in the distribution of resources cannot under any circumstances be pardoned. However, when examined in the light of the vision of transcommunality, it appears that all our efforts to solve this social ill may have been directed more at treating the symptoms instead of the causes. And the causes are in dire need of addressing.

According to how issues are normally reasoned out and settled, the ethnic group's complaint about their being shortchanged on the benefits of resources in the Solomon Islands is legitimate. However, when viewed through the lenses of transcommunality, the unequal distribution of resources is only the symptom of a much bigger problem that is already deeply entrenched in the sociocultural fabric of society. The problem is escalating societal homogenization. As mentioned earlier, escalating societal homogenization is especially problematic because of its uniformly Anglo-European orientation. More specifically, sociocultural homogenization as it is being experienced in the Solomon Islands has created the problematic twin process or phenomenon of *massification*. Under massification, two processes or forms of drastic societal change are occurring simultaneously. In the first process, the indigenous populations are being deculturalized or deconditioned from heterogeneity in such areas as taste, expectation, behavior, culture, identity, knowledge, and the like. Along with this deculturalization, which in principle is deheterogenization, comes the second process, which is a resocialization or reconditioning that strongly emphasizes uniformity or sameness in taste, expectation, behavior, culture, identity, and so forth. The result is de-authenticity, which translates as externally forced homogeneity. In the language of the Kwaralae people of Malaita, Solomon Islands, this pseudo-westernization is referred to as *tua malafakalanga*, literally, "living in imitation of life brought by the ships" (Gegeo 1998, 1994).

Several issues are problematic about forced homogenization as experienced through the massification of national taste, expectations, identity, and ideology. In terms of taste, for example, resources are likely to be consumed at such a high rate or in such mass quantities that they are quickly exhausted. Moreover, the pressure from mass consumption also means that resources—e.g., the forest—are never given enough time to rejuvenate themselves before they are used again, if they have not already been used to extinction the first time around. This is a particularly serious problem in island environments—as exemplified by the Solomon Islands—where the land mass is so small and the ecology so fragile that it can be easily destroyed. Sociocultural homogenization also means that some people will master the habits and tastes of the new social formation so well that they will always out-compete others, which in essence means consuming a higher percent of the resources. The rise of interethnic tension and eventual violence, as the case is today in the Solomon Islands, is inevitable.

In contrast, in a situation where heterogeneity defines social ontology, these problems can and do occur but on a relatively smaller scale. One reason is that heterogeneity itself can function as a kind of balancing social force that ensures an equilibrium of coexistence between and among human groups. Some examples from Solomon Islands indigenous cultures will help to clarify how this works. Before and during the early decades of westernization, every tribal group in the Solomon Islands had taboos that involved refraining from eating or coming into contact with certain types of fish, birds, animals, plants, etc. Some tribal groups overlapped in the observation of such taboos. The role played by cultural heterogeneity as a balancing social force as seen through these taboos is through the exchange of food. Thus, for example, tribe X would exchange foods forbidden to its members for foods from tribe Y that its members could eat, and vice versa. This fundamental interdependence necessitated the unconditional bridging of interpersonal relationships and, hence, human social coexistence, which lies at the heart of transcommunality. "Unconditional" does not mean that the circumstances surrounding the ceremonial bridging of fractured relationships were always harmonious. It means instead that community members always felt personally obliged to repair them. This is in contrast to acts of damage repair that are mechanical, which means they are devoid of the love and the caring embedded in doing something as part of one's engaged social activism.

Interestingly enough, when Solomon Islanders talk about the pain and suffering caused by the current interethnic violence, they repeatedly comment that they wish they could bring back the days when resources were exchanged and shared rather than fought over in the civil war now being waged. These comments are not an unfounded nostalgic longing for a past that never existed. I grew up in a rural village in the Solomon Islands in the late 1950s and early 1960s, and I can recall those days vividly. I can still remember, for example, the many times I was sent by my parents with fish to give to our neighbors in our village, and returned to our house carrying corn, sugar cane, taro, yams, cooked pork, pineapples, and other food items given by the neighbors in appreciation of the fish. We did not see these as "exchanges" as often portrayed by anthropologists; nor did we have a name for this customary social sharing. In our culture, to name these kinds of everyday village routines would be tantamount to distancing ourselves from one another, because naming, for us, usually means the creation of identity that implies some degree of separation.

Instead, we unconditionally engaged in the routines simply as intrinsic features of the social coexistence and inclusive difference by which village ontology was defined. From the perspective of transcommunality, these seemingly mundane cultural routines spoke strongly to the power of heterogeneity where, unlike in homogeneity, competition for resources which breeds hostility was for the most part absent.

It is perhaps important to emphasize that when transcommunalists call for the respect and conservation of heterogeneity, they do not necessarily mean a wholesale abandonment of homogeneity. Some degree of homogeneity is necessary, such as having certain international languages with which the mass of the people can communicate. The kind of homogeneity against which transcommunal activists argue is the crushing kind being currently promoted through globalization which, contrary to what the promoters believe, thus far has caused far more fragmentation in interpersonal relationships and communities around the world than cooperation and unity. In light of this, a more workable model would be one that embraced the positive aspects of both homogeneity and heterogeneity.

In any case, like any new theory or model that challenges the cultural conventions by which we run our community and societal affairs, transcommunality is likely not to sit well with a lot of people. Some people may take it to be simply another form of the abstract and utopian daydreaming for which academics are famously known. Other people may shrug it off as simply a romantic call for a return to a primordial past that never existed, or that, if it did exist, would no longer be relevant. To make these kinds of charges is, of course, to miss the important message of transcommunality and hence the potential it has for transforming our thinking about and the approaches we should take toward solving current social problems. Luckily, John Brown Childs anticipated such charges and has eloquently responded to them in this book, drawing both from his own community-based research and his cultural heritage and ancestry that embraces African American, Native American, and Pacific Madagascan. Transcommunality is a powerful visionary line of thinking which deserves both the intellectual and practical engagement of every person who is committed to finding alternative ways to liberating ourselves and our communities from the tyranny of persistent social inequality.

References

Childs, John Brown. 1998. "Transcommunality: From the Politics of Conversion to the Ethics of Respect in the Context of Cultural Diversity—Learning from Native American Philosophies with a Focus on the Haudenosaunee." *Social Justice*, 25(4).

———. 1994. "The Value of Transcommunal Identity Politics." *Z Magazine* (July/August): 48–51.

Dunning, John H., and Khalil A. Hamdani, eds. 1997. *The New Globalism and Developing Countries*. New York: United Nations University Press.

Gegeo, David Welchman. 1998. "Indigenous Knowledge and Empowerment: Rural Development Examined from Within." *Contemporary Pacific*, 10(2): 289–315.

———. 1994. *Kastom and Bisnis: Toward Integrating Cultural Knowledge into Rural Development in the Solomon Islands*. Unpublished dissertation, Department of Political Science, University of Hawaii at Manoa.

Hall, Stuart. 1995. "New Ethnicities." In *The Postcolonial Studies Reader.* Ed. Bill Ashcroft et al. New York: Routledge.

Herman Gray

Transcommunality

Politics, Culture, and Practice

THE LATE 1960S are seen by many on both the left and the right as the origin of the downward spiral into identity politics, tribalization, and balkanization from which we have yet to recover. Cultural differences and the struggles for recognition and representation that they produced were neither an unhappy accident of history nor a mere cheering fiction. Difference remains a powerful principle of belonging, identification, membership, and struggle. Thus, "identity politics," which is organized around cultural difference, is a highly contested conceptual, political, and emotional terrain. For some, like critical theorists and neomarxists, difference and the politics of identity that it generated are stubborn premodern impediments to a grand vision of and commitment to a universal modernist ideal of social justice crafted from alliances across recognizable but insignificant distinctions of race, gender, class, and sexuality. For others, like contemporary scholars of color, they are the social basis of contemporary struggles and politics, and the cultural terms in which they are fought. For still others, like poststructuralists, the positions and terms of the debate are the problem. Poststructuralists urge a critical examination and destabilization of the very categories through which we imagine the world (of difference), setting our conceptual sights toward the imagination of

new categories and social relations that move entirely away from
identity, coherence, essences, and subjects.

Debates over diversity, multiculturalism, identity, the prospects
for united struggles for social justice, and visions of the unities
required for effective struggles are still mired in internecine bat-
tles over how to make politics (and what are the politics that
matter). These debates also flourish in a moment of great and persistent contradiction. Global tendencies toward dispersion, migration, travel, and movement of culture, information, people, and
subjectivities occur at the same time as pressure mounts toward
centralization, monopoly, and the concentration of the world's
resources in the hands of fewer and fewer of the world's people.
New geopolitical and administrative units and larger more complex economic entities appear which exert pressures toward the
global and the transnational. At the same time, our lived experiences are simultaneously tugged by the increased significance of
local ties of distinction (based on differences of language, tradition, race, and ethnicity) and community.

Cultural Politics and the Potential of
Transcommunality

> By *transcommunality* I mean the constructive and developmental
> interaction occurring among distinct autonomy-oriented commu-
> nities and organizations, each with its own particular history, out-
> look, and agenda.
>
> —Childs, herein

Can John Brown Childs's concept of transcommunality enrich
the terms within which we think and imagine cultural politics?
Needless to say, I think so. This potential articulation is formed
out of a necessary conceptual affinity between identity and culture. It is an articulation where culture (most specifically popular
culture, commercial culture, and representation), like identity, is
both the object of much intellectual dispute and a socially rich and
politically productive site of social practices that matter—practices
that, as Stuart Hall suggests, can help change the balance of power
in ways that matter.

What are the specific epistemological, social, and historical conditions necessary for thinking cultural politics through the logic of transcommunality in ways that get beyond the territorial disputes of identity politics? Specifically concerning cultural politics, the ideas gathered around the concept of transcommunality intersect and engage with a number of strains associated with interventions from cultural studies, critical theory, the study of popular culture, and concerns with the politics of representation. Like the concept of identity politics, culture (and cultural politics) is a conceptual and political site of some serious boundary disputes: about "real" politics (as opposed to cultural politics), structural forces like the economy (as opposed to cultural expression like representation), actual embodied subjects (as opposed to discursive and performing subjects). I point to these territorial disputes not to rehearse them yet again but simply to highlight how unproductive they are. Conceiving of opposition in this way elides what I take to be a necessary affinity between the categories of *culture* and *identity politics* and *representation*.

Taking as a starting point Childs's specification of transcommunality with which I opened this section, it is clear to me that the concept of transcommunality at the very least helps to sharpen our engagement with the politics of difference; difference is inevitably the terrain on which social struggles—whether cultural struggles to construct communities of affiliation or social struggles over the distribution of material resources through appeals to the state—occur. That is, there is no necessary conflict between a logic that presses toward increased differentiation, fragmentation, and localism, and a logic that simultaneously pulls us outward toward increased connectedness and linkage. These are responses to the recognition and intractability of living in a social world of differences.

One of the implications of thinking through the potentialities of transcommunality is epistemological. Notions of subjects, belonging, autonomy, spheres (multiple, counter, and alternative) of public life, and culture can no longer be imagined only in terms of European universalistic philosophical traditions that are the products of a specific position in and experience of modernity.

Epistemologically, Childs proceeds from local indigenous cultural practices, cosmologies, and traditions that were generated from a particular set of circumstances and articulations. There is great potential here, particularly as a matter of engaging with and understanding how ideas get taken up, circulate, and become hegemonic as common sense. We might well see this concept (and the roots of its evolution and specific application) very much within the rubric of the history of ideas, the history of knowledge, even the sociology of knowledge. Accordingly, we might view the epistemological foundations and circumstances out of which the idea of transcommunality develops in relationship to those projects that have now become canonical certainly within sociology—for example, the work of Marx, Durkheim, and Weber. Like the members of the indigenous communities in North America, these bourgeois male European intellectuals were profoundly concerned with issues of conflict, social change, social engineering, the division of labor, exploitation, social justice, and freedom.

Adding this comparative dimension to thinking about different kinds of knowledge is a productive means of contesting, struggling over, and otherwise engaging modernist canonical projects without falling into an either/or, essentialist, or utopian position with respect to alternative possibilities. This is indeed a matter of cultural politics; it goes to the heart of concerns about identity, subjectivity, and difference. Working through traditions that parallel, annex, modify, and in some cases offer alternatives to Euro-modernism affords us the opportunity to pose questions about knowledge, identity, and culture, without the superficial and tired moves that reduce these complex engagements to issues of discursive replacement and reinscription of hierarchy. Locating the philosophical and epistemological roots of transcommunality in a historically specific time and place adds a productive comparative dimension. It lets us identify another body of practices and traditions that give us yet another opportunity to ponder, as Clyde Taylor and Paul Gilroy have done, how those other than European modernists conceived, grappled with, and developed solutions to those circumstances and encounters with modern societies in other places and spaces.

The epistemological potentialities for thinking about cultural politics through the category of transcommunality can be appreciated in two ways most immediately. One is specifically in terms of modern therapeutic discourses that—in our media-saturated, commodified public cultures—locate the nature of conflict and social crisis (and their amelioration) in the modern subject. The other potential is in terms of the practical requirements for engaging principled social (change) action through the recognition of difference.

Childs offers transcommunal thinking and practice as a structural and collective response or strategy to social conflicts and tensions that culturally take the form of violent confrontation, territorial disputes, and struggles over scare resources by different communities distinguished by cultural difference of class, race, sexuality, and tradition. In late modernism, one response to these socially and culturally based tensions and conflicts is of course the popularization—through television specifically directed at the poor and more selectively the middle class—of the self-help publishing industry, and counseling movements of one kind or another, and what is popularly called therapeutic discourses. Whereas transcommunality recognizes these forms of social conflict as socially based, popular self-help therapies locate them in the individual background, personal circumstances, or impaired psychic and emotional life of individual subjects. This is especially the case in matters of personal identity—appearance, health, relationships—as well as social issues—teen pregnancy, youth violence, and poverty. Much of the pop therapeutic discourse cordons off the impaired individual from the social life (and influence) of the community and social relations found there. In the case of poor and minority communities, the communities themselves are thought to be impaired and in need of a collective dose of self-help therapy. According to this discourse (with selective emphasis and applications by class), the problem and thus the solution to what ails us individually and collectively is to be found in the identification of disease, pathology, will power, character, personality, or values. If the impaired or faulty subjects are beyond restoration and repair, they must be cordoned off and expelled from the social body, to be contained and warehoused with heavy doses of regulation, discipline, and surveillance. In the case of the poor and the middle class who are redeemable, the discourse of self-help and pop therapy aims at transformation and fortification with the necessary social and cultural skills to take on a hostile world and survive.

By contrast, the view of the subject implicit in transcommunal cultural practice emphasizes the possibilities of social transformation, collective action, and community influence and responsibility. The political commitments that result are necessarily aimed at transforming the social world, the social body, and the individual.[1] The social benefits of collective social action and engagement are more lasting and effective than those fashioned on a model of individual isolation, fortification, and transformation. There is more than a hint of this way of thinking about conflict resolution in the idea of reconciliation and transformation being attempted on a large scale in Latin American, Africa, and Eastern Europe. The gain offered by transcommunality is its applicability to different levels, sites, contexts, and kinds of conflicts—from gangs to nation-states to ethnic and racial groups.

On the question of the practical requirement necessary for sustained and engaged politics in the age of media, representation, difference, and identity, Stuart Hall has argued that it is pure folly, to imagine a cultural politics where identity will insure allegiance, loyalty, and commitment to the "right cause." Central to Hall's formulation is a theoretical and political reckoning with the intractable nature of politics fought on the terrain of media and representation; hence he turns to indeterminacy and contingency as a hedge against an essentialist cultural politics of identity. Transcommunal thinking displays a similar reckoning with the limitations of identity (as opposed to difference) in its advocacy of engaged and disengaged flexibility, its commitment to the practical utility of short-term goals, and its encouragement of a long-term vision of what is possible and desirable. This critical practice requires political and organizational flexibility (which as Childs notes is not the same as the absence of a principal political position). It seems to me that these qualities express in practical and strategic terms what Stuart Hall elaborates theoretically as contingency and indeterminacy. Regardless of how and at what level we apply it, this very flexibility enables the kind of political practice that can identify and build or (re)articulate opportunities for cooperation (since deeply entrenched political positions and conceptions of subjects in this formulation do not really matter and thus pose little if any threat to identities per se or the politics that are built on their recognition).

This quality of flexible engagement seems to have much in common with the concept of articulation so central to theorizations of cultural studies and new social movements (both in the sense of linkage and expression). The capacity for potential alliances, quick responses, and mobilizations of various sorts does not reside in enduring commitments to change built on the basis of entrenched wars of maneuver, as opposed to wars of position. The strategic and flexible engagements of transcommunal politics are truly wars of position in the best sense.

But the concept of articulation (in the sense of linkage) brings into sharper relief some of the potential limits, even problems of pragmatic flexible engagement. How does transcommunal action, for instance, guide us through the theoretical and practical thicket of multiple shifts in local circumstance, context, and interorganizational dynamics that may weaken (or strengthen) commitments to alliances, mobilization, cooperation, and support that are part of the social fabric and cultural understanding of members? (One might argue that this is precisely what happened within SNCC in the late 1960s when the organizationally disciplined multiracial alliance under the leadership of Bob Moses was displaced by what many would call the radical identity politics of black power advocated by Stokley Carmichael.) Are such alliances, actions, and possibilities equally effective and productive under the pressure-cooker conditions of social crisis? Do the results of effective alliance building and cooperation produce the very conditions (occasionally even successes) that erode or undermine transcommunal forms of organization and practice and ultimately community?[2]

Such questions prompt me to ponder the limitations of thinking about community as a finished, bounded, ideal unit of social life. Rather, through its theorization of flexible engagement, at the very least transcommunality encourages a way of thinking about community as a dynamic process fashioned out of constantly shifting relations, positions, interests, and circumstances. This perspective on community is in marked contrast to those that see communities as simply marked by identifiable signifiers of difference, as bounded territories that are to be contained, regulated, and disciplined.

Transcommunality and Culture

> Transcommunality must be distinguished from an inward-focused identity politics ... that consciously cuts its participants off from contact with others in the name of racial, ethnic, or ideological claims of purity.
>
> —Childs, herein

Insofar as culture is concerned, the concept of transcommunality is suggestive at least on the question of public space and the kinds of cultural practices that occur within those spaces. The formulation that has contributed most to my thinking about the relationship between transcommunality and cultural practice is the work of Dorine Kondo, Lisa Lowe, Robin D. G. Kelley, and George Lipsitz. In *Dangerous Crossroads,* Lipsitz identifies the political dangers and opportunities of commercial popular culture, most notably popular music, for constructing new forms of belonging and social relations that do not have to come at the expense of social location, cultural identity, and the recognition of difference.

Lipsitz is especially concerned with the ways in which commercial culture provides the routes along which specific cultural practices travel, are aligned with, and help establish new forms of community, affective identification, and belonging. But as he is quick to indicate, while such identifications are ideally forged on the basis of mutual respect for differences in location, tradition, and circumstance, forms and commercially mediated expressions of difference are also the basis for conflict, competition, and struggle over the particularity and exclusivity of difference. Thus Lipsitz tries to underline the danger as well as highlight the opportunity of the politics of culture alluded to in the title of his book. Despite such danger, the potential gain is worth the risk; the local and specific circumstances of people's everyday lives are enriched and potentially transformed on their own terms through their encounters, transformations, and desires. Lipsitz uses the concept "intercultural communication" (a term with obvious affinity to transcommunality) to describe this process of contact and exchange.

In the realm of commercial culture and popular practices, the most obvious example of transcommunal intercultural communication is the soundtrack of the postmodern urban world: Hip Hop. Hip Hop is a commercial form fashioned from a specific confluence of social, cultural, and historical articulations that brought together different subjects, traditions, and narratives, recombining them so that they spoke to the specific and local circumstances out of which they were fashioned. At the same time, as a popular commercial form, Hip Hop travels widely—across different social, geographic, media, and discursive spaces—adapting as it is adapted, recombining as it is itself recombined, to speak to local and specific conditions at the same time as it continues to signal identification and belonging to a global imagined community.[3]

In commercial popular forms such as Hip Hop, we see the importance of attachments to place that commercial popular music both undermines and reinforces, as Lipsitz has noted. The point is that distinctive geographical boundaries and specific locations are important but no longer the only condition out of which cultural identities, social belonging, or potential alliances are forged. As Dorine Kondo shows in her study of Japanese fashion and Asian American theater, media and global commodity culture produce infinite possibilities for mixing and remixing identities and identifications. Although the endless slide toward relativism (or the imposition of what Gilroy calls ethnic absolutism of popular music) is possible, I am much more interested here in the ever widening set of resources that this circulation of popular music offers for crafting notions of self, belonging, and identification that challenge and oppose those imposed by the powerful over the weak.

This specific and particular use of commercial music within the space of popular culture is one of the ways that the ethos of transcommunality is productively aligned with cultural politics. Put another way, the role of commercial popular culture in the production of transcommunal alliance demonstrates just how distinctive groupings and collectivities come together, respect differences, and yet build alliances over concrete material concerns with a shared sense of purpose.

Whereas Childs's concept of transcommunality insists on the productive potentialities of a respect for difference, Lipsitz's critical discussion of intercultural communication in commercial culture at the very least encourages us to get beyond angst at identity and difference, and beyond suspicion about the inherent dangers of popular commercial culture. These suspicions are deeply rooted in a conception of difference and commercial culture as always ready sources of superficial politics, weak alliances, and impediments to real change. Popular culture, difference, and identity constitute the soft underbelly of real politics in a global world. Both Lipsitz and Childs encourage a conception of identity, difference, and the popular as an important cultural terrain (not to be eliminated, managed, or repressed) on which critical understandings and engagements with the social and the political (in whatever shape and form) are expressed. In this respect, the popular is an important site for crafting identification and belonging, the stuff out of which alliances and articulations are built and struggled over.

The potentiality of transcommunal politics operates most productively in the spaces of cultural practices imaginatively fashioned from critical engagement with and transformation of the cultural resources at the level of everyday life. When we give critical recognition to and engage with the politics and practices generated in such spaces, we neither privilege struggles for culture and identity nor avoid struggles for the environment, the redistribution of resources, and social justice. Rather, such recognition broadens the concept of the political, and most especially the conception of the social and cultural terrain on which such struggles take place. By this broadening, we avoid the pitfall of retreating into the narrow and protective quarters of difference and identity as enclaves and zones that need to be barricaded and protected from leakage, dilution, and contamination. The space of the popular—including commercial culture—is the public space of the dialogic, where different groups, cultures, and social formations meet in momentary articulations where they engage, borrow, compare, expand, and modify cultural practices.[4] As Lipsitz is the first to recognize, staging these encounters at the sites of commercial media and popular culture brings with it danger as well opportunity. As I have already noted, this quality of contingency and indeterminacy necessitates a vision of politics that transcends the limits of innocence and romanticization too easily and often associated with the popular.

Transcommunality and Practical Action

> Transcommunal identity politics celebrates and asserts distinctive and essential community/organizational allegiances that can serve as multiple bases for common action with others.
>
> —Childs, herein

Along with the centrality of popular culture in the production and constitution of dialogic counterspheres and spaces where transcommunal practices and alliances occur, I want to make two final points about transcommunal politics and culture. The first is the recognition that the state is no longer the privileged and primary object of political struggle. The second is the necessity of thinking about modernist categories of universal subjectivity—in this case the urban working class—through the specificity of identity and difference. In both cases, the work of Lisa Lowe and Robin Kelley can be joined to that of John Brown Childs.

New social movements based on identity, identification, and belonging are characterized by their move away from exclusive focus on the state as the primary site of claims for recognition and representation. The increasing corporate mobility, strategies of flexible production, decentralized administration and management, and increasing velocity of information flows have produced new configurations of home, the local, displacement, and movement. At the same time, they have created openings for new real and imagined communities of belonging and affiliation. Such developments require new thinking and rethinking about politics, community, and publics. Transcommunal politics of engagement seem perfectly suited to these shifting conditions and thus may offer productive strategies, the identification of new sites, and conditions of possibility for a politics and practice suited for the conditions of global capital, mobile information, labor, and technology.

Some indication of what these actual practices might look like in the form of effective and productive locally based politics is offered by Robin D. G. Kelley's account of multiracial urban-based social struggles in the university (clerical workers, graduate teaching assistants, janitors), public transportation (bus riders, city employees), and the hotel and leisure industry (housekeepers, kitchen staffs). Kelley insists that these struggles, the articulations out of which they come, and the alliances that they produce are expressions of new conceptions of social and political identities and struggles. In the case of Asian and Mexican immigrant women in sweatshops, Lisa Lowe has shown that sustained struggles over working conditions, wages, and dignity are fashioned out of alliances across race, class, immigration status, ethnicity, and gender. Political struggles such as those described by Lowe and Kelley are transcommunal in that they do not pose class and identity as distinctively opposed binaries in a zero sum game of real politics. According to Lowe and Kelley, these are new class struggles which take the specific form of visible and discernible identities that are not posited as universal signifiers of collective identity or essential working-class subjects.

The powerful examples offered by Lowe and Kelley of new forms of class struggle, by Childs of conflict resolution and community-based mutuality, and by Lipsitz of new forms of imagined community constructed in and through commercial culture all suggest concrete ways of how transcommunality might be productively linked to continuing concerns with analytic and political matters of culture. Moreover, these examples serve as the basis of an engagement with conceptions of difference and identity that neither lapses into romantic longings for essentialist notions of politics nor raises excessive anxiety over politics made at the site of culture and identity.

When placed in conversation with the work of scholars like George Lipsitz, Lisa Lowe, Robin D. G. Kelley, Stuart Hall, and others, transcommunality is immediately enriched and its possibilities and applications extended. It is the basis of incisive critiques of static and hegemonic epistemologies and politics, especially those invested with commitments to already finished conceptions of appropriate subjects, politics, sites, and struggles. Social and cultural struggles of all sorts are being waged by social formations constituted by poor people, working people, immigrants, youth, and women whose struggles for recognition, belonging, and social justice are organized through distinctive differences and identities that matter.

Notes

1. The questions of by what criteria, in what direction, and through what means could be more carefully developed and productively put in conversation with the critical theories of Juergen Habermas and Zygmut Bauman.

2. The work of urban anthropologist Stephen Gregory on community organization, class, and race politics in the borough of Queens is very suggestive on this point.

3. To illustrate a typically transcommunal moment of intercultural communication: On a recent trip to Christchurch, New Zealand, it was recommended that my colleague John Brown Childs and I visit a night spot we were told was frequented largely by young Pacific Islanders, Maori, and Samoans. As the evening progressed, the place included

whites as well. By the time the evening was in full bloom—music blast-
ing, people dancing—and the ambience of place was fully apparent, I felt
a very strange sense of familiarity and difference at the same time. These
young people were dressed in Hip Hop fashion and listening to the music
of Tupac, Biggy Smalls, Dr. Dre, and Latifah, and yet they were distinctively Pacific Islanders. They were not trying to be American, black,
or western, and yet it was the music of black and brown working-class
urban America that created the space for this transcommunal moment.
(I should note that the club was owned and managed by a black Cuban.)

4. Here I do not mean the distinctive public sphere of rational communicative action in a Habermasian sense, but a public sphere where the
form and content of speech include media images, sound, memory, and
affect as the basis for intercultural communication.

5. For further readings on these topics see Robin Kelley's *Race Rebels:
Culture, Politics, and the Black Working Class* (New York: Maxwell Macmil-
lan International, 1994); George Lipsitz's *Dangerous Crossroads: Popular
Music, Postmodernism, and the Poetics of Place* (New York: Verso, 1994); and
Lisa Lowe's *New Formations, New Questions, Asian American Studies* (Dur-
ham, NC: Duke University Press, 1997).

Sofia Quintero

One Love

Transcommunality among the
Hip Hop Generation

> Most people in the United States can't comprehend the
> world power of rap, and don't care to believe it. In 1994,
> when Public Enemy did our latest European tour in
> Budapest, Hungary and Zagreb, Croatia, people were
> traveling by the busloads from former Eastern Bloc
> countries to check out the show and invite us to their
> countries to perform.... When I was in Brazil, I swore
> I was in Oakland. It's like a tropical Oakland.
>
> —Chuck D with Yusuf Jah,
> *Fight the Power: Rap, Race and Reality*

THE IDEA of transcommunality expressed by John
Brown Childs comes at a most opportune time for the Hip Hop
nation. As chronicled by the recent media attention to the activism
of Hip Hop artists,[1] more headz are getting their politic on.
Whether it's graffiti writers tagging "No More Prisons" on side-
walks throughout the nation or independent record labels such
as Raptivism Records and Clockwork Productions releasing
socially conscious music, the progressive citizens of the Hip Hop
community are determined to return the subculture back to its
roots in resistance. Such efforts raise awareness of and create

opportunities for collaborating across differences in pursuit of social and economic justice. As artists inspire and activists organize, transcommunality offers a powerful approach for overcoming the various tensions and threats that presently exist in Hip Hop subculture.

In his "First Words" in *Transcommunality*, Childs describes the "rushing toward mindless materialism, propelled by powerful, unfeeling economic syndicates that uproot body and soul." Nowhere is this state of affairs more true than among the Hip Hop generation. For all the rhetoric of Hip Hop's appeal to and, as a consequence, ability to bridge peoples throughout the world, the only arena in which such cultural transcendence inarguably has occurred has been the consumer market. The ever increasing commodification of Hip Hop subculture—its transformation from participatory process to consumed product—demands and foments individualism, competitiveness, and other tenets of the marketplace that diametrically contradict those critical to social justice.

Quite a departure from Hip Hop's humble yet rebellious origins. Having its cultural roots in African-influenced practices such as Brazilian capoeira to Egyptian hieroglyphics, Hip Hop evolved from the souls and through the bodies of African American and Latino youth of the South Bronx during the late 1970s, a period of extreme political disfranchisement and economic devastation.[2] Understandably, many romanticize its emergence. Visualize these young people, they say, with no access to opportunity—be it economic, educational, or artistic—creating something from nothing, relying on little more than their own bodies to express themselves creatively and find meaning amidst squalor. While such idyllic descriptions are not untruthful, they underemphasize the revolutionary elements that existed in Hip Hop from birth. Perhaps when taggin' up on a subway train or highway overpass, the graffiti artist did not consciously set out to challenge the notion of private property. Maybe the breakdancer who rolled out his linoleum on the street corner did not deliberately seek to push the definition of public space. But given the increasing acts of police repression that usually accompany the calculated destabilization of urban communities of color, it is no less possible to acknowledge the revolutionary spirit that burned among Hip Hop's earliest practitioners than it is to deny the intended rebelliousness in the lyrics of today's emcees.

So far Hip Hop has come from the days when rappers and breakers earned money with their talents by passing a baseball cap among appreciative spectators. In 1999, one out of ten albums sold were recorded by rap artists to the tune of $1.4 billion.[3] Estimated as a $5 billion market in 1996,[4] Hip Hop fashion sales continue to explode. FUBU—the nation's largest urban apparel company, with its $115 baseball jackets and $67 baggy jeans—made $300 million in 1999, up from $3 million only three years earlier.[5] Increasingly, Hip Hop clothing lines like PHAT Farm and Sean John are cited as factors in the financial descent of fashion giants like Tommy Hilfiger and Donna Karan, mainstream designers for the affluent once popular among Hip Hop celebrities and their fans. While still punishable by law (and beating by the police) in the streets or rail-yard, graffiti on the SoHo gallery circuit finds wealthy patronage. A culture that once only thrived underground now commands significant attention from the fourth estate; Hip Hop not only garners the attention of the likes of the *New York Times*, *Wall Street Journal*, and *Nightline* but also spawns innumerable outlets devoted to its coverage from magazines to websites. Consider *The Source*, a popular Hip Hop magazine that enjoys a passalong rate of approximately one purchase for as many as fifteen readers—at least three or four times higher than the average magazine industry rate.[6] The magazine recently launched its own annually and nationally televised awards show.[7]

With the exception of a few individuals, however, this commercial success has meant little to the social, political, and economic advancement of the communities who create Hip Hop nor those who consume it. It serves as a prime conduit—mostly through rap music and videos—for the international marketing of expensive clothing, toxic consumables, and luxury items to those who can afford them the least economically, politically, and spiritually. To their detriment, individuals compete to outdo each other at the only practice of value—consumption. As Lipsitz wrote:

> Although irrefutably ironicized, preoccupations with power, appearances, and property in hip hop sometimes makes it hard to tell the difference between critique and collaboration. As Greg Tate has shown repeatedly through his exemplary coverage of hip hop, sexism, homophobia, and materialism loom so large in youth culture, even within performances that are clearly culturally and politically radical in other ways, that it is difficult to imagine how all the insight, energy, and inspiration flowing through youth culture can become a part of social change rather than merely presenting a picture simulating it.[8]

At the community level, the commodification of Hip Hop has done more to exacerbate racial tensions than it has to foment crossracial interaction. The more prevalently and narrowly it is perceived as a means toward economic affluence, the more frequent and vehement the jockeying to "own" it. An example of this is the growing debate on the "race" of Hip Hop. On one extreme is the quixotic insistence that Hip Hop was a multiracial phenomenon from its inception, evolving from the interaction between and participation by people of all races. Pointing to white graffiti artists and Latino breakdancers, those who cling to this utopian view frequently seek to extend "ownership" of Hip Hop to a multiracial sea of hands. They misunderstand the inadvertent racism that lies in the idealistic naïveté of overlooking its predominantly African roots and deemphasizing its obvious and persistent African American presence.

At the other end of the debate are those who are equally mistaken in their nationalistic zeal to cast Hip Hop as a purely African American innovation with little regard for the role that geography and class played in its development. Justifiably angry that the exploitation of African American talent largely occurs at the hands and to the benefit of a few white men, they jealously guard Hip Hop from "outsiders" whose participation, consumption, or appreciation they dismiss as cooptation even when there is no material gain for doing so. Recognition of the participation of Latinos in the evolution of Hip Hop—particularly Puerto Ricans in New York City—are rare and grudging.[9] They attribute particular styles of dress, language, and conduct as proof of black ownership, failing to realize not only that much of what they define as black can be more appropriately called urban, but also that the danger lies in certifying blackness in such narrow, even stereotypical ways.

This debate exemplifies what Childs calls the "politics of conversion" that exists within the Hip Hop community today. One need only scan the message board on a Hip Hop website and observe how vigilantly the disputants try to convince others that their perspective is the truth. Ironically, they frequently lace their arguments with contradictory statements, wavering between rebuking each other for not knowing the "truth" about Hip Hop's origins and paying homage—with slogans like "One Love" and "It's all good"—to a mythical, unified, Hip Hop nation.

The truth lies not only between the two extremes but also in the fact that had not corporate interests sought to commodify Hip Hop subculture, such a debate might be nonexistent. The emergence of Hip Hop—a subculture born in resistance to the oppressive conditions of the dominant society—was a transcommunal experience. It brought together African American, Latino, and white youth at a time when their common socioeconomic reality did not.

Furthermore, the cultural roots of their practices and the identities of the participants were less important than the practices themselves. In fact, each individual not only enjoyed the autonomy to participate as she or he saw fit, but such "unique essence of being" was encouraged. The diversity was deemed to add value to the collective experience.

Herein lies the transcommunal principle of "creating cooperation that draws from diversity rather than bypassing it." Had Hip Hop remained in this cultural realm, would there be such a compelling need to claim ownership of it? Utilizing a transcommunal paradigm, activists among the Hip Hop generation may be able to revive Hip Hop as a form of cultural activism, recapture its power to challenge oppressive concepts and structures, and seize the opportunities it creates to bring together different communities to promote social change.

As it stands now, however, Hip Hop as commodity does the contrary. Hip Hop is becoming the vehicle of choice for orienting youth—particularly but not exclusively those of color—into a value system that runs counter to their advancement. This orientation includes:

- *The increasing prevalence of an "I do my thing, you do yours" mentality.* Contrary to the transcommunal method of encouraging positive interaction by honoring diverse viewpoints toward a shared experience of social justice, this attitude reinforces individualism, promotes competition, undermines community, and ignores accountability toward the common yet exclusive objectives of personal wealth and influence. That is, in order to be left to do "my thing" unchallenged, I must accord you the same. Frequently, this tenet is expressed with a spirit of acceptance for different styles and agendas, but if truly rooted in an ethics of respect as portrayed, clashes between "my" thing and "your" thing would less often culminate in verbal attacks and physical violence.

- *The depreciation of "the community" in strictly economic terms.* Most Hip Hop artists constantly use terms like *community* or *people* as a broad euphemism for fans, investors, and others whose support keeps them financially afloat. Indeed, their most meaningful sense of affiliation shrinks drastically to those with whom they are financially interdependent, such as label mates and crew members. They expect support from "the community" in the form of record or ticket sales and return it with symbolic public appearances and modest financial donations.

- *A redefinition of authenticity that grows more negative and exclusive.* For there to be the hegemony of the few, there must be homogeneity among the many. This is increasingly evident in Hip Hop by the dominance of gangsta rap, with its oppressive demands for conformity. Today a "legitimate" head exploits women, terrorizes gays, loathes whites, enjoys violence, avoids politics, and eschews spirituality, otherwise he's not "keepin' it real." Identity difference or ideological dissent is unacceptable, for what is "real" has already been definitively determined by the few whose continued supremacy depends on widespread concession to their "truth." All who aspire to join the ranks of the powerful (or at least hope to avoid their wrath) would do well to accept their position.

From these phenomena emerges that homogenizing unity which not only breeds a politics of conversion among the Hip Hop generation but also a culture of self-destruction of the masses cloaked by the celebrated success of the few.[10]

All this amidst a pleasing rhetoric of Hip Hop's crosscultural appeal and multiracial practitioners. If activists in the Hip Hop community can incorporate the principles of transcommunality into their work, perhaps they can counter these commercial forces and return Hip Hop culture to its radical origins. In the introduction to *Transcommunality*, Childs writes, "Transcommunality emphasizes a constant process of negotiational construction of organization among diverse participants, rather than an imposed monolithic system [recognizing] that dispute and difference ... must be accepted as a basic aspect of the 'human condition' rather than being constrained." To some extent, Hip Hop was once such a process, and in some oases of hopeful struggle, it still provides opportunities for this "method that allows for a high degree of diversity, autonomy, and coordination of its participants." In whatever ways we do or hope to use Hip Hop to promote social change—raising awareness of social issues, communicating alternative analyses of persisting injustices, drawing resources to build institutional responses, inspiring individual transformation and collective action—we must adopt a framework that honors and maximizes its multicultural appeal. Mere recognition has been an insufficient strategy for realizing Hip Hop's potential. By bringing a more reflective and strategic perspective to our work—

a transcommunal one—people of conscience in the Hip Hop community can reappropriate and connect the multifaceted base of diverse peoples that commodification has built, and then move toward radical change. And we should if the phrase "One Love" is to hold any real meaning.

Notes

Epigraph: Chuck D with Yusuf Jah, *Fight the Power: Rap, Race and Reality* (New York: Delacorte Press, 1997), 110–111.

1. For example, see Angela Ards, "Rhyme and Resist: Organizing the Hip Hop Nation," *The Nation,* 26 July/2 August 1999; Jon Caramanica, "It's Nation Time . . . Again," *Village Voice,* 1–7 September 1999; Lisa Sullivan, "20 First Century Hip Hop: Puff or Politics," *Horizon,* October 1999; Peter Noel, "Bring the Noise," *Vibe,* August 2000.

2. This is eloquently and thoroughly described by Tricia Rose, *Black Noise: Rap Music and Black Culture in Contemporary America* (Middletown, CT: Wesleyan University Press, 1994), 21–61.

3. Laura Goldstein, "Urban Wear Goes Suburban," *Fortune,* 138(12) (1999).

4. Karen Hunter, "Fubu Fitted for Success: Taking Urban Gear to Top through Macy's," *New York Daily News,* 11 November 1996.

5. Goldstein; Judith Schoolman, "Low Profits Hit High Fashion Bigs," *New York Daily News,* 7 February 2000.

6. Rose, 8.

7. For example, listen to Mos Def, "Hip Hop," *Black on Both Sides,* Rawkus Entertainment, 1999.

8. George Lipsitz, "We Know What Time It Is: Youth Culture in the 90s," *Center for Puerto Rican Studies Bulletin,* 5(1) (Winter 1992/93): 17.

9. Juan Flores, "Puerto Rico Rocks: New York Ricans Stake Their Claim," *Droppin' Science: Critical Essays on Rap, Music and Hip Hop Culture* (pp. 85–105), ed. William Eric Perkins (Temple University Press, 1996); and Juan Flores, "Puerto Rican and Proud, Boyee!: Rap, Roots, and Amnesia," *Centro Journal,* 5(1) (Winter 1992/93): 24–25.

10. For example, listen to Dead Prez, "Hip Hop," *Let's Get Free,* Loud Records, 2000.

John D. Brewer

Transcommunal Practice in Northern Ireland

THE FAMILY HISTORY that John Brown Childs sets down in *Transcommunality* leads effectively to the case made for Native American peace making, which itself is interwoven with the case made for transcommunality as a peace-making technique. The movement is between the general and particular, between local family history and abstract peace-making skills. Regarding transcommunality as a peace-making approach, I would raise a few points for general discussion.

To what extent is Native American peace-making special or unique? Anthropological evidence shows that many preindustrial societies had formal and institutionalized mechanisms for conflict resolution. This is part of the social condition according to Durkheim's account of Native Australians, for without it, conflict would subsume the group. Sometimes these mechanisms institutionalize ways of conflict—identifying ways of doing "war" in a controlled manner—such as many groups in the South Pacific with strong cultures of violence (Borneo and Indonesia, for example); sometimes they institutionalize ways of peace making. The latter is characteristic of the Native American tradition Childs describes. There are, of course, other ethnic groups with similar peace-making traditions.

Another point worth discussing is that the nature and depth of the conflict affects the possibilities for peace making. Some social cleavages around which there is conflict are all encompassing, taking in someone's very ontological security and sense of identity. Other conflicts involve issues around which one does not invest the same meaning. Some separate single-issue conflicts can be deep (neighbors quarrelling over the height of trees on their shared border), but rarely do they assume the importance and self-defining character as conflicts which shape someone's whole identity. The latter are less likely to be pluralist, in that lines of cleavage around which there is conflict do not undercut one another but coalesce around an all-encompassing cleavage. Peace making is harder with this kind of conflict.

Interethnic conflict is an example where peace making is most difficult. Peace making among Native Americans was surely facilitated by its occurring in the context of a shared ethnic identity and culture, with tradition defining institutionalized ways of peace making. It might thus not be relevant as an example of a peace-making technique used to deal with conflict between ethnic groups where there is no shared culture or tradition. Of course, this is where transcommunality comes in as an attempt to bridge different ethnic cultures.

The spirit of transcommunality can be succinctly summarized: dialogue; finding common, shared ground; flexibility in approach. These are features of the conflict resolution literature widely known thus far. Thus, it is important to stress what is special about transcommunality. I'm not sure that it is sufficient to say that its distinctive feature is to recognize, endorse, and permit the validity of the combatants' culture and ethnicity, since this is something that Archbishop Tutu and Nelson Mandela advocated as a lesson from the South African peace-making experience. In other words, the notion of transcommunality may benefit from being located in the context of similar peace-making approaches. This would allow a wider comparative focus than just the Native American case. I think the South African case is particularly instructive.

The conditions that Childs cites as necessary for transcommunality to work read as if there is already willingness on the part of the combatants to find a resolution to the conflict, and that the notion is best understood as an approach to peace making when sides are looking to agree or there are at least some people prepared to enter discussions to look for an agreement. Some conflicts—notably that in Northern Ireland—are intractable because there is no willingness to find a solution, or those that are willing have insufficient support behind them. It is worth laying out what transcommunality can do in these situations, although Childs rightly points to one dimension of this problem, namely the accusation that peacemakers (transcommunalists) can be portrayed as traitors. There are, however, other dimensions where transcommunality might make a contribution, if only to have it stated that features of transcommunality are important, such as dialogue, shared understandings, and respect for the validity of one's own and the other's position.

Archbishop Tutu once said that peace required someone to understand the position of his or her enemy. This is something beyond dialogue—it is about recognizing the fears, anxieties, hopes, and aspirations of one's opponent. It strikes me that transcommunality is distinctive because it is more than just about dialogue—it is about according the position and identity of one's opponent the same validity and respect as one's own, and about building peace in such a way that does not require you or your "enemy" to give up on that identity. The Northern Irish peacemakers call this "mutual recognition," and while we practice it less than we preach it, true peace making requires it to be lived daily and constantly. This is something that transcommunality stresses, which illustrates its value as an approach to peace making.

Bettina Aptheker

Transcommunality as Spiritual Practice

WE ARE in a campground owned by the Tohono O'odham people. It is in Arizona at its southernmost point, about forty miles from the tribal headquarters in Sells. We are fifty years old, a lesbian couple. I am Jewish; my partner is of German heritage. The park caretaker, Mario Puella, greets us. We shake hands. He is driving a king-cab pickup truck with oversized tires and four-wheel drive. He is accompanied by Ramsey, a Blue Hill dog, a breed favored by the Tohono O'odham for its shepherding skills. Mario says it is fine for us to stay, and we fill out the appropriate forms. The charge is $5.00 per day. He tells us that the flush toilets are hopelessly clogged and there is no money for repairs. He points to a pit facility. "O.K.," we say. We have become accustomed to even more "primitive" means in our years of camping in remote areas. Mario tells us that there is a mountain lion in the area. If he comes nearby, we are advised to get into our vehicle. This seems like excellent advice. Mario laughs with us, explaining, "We don't want to hurt him, but we keep track of him. He has a range of maybe twenty or twenty-five miles. Be careful."

This desert land is all rugged cliffs and jagged peaks and red rock formations. Baboquivari, sacred mountain of the Tohono O'odham, towers above us. Mesquite, pear cactus, barrel cactus, sagebrush, and saguaro fill the valley. Only a few miles away is the

Mexican border, an imaginary line cutting through mountains and ravines, with its periodic checkpoints at accessible crossings.

We stay a week. We are alone in the campground. Most days Mario comes by to check on us. He wants to be sure we are all right. We begin to visit with him, offer him tea. He is in his mid-twenties, chunky, well-built, with bronze skin, jet black hair, round face. He is wearing a very clean, tattered T-shirt that gives the word "threadbare" new meaning. He has an easy manner, speaks respectfully of the elders, tells us of an oasis with oak trees and lush grasses and a stream. We find it, savor its sweet waters and cool air. Later he tells us about Baboquivari, and sacred dances. One night we hear the drumming. Another night, mountain lion prowls the ravine just below our campsite. Twigs snap, leaves crackle. There is a low, primal growl. We enter our vehicle, as advised.

Mario explains the effects of poor diet and government rations on his people. A huge percentage of the Tohono O'odham have diabetes. The day we are to leave, Mario writes each of our names on a special form, signs it, and hands it to us. "In case you are stopped by the Border Patrol," he explains. We point to our white skin. "They won't give us any trouble," we say, suddenly thrust back into the reality of U.S. racial politics, enraged that Mario's people are subjected to constant harassment by the Border Patrol. We learn that at the end of the U.S. war with Mexico, the Gadsden Purchase and the Treaty of Guadalupe Hidalgo settled a border that split the Tohono O'odham Nation, without any consultation or regard for them. It was as though they did not even exist. Families were split, half in Mexico, half in the United States. Poverty on both sides of the border. Genocide on both sides of the border. In the 1970s the Tohono O'odham Tribal Council successfully challenged both governments, and the result was a tearing down of the border on tribal lands. Mario's forms as we leave the tribal land in case we are stopped by the Border Patrol now take on a different meaning. His is an act to affirm the sovereignty of the Tohono O'odham. His action and their struggle are ineluctably marked by this history. It is a struggle for sovereignty, self-determination, cultural integrity, a restoration of the naming of a people because the Tohono O'odham are known among white people as the Papago. It is a struggle, too, for the restoration of language, adequate medical care, water rights, a proper traditional diet, education, and land rights, and interventions against domestic violence and alcoholism.

We see a people rebuilding, reconstituting themselves. Theirs is a struggle, very much as John Brown Childs has observed about his own ancestors, the Haudenosaunee, and it reflects Native American history more generally. It is not based on class and individual human rights but, as Childs notes, "on community-based land, self-determination, and spiritual power." Childs says, speaking of the Haudenosaunee, "The land, which is ancestral, is a place of spiritual strength and renewal." From this epistemological and spiritual space, Childs extrapolates a theory and praxis of transcommunality to reduce gang violence in our urban centers and simultaneously address the grievances of oppressed peoples, building coalitions among diverse cultural and racial groups.

Respectfully and cautiously, using the historical example of the Haudenosaunee people who are among his ancestors, Childs posits his basic principles of respect in words and deeds, shared practical action, constructive disputing so that differences are not sublimated or diluted by mere slogans of solidarity. There is the conscious building of interpersonal relationships, and the restoration of harmony. Rooted in an indigenous worldview drawn from the historical record of the Peacemaker and his co-worker Hiawatha, who forged what Europeans came to call the Iroquois Confederacy, Childs emphasizes the mutually reinforcing practices of redemption, reconciliation, and the restoration of balance and harmony among and between peoples.

The archive from which Childs builds his transcommunal model represents the Mother of the Nations as a co-worker to the Peacemaker, and I wonder why they are not simply the Peacemakers, co-equal in their historical placement. Powerful stories elaborate the significant advice and inspiration given by the Mother of Nations to the Peacemaker. I think about the problem of archives, and the interpolations we make from them in the context of a white society that is so intensely unbalanced and misogynist.

Words matter. Naming is crucial. Childs reports that the Mother of the Nations tells the Peacemaker his words are good but asks what form his words will take in the world. In the indigenous view in North America, as I understand it, balance is at the promotional heart of harmony, and gendered representations form precisely the core metaphors of balance; for example, Mother Earth and Father Sky are co-equal and absolutely interdependent. Because of this the Haudenosaunee had a significant influence on early Euro-American feminists, including Elizabeth Cady Stanton and Matilda Joslyn Gage. Gage became an honorary member of the Iroquois nation (Wagner, 2002).

Tremendous wisdom, flexibility, strength, and resilience are drawn from such an indigenous worldview. As Childs accurately assays: "Many Europeans habituated to authoritarian, male-dominated societies ... were often baffled by this grassroots democratic system [of the Haudenosaunee] ... that strenuously sought to avoid anger and violence by emphasizing compassion, clearheadedness, and consensus." I think how much of the European violence against indigenous peoples was also explicitly a violence against women, a violence rooted in misogynist practices that could not and would not tolerate cultures based on an integral equality/balance between women and men (Smith, 1995).

And I am back to the Mexican border as location and metaphor. Rooted in white supremacy, Euro-Americans have at once expanded borders to suit their own imperial designs, and barricaded borders to insulate themselves against "foreign" or "alien" encroachment. Almost always the perceived peril comes from people of color. The "Yellow Peril" of the late-nineteenth century, with its exclusion laws, is easily paralleled to the current, hysterical militarization of the U.S. border with Mexico, La Migra, raids of predominantly Latino communities and sites of employment, and the police killings of African and Haitian immigrants in New York City. Our country is riddled with violence. Commentators (usually white and male) ponder its causes, while it remains perfectly obvious that the varying configurations of racism, misogyny, homophobia, and class inequities account for most of it. The Haudenosaunee beckon us toward a radically different process by which to resolve conflicts and restore peace.

Borders are inventions of the mind. There are borders of intransigence, hierarchy, and exclusion. There are borders born of integrity, sovereignty, and self-determination. Borders can provide sites of balance and respect, or they can be sites of invasion and humiliation. For the Haudenosaunee, as I understand their cosmology, all of life is interconnected and interdependent, and the accepted binary oppositions of western thinking (animate/ inanimate, sacred/profane, male/female, black/white, spirit world/material world) do not exist as oppositions at all. The Earth herself is alive; all that exists are varying forms of energy and "intelligence manifesting in different ways," as Native American writer Paula Gunn Allen (1986, 60) expresses it, each an essential part of the other. Borders can be permeable or impenetrable depending on what is appropriate. The point is to sustain a system of balance and harmony in which all can be held with respect. For the Haudenosaunee, the capacity of the Longhouse is infinite. In contrast, the western dualisms produce and reinforce illusions of separation and hierarchy. These, in turn, produce the impulse toward domination and violence.

In developing a model of transcommunality as a strategy for progressive political organizing, John Brown Childs proposes to honor cultural difference (so as to counter the terrible effects of racism) while simultaneously enforcing a process for mutual respect, the resolution of conflict, and the lessening of violence. For such a process to succeed, it must necessarily personally transform its participants. That is, once grounded in the kind of spiritual practice of transcommunality which Childs articulates, a dialectical relationship between political organizing, conflict resolution, and personal, spiritual transformation is set in motion. For the one to succeed, the other must be engaged. They are simultaneous and mutually reinforcing. Likewise, participants must learn to model the balance for which we/they strive in their daily practice, in their personal relationships, and in their actions, so that, for example, modern "peacekeepers" are both male and female, interracial, and intercultural. Liberation requires a mutually reinforcing process of political, personal, and spiritual transformation.

To be sustained, spiritual practice requires a training of the mind, a quieting of its fierce and egocentric storms. I have found examples of this practice from many different spiritual traditions. Ultimately it is transnational and transcendent. For example, a Jewish prayer for the Sabbath invites us to "Listen":

> In the clearing, where the mind flowers
> and the world sprouts up at every side
> listen
> for the sound in the bushes
> behind the grass. (Falk, 1996, 102)

A Tibetan Buddhist instruction counsels the practitioner:

> Transcend boundaries of kinship by embracing
> all living beings
> as one family of consciousness. (Hixon, 1993, 251)

Ultimately, transcommunality is a political practice that inspires, requires and is sustained by a spiritual one in which self-love and transcendent love are mutually inclusive.

Ceremony, a novel by Native American writer Leslie Marmon Silko, illuminates these ideas. In the Navajo nation at the end of World War II, Tayo, the novel's central figure, a veteran of the war in the Pacific, must find a way to heal from what western doctors diagnose as "battle fatigue." He is enveloped in a white fog–like existence, continually nauseated and vomiting. War is the ultimate expression of separation because it demonizes "an enemy" who must be destroyed. At the literal center of the novel is a story of the "witchery," which describes precisely the coming of European colonizers and the separations they enforce:

> Then they grow away from the earth
> then they grow away from the sun
> then they grow away from the plants and animals
>   They see no life
>   When they look
>   they see only objects.
> The world is a dead thing for them
> the trees and rivers are not alive
> the mountains and stones are not alive.
>   The deer and bear are objects
>   They see no life. (Silko, 1977, 135)

Tayo's loss and suffering, grief and fury move him between drinking binges and senseless violence with his war buddies on the one hand, and the Dine spiritual path on the other. Through the healing powers of the creatrix Spider Woman, who manifests in a variety of female forms, and the wisdom of Navajo elders, Tayo gradually heals, regains his balance, and reunites with the land and with the constellations (that is to say, with Mother Earth and Father Sky).

The dialectics of transcommunality require a process of personal transformation, and personal engagement in a healing process. Childs implies this when he notes that Haudenosaunee chiefs were expected to rise above insults or other offenses directed at them. This is very hard to do without a strong spiritual practice and firm motivation. Likewise, Childs quotes Abenaki writer Joseph Bruchac on the "strong tradition of redemption among native people," and their belief that what Europeans term "evil" is "a twisting of the mind."

The Haida artist Bill Reid carved a massive sculpture, "The Raven and the First Men," from a block of laminated yellow cedar. It occupies a whole room at the Museum of Anthropology at the University of British Columbia in Vancouver. You enter and circumambulate the sculpture, viewing it from many different angles and sides. In many Northwest indigenous cultures, Raven figures prominently as Creator and as the transformer. Reid's Raven appears in the stylized representations characteristic of the totem. He is perched atop a clamshell. The shell is being pried open by human beings in varying states of infancy and duress. While most are trying to climb out, others are scrambling back in. The sculpture depicts an episode from a nineteenth-century Haida story. In Reid's contemporary incarnation, it takes on a broad, universal representation of the human condition. All the human forms are in the clamshell. To emerge they must transform themselves from infancy with its insatiable needs and wants into adulthood with its potential for selfless and compassionate communality. Raven is the transformer, a representative from the Spirit world functioning in much the same way that Spider Woman does in Silko's *Ceremony*.

I have shown a photograph of Reid's sculpture to many different audiences in my travels in an effort to explain the process of transformation it represents. Nobody among non-Native peoples accepts it. Everyone argues with me. Raven is the oppressor, forcing the clamshell shut, while humans struggle against him to free themselves. This is a political model to which we are very attached because it places responsibility for our suffering on someone else. It is a model that designates the oppressor as Other, outside ourselves, to be opposed, defeated, crushed, destroyed. Do we not see the paradox? In doing this we are replicating the western process of separation that created the systems of domination in the first place.

Each of us can occupy an oppressor position, depending on the historical moment and our positionality. For example, white women are simultaneously oppressed as women and oppressors when they align themselves with racism and reinforce racist practices. Black men are likewise simultaneously oppressed by racism and oppressors of women whom they subordinate. Chicano people are oppressed as a group, but they can also be oppressors when manifesting anti-Semitism toward Jewish people. African Americans who are light-complected and assume racialized privileges can be oppressors of people of color. We can go on with this almost indefinitely, and I am not singling out any particular group.

I am trying to show that each of us can occupy a hierarchical position reinforcing the institutions of power and privilege that pervade the social order. The only way out of this is to uproot the process itself.

Liberation requires a mutually reinforcing process of political, personal, and spiritual transformation. The beauty of the Haudenosaunee model of the Longhouse is precisely in its uniting these apparently disparate qualities into a wholeness for the practice of balance in everyday living.

References

Allen, Paula Gunn. 1986. *The Sacred Hoop: Recovering the Feminine in American Indian Traditions*. Boston: Beacon Press.

Falk, Marcia. 1996. *The Book of Blessings: New Jewish Prayers for Daily Life, the Sabbath, and the New Moon Festival*. San Francisco: Harper.

Hixon, Lex. 1993. *Mother of the Buddhas: Meditation on the Prajnaparamita Sutra*. Wheaton, IL: Quest Books.

Silko, Leslie Marmon. 1977. *Ceremony*. New York: Penguin Books.

Smith, Andrea. 1995. "Christian Conquest and the Sexual Colonization of Native Women." In *Violence against Women and Children: A Christian Theological Sourcebook*. Ed. Carol Adams and Marie Fortune. New York: Continuum Publishers.

Wagner, Sally Roesch. 2002. *Sisters in Spirit: Haudenosaunee (Iroquois) Influence on Early American Feminists*. Summertown, TN: Book Publishing Company.

About the Contributors

BETTINA APTHEKER is Professor of Women's Studies at the University of California, Santa Cruz. She is the author of *The Morning Breaks: The Trial of Angela Davis; Tapestries of Life: Women's Work, Women's Consciousness, and the Meaning of Daily Experience;* and *Woman's Legacy: Essays on Race, Sex, and Class in American History.*

JEREMY BRECHER is a historian with a Ph.D. from Union Graduate School. His books include *Strike!; Brass Valley: A History from Below; Global Village or Global Pillage;* and *Globalization from Below: The Power of Solidarity.* Brecher is the Humanities Scholar in Residence at Connecticut Public Television and has written scripts for several documentaries including *Rust Valley, The Amistad Revolt,* and *The Roots of Roe: Schools in Black and White,* for which he won two Emmy Awards and the Edgar Dale Screenwriting Award.

JOHN D. BREWER, Professor of Sociology at Queen's University, Belfast, and Fellow of the Royal Society of Arts, is the author of twelve books on topics such as ethno-religious conflict and policing in divided societies. He writes extensively on South Africa and Northern Ireland. Among his works are *After Soweto: An Unfinished Journey,* and *Anti-Catholicism in Northern Ireland: 1600–1998, The Mote and the Beam* (with Gareth I. Higgins).

GUILLERMO DELGADO-P. is an Andean anthropologist who teaches in the Latin American Studies Department at the University of

California, Santa Cruz. He is the editor for the online Bolivian Research Review (<www.bolvianstudies.org>) and serves on the steering committee of the Chicano/Latino Research Center (CLRC) at Santa Cruz. Along with his colleagues John Brown Childs and Renya Ramirez, he coordinates the Interethnic Research Cluster of CLRC.

ARIF DIRLIK is Knight Professor of Social Science and Professor of History and Anthropology at the University of Oregon. His latest books include *Postmodernity's Histories* and two edited volumes, *Chinese on the American Frontier: History after the Three Worlds* (with Vinay Bahl and Peter Gran), and *Places and Politics in an Age of Globalization* (with Roxann Prazniak).

DAVID WELCHMAN GEGEO holds a Ph.D. in political science from the University of Hawai'i and teaches in the Liberal Studies Institute at California State University, Monterey Bay. For the past twenty years he has been conducting research and publishing on his own people, the Kwara'ae of Malaita in the Solomon Islands, South Pacific.

HERMAN GRAY is Professor of Sociology at the University of California, Santa Cruz. He is the author of *Producing Jazz* (Temple University Press) and *Watching Race: Television and the Sign of Blackness*. Gray publishes widely in the areas of media studies, cultural politics, and the representations of African Americans.

RENATE HOLUB teaches social theory and comparative European studies at the University of California, Berkeley, where she directs the Program in Interdisciplinary Studies. She is the author of *Antonio Gramsci: Beyond Marxism and Postmodernism*.

SOFÍA QUINTERO was named by *City Limits* as one of the "New School of Activists Most Likely to Change New York." Quintero is an activist, teacher, writer, speaker, and comedienne who strives to apply her creative abilities in popular media to promote social justice. She teaches a course at the Brecht Forum on the politics of Hip Hop, called *From Getting Paid to Getting Free*.

ANDREA SMITH (Cherokee) is Assistant Professor of American Culture and Women's Studies at the University of Michigan. She is a co-founder of the Chicago chapter of Women of All Red Nations and Incite! Women of Color Against Violence.

STEFANO VARESE, Peruvian anthropologist, is Professor of Native American Studies at the University of California, Davis. He is the author of numerous works, including *Salt of the Mountain: Campa Ashaninca History and Resistance in the Peruvian Jungle,* and is editor of the book *Pueblos Indios, Soberania y Globalismo.*

HAYDEN WHITE is University Professor Emeritus, History of Consciousness Department, at the University of California, Santa Cruz. His numerous publications include *Tropics of Discourse: Essays in Cultural Criticism* and the *Content of the Form: Narrative Discourse and Historical Representation.*

Index

136–37; contrasted with transcommunality, 199–200; as flawed basis
for global conflict resolution,
185–87
European Union, 149
Exxon, 176
EZLN. *See* Zapatista movement

Fanon, Frantz, 87n. 15, 149, 153;
Black Skins, White Masks, 153
fascism, 166
fashion industry, 205, 213
feminist activists, influenced by Haudenosaunee, 225
feminist theoreticians, 110, 153
feminization of labor, 110–11
First Nations Development Institute,
29
Fiumara, Gemma Corradi, 21, 85n. 2;
The Other Side of Language, 85n. 2
Five Nations, the. *See* Haudenosaunee
flexible associations, 68–72, 127,
202–3. *See also* Congreso Nacional
Indígena; engaged/disengaged
organizational flexibility; Hau-
denosaunne; transcommunality
Flores, Juan, 218n. 9
Forbes, Jack, 29, 84n. 4
forgiveness: in Haudenosaunee
thought, 62; in Indigenous
thought, 64–66
Formalist–Substantivist debate in
anthropology, 131–32
fractum model of organization:
as alternative to transcommunal
mosaic model, 166–70; defined
167
free-determination, as concept in
Indigenous activism, 28, 36, 85n. 6
freedom, 54–55, 149
free market, 10
free trade, 37
Freidman, Jonathan, 38–39
Frye, Hardy, 107
FUBU clothing, and Hip Hop culture, 213

Fuentes, Carlos, 37, 85n. 2
Fukuyama, Francis, 107
Fundamentalism, western secular
forms of, 148–49

G7 countries, 152
Gadsden Purchase, 223
Gage, Joslyn Matilda, 225
Galeano, Eduardo, 84n. 3
Geertz, Clifford, 85n. 1
Gellner, Ernest, 84n. 2, 148; *Postmodernism, Reason, and Revolution,* 148
Gemeinschaft. See community
gender, 41–42, 111, 158, 163, 174,
208–9, 224–25; and capitalism,
178–79; and Haudenosaunee,
54–55. *See also* feminist activists;
feminist theoreticians; feminization of labor; women, of color;
and specific writers
Gesellschaft. See society
ghetto peacemaking (U.S.), 12, 58–59,
65–66, 74–75, 106
ghetto warfare (U.S.), 44–45, 106
Gilroy, Paul, 86n. 11, 200, 205–6
Gitlin, Todd, 177
global civil society, 151
global cooperation, 8, 10–12, 76–72.
See also global homogenization,
globalization from below as counterforce to; transcommunality
global elites, 151–53
global fragmentation, 8, 10, 120–21
*Global Gamble, Faustian Bid for World
Domination, The* (Gowan), 151–52
global homogenization, 8, 9–10,
137–38, 153, 170–71, 178; globalization from below as counterforce to, 157–65; Indigenous activism as counterforce to, 33–39;
Islam as counterforce to, 154, 171;
media sites of resistance to, in
Brazil, Egypt, Hong Kong, India,
Iran, and Mexico, 154–55
*Global Visions: Beyond the New World
Order* (Brecher, Childs, and Cutler), 103

global intellectuals, 149
global public sphere, 149–50
globalization, 8, 9–10, 105, 120–21,
   133, 162. *See also* capitalism; colo-
   nialism; imperialism
globalization from below, 157–164;
   transcommunal aspects of, 158–59,
   162–64
Goldstein, Judith Schoolman, 218n. 5
Goldstein, Laura, 218n. 3
Goldtoes (cultural activist), 74–75
Gorz, André, 41–42
Gowan, Peter, 151–52; *The Global
   Gamble: Faustian Bid for World
   Domination,* 151–52
Gramsci, Antonio, 87n. 16, 106,
   151–53
Grand Council of the Cree of
   Québec, 30, 36
Gray, Herman, 83n. 3
Great Council of the Haudeno-
   saunee, 53–54
Great Law of Peace, 51–52, 56
Green Party (Germany), 73
Gregory, Stephen, 209n. 2
Grindre, Donald, 48
Guatemala, 8, 40

Habermas, Juergen, 147–50, 154,
   209n. 1
Haida people, 228–29
Haiti, U.S. intervention in, 103
Hall, Stuart, 202–3
Hamer, Fannie Lou, 40
Hastie, Roberta Childs, 15
Hastie, William Henry, 15–16
Haudenosaunee (Five Nations, Iroquois Confederacy, League of the
   Iroquois, Six Nations), 18, 46–56;
   and anger management, 53–54;
   and boundaries as positive, 70; and
   condolence for loss of life, 62;
   and constructive disputing, 53–54;
   and coordinated autonomy of
   social units, 49–56; and cycles of
   vengeance being stopped, 50–51;
   and diversity as unity, 52–54; and

engaged/disengaged social organization, 71; and flexible associations, 49–56, 71–72; and forgiveness, 62; and freedom, 54–55; and
   Great Council, 53–54; and Great
   Law of Peace, 51–52, 56; and Hiawatha, 50–51, 65, 88n. 2; and households as foundations of society, 54;
   influence on Euro-American feminist activists, 225; influence on U.S.
   Constitution, 88n. 3; and interpersonal relations protocols, 57–58;
   and kinship, 55–56; and longhouse
   model for the society, 47–48, 54,
   56, 68–69, 230; as model for transcommunality, 46–51, 57–75; and
   the Mother of the Nations, 57, 61,
   224–25; and Onondaga central
   meeting place, 52–53; and peace,
   50–51, 54, 56; and The Peacemaker, 50–51, 52–54, 61, 65,
   224–25; and personal transformation, 64–66; and pragmatism,
   61; and respect, 57, 61, 224; and
   Thadodaho, 52–53, 65; and Tree of
   Peace, 52; and visionary thought,
   51–52, 67–68; and women as leaders, 53–55
Hawai'i, Indigenous activism in,
   29–31, 63–64, 69–70
Hecht, David, 42
Hernandez-Avila, Ines, 31
Hiawatha. *See* Haudenosaunee
Hip Hop culture, 212–15; and African
   Americans in South Bronx,
   214–15; African influence on, 212;
   and Brazilian capoeira, 212; commodification of, 212–16; and community, 214, 216–17; as global
   imagined community, 205–6; as
   mythic nation, 215; and Puerto
   Ricans in South Bronx; 214–15;
   race origins debate in, 214–15;
   racial tensions in, 212; transcommunal origins of, 215
historic bloc: as Gramsci's concept,
   152–53

246 Index

shantytown organizations, 41–45; in Africa, 42; and class, 41–42; and emplacements of affiliation, 44; in Latin America, 42–43; and leftists, 41–42; in the U.S., 42, 44–45
shared practical action. *See* transcommunality
Shiva, Vandana, 9, 158–59
Siberia, 9
Sidiki, Jitu, 58
Sikkink, Kathryn, 159
Silko, Leslie Marmon, 227–28, 229; *Ceremony,* 229
Simone, Maliqalim, 42
Sioui, Georges, E., 46, 47
Six Nations, the. *See* Haudenosaunee
Sky Father, 29
Smith, John, 16
Smith, Wadada Leo, 70–71
SNCC. *See* Student Non-violent Coordinating Committee
socialism, 123–25. *See also* the Left; Marxism
social justice, 151
society, distinguished from community, 129, 166
Solomon Islands, 190–95
Source, The (Hip Hop magazine), 213
South and Meso-American Indian Information Center, 34–35
South Bronx, N.Y.: grassroots activism in, 212–13; Hip Hop origins in, 212–13
South Central Los Angeles, Calif., and transcommunal cooperation, 74, 110
Southwest Network for Economic and Environmental Justice, 87n. 1
sovereignty. *See* Indigenous activism
Soyinka, Wole, 63
spaces of public action, 123–26, 147, 167, 172, 207. *See also* place-based politics; territory
Spider Woman, 229
spiritual power, in Indigenous activism, 28, 31, 36, 226–27. *See also* place-based politics; territory

Stanton, Elizabeth Cady, 225
State, the, and political struggle, 207–8
state socialism, 123–25
Stevenson, Winona, 47
Stop the Violence/Institute the Peace, 58
Student Non-violent Coordinating Committee (SNCC), 107, 113–14, 203
Substantivist-Formalist debate in anthropology, 137–38
Sumner, Charles, 15
Sundance Ceremony, 142
Swamp, Jake, 47
sweatshops, 110, 131, 208
Sweets, John F. 87n. 1

Takagi, Dana, 103
Taylor, Clyde, 200
Tchou, John Kuo, 87n. 1
Tecumseh (Shawnee leader), 46
Tehanetorens (Haudenosaunee writer), 50
Temuco-WallMapuche Declaration on the North American Free Trade Agreement, 37–39. *See also* Mapuche people; North American Free Trade Agreement
territory, 28–31, 35, 112, 129–43. See also Indigenous activism; place-based politics; spiritual power
Thadodaho (Onondaga/Haudenosaunee leader), 52, 65. *See also* Haudenosaunee
Thancoupie (Australian Indigenous activist), 31
theraputic discourses, 201–2
Theresa Hotel (Harlem), Fidel Castro and Malcolm X meet in, 114
Third World, and transcommunality, 189–90
Tocqueville, Alexis de, 19; *Democracy in America,* 19
Todorov, Tzvetan, 23
Tohono O'Odham people (Papago), 222–24